Dr. Janss,

After our conversation the last time I thought you might enjoy reading an expanded version of the engagement model. Thank you for your interest in our work.

Best regards,

Donna de St. Aubin

Attract, Engage & Retain Top Talent

50 Plus One Strategies Used by the Best

by
Donna de St. Aubin
&
Brian J. Carlsen

AuthorHouse™
1663 Liberty Drive, Suite 200
Bloomington, IN 47403
www.authorhouse.com
Phone: 1-800-839-8640

First published by AuthorHouse 10/17/2008

ISBN: 978-1-4389-2409-0 (sc)
ISBN: 978-1-4389-2410-6 (dj)

Library of Congress Control Number: 2008909836

Printed in the United States of America
Bloomington, Indiana

This book is printed on acid-free paper.

This publication is designed to provide accurate and authoritative information
in regard to the subject matter covered. It is sold with the understanding
that the publisher is not engaged in rendering legal, accounting or other
professional service. If legal advice or other expert assistance is required,
the services of a competent professional person should be sought.

From a Declaration of Principles Jointly Adopted by a Committee of the
American Bar Association and a Committee of Publishers & Associations.

About the Authors

Donna de St. Aubin's human resource and management expertise spans more than 25 years and includes executive human resource positions in the health care, manufacturing, financial and insurance industries.

In addition to her experience in human resource management, planning and internal staffing, Ms. St. Aubin has also been involved in major corporate mergers, acquisitions, divestitures and consolidations.

Ms. St. Aubin develops executive and leadership processes to attract, engage and retain top talent. This includes defining leadership attributes, change management, building global leadership brands, evaluating organization effectiveness and creating workforce strategies.

A frequent speaker before industry and management groups, Ms. St. Aubin has taught at the University of Colorado and the University of Wisconsin Executive Management Institute. She is a past faculty member of the Keller Graduate School of Management, and is a long-standing faculty member of the Graduate School of Banking at Colorado.

Ms St. Aubin is a co-author of the book *50 plus one Tips When Hiring & Firing Employees* (Encouragement Press, ©2006)

Ms. St. Aubin received a M.B.A. from Northwestern University, Evanston, Illinois and a B.A. from the College of St. Catherine, St. Paul, Minnesota. She is a member of the Human Resource Planning Society, ASTD, Human Resource Management Association of Chicago and the National Association of Women Business Owners (NAWBO). She is also active in church and community organizations.

Brian J. Carlsen has over 15 years experience in corporate training and organization development. His experience centers around facilitating leadership and interpersonal skill training, planning and facilitating meetings, coaching executives and teams, and developing effective programs for learning and change.

Brian's role for St. Aubin, Haggerty & Associates is one of providing training design, coaching and classroom facilitation expertise. Brian has developed and delivered training in leadership and supervisory skill areas such as performance management, organization and team leadership, career management, facilitation skills, listening skills, business ethics, effective presentation skills, decision-making and problem solving, selling skills and creativity. He has facilitated small and large group meetings to do strategic planning, make decisions, and build teams. Brian has also facilitated experiential outdoor education, team-based executive sales simulations, and has served as master instructor to certify other trainers. He is a certified facilitator of Myers-Briggs Type Indicator* and Extended DISC*.

Mr. Carlsen received his B.A. degree in History and English from Augsburg College, Minneapolis, Minnesota. He received his M.Ed., Business Education-Training and Development from the University of Minnesota. Brian is a member of the American Society of Training and Development (ASTD), is listed in *Who's Who in American College and University Students* and has been quoted in a *Fast Company* Magazine article on Executive Presentation Skills.

Acknowledgements

This book reflects the ideas and contributions of a number of individuals. There are four in particular who have helped in special ways to translate our ideas into the finished product. They include:

- **Sara Stutz,** a student athlete at Northwestern University who while serving her practicum with St. Aubin, Haggerty & Associates, Inc., gathered research to support a number of the topics that we have written about here.

- **Jerry Orf** collected research, helped to craft and fill out a number of chapters while also reviewing drafts and making helpful suggestions for finalizing concepts.

- **Monica Gavino** who not only wrote the chapter, *Sustaining a Climate of Respect and Inclusion,* also provided research and collaboration in the development and field testing of key models used in the book.

- **Dana Savocchi** who had the task of working with us over the past year to project manage the on-time completion of this book, making it ready by reviewing and providing first editing of all chapters before submission to our editor and publisher.

We also appreciate our clients who have trusted us to help guide their journey to attract, engage and retain top talent. Their stories are found throughout this work and helped to add reality to the research and models presented.

Table of Contents

Introduction

Leaders of great organizations have learned the strategic worth of sustaining a full and ever developing talent pipeline and of unleashing the real desire all talented people share to contribute value. It starts with attracting and hiring the best talent for your enterprise. You are known as a magnet for talent by establishing an appealing employment brand. An organization with a superior employment brand is one whose leadership and workforce behaviors match the company brand. This means that the value proposition for the business is reflected in the actions of the employees at all levels of the organization. We know from recent organizational studies that productivity, earnings and return on investment is superior in organizations with strong culture and employment brands.

Even for organizations that attract the right talent, the challenge remains to engage them in their work and to retain them longer than the competition. Engaged and committed employees are proud to work for their employer, are dedicated to the organization and willing to give the extra effort necessary to achieve the goals of the enterprise. Engagement is a leading indicator of financial performance. Companies that increase their engagement levels can expect to significantly improve their subsequent financial performance.

Two studies conducted by Towers Perrin–ISR, a Chicago-based HR research firm, resulted in these findings:

- A 52 percent difference in 1-year performance improvement in operating income between companies with high vs. low employee engagement. (High engagement companies improved 19.3 percent. Low engagement declined 32.7 percent.)
- A 13.2 percent improvement in net income growth over a one-year period for companies with higher employee engagement.
- A 5.75 percent positive difference in operating margin and 3.44 percent positive difference in net profit margin of high vs. low employee engagement companies.

Forward-thinking leaders have discovered that an opportunity exists to thrive in the competitive marketplace by better engaging the hearts and minds of employees– and in *Attract, Engage & Retain Top Talent* we explore a myriad of approaches to go about doing just that. The ideas within these pages emerge from experiences and lessons learned from organizations seeking to excel by unleashing the talent of their people. As you seek to undertake talent pipeline initiatives, remember that no organization can or should do everything. It is important to deeply understand the unique leadership strengths of your organization, strategic business drivers, market demands, differentiating competencies and workforce requirements in order to craft your unique approach to attract, engage and retain the talent that is needed to accelerate success.

Leadership is both art and science. Building your organization into a preferred employer with an engaged workforce and a culture that retains the right people doing the right things requires inspiration and hard work. We hope that this book will serve as a blueprint or at the very least an idea generator for the creation or re-creation of your desired place to work.

Donna de St. Aubin

Brian J. Carlsen

plus one
Engage & Retain Through the Employee Life Cycle

After working for the last 20 years with clients who have a desire to impact their organization's performance through positive and meaningful employment practices, and through our own and others' research, St. Aubin, Haggerty & Associates, Inc. has developed the following model for engaging and retaining talented and satisfied employees.

Figure 1.1

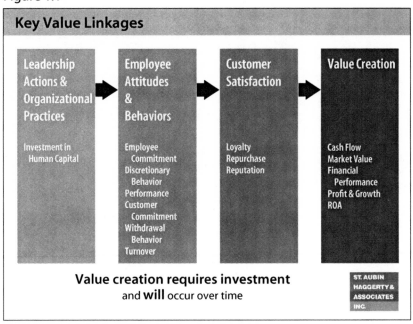

The Key Value Linkages Model and existing research suggest that investments you make in your employees (pillar one) strongly influence how employees feel and what they believe about the organization, which directly influence their behaviors (pillar two). When these feelings and beliefs are positive, customer relations and retention are improved (pillar three) and enterprise value is created over time (pillar four). Conversely, when leaders do not drive practices that attract and more fully engage talented employees, the likelihood of high organizational resilience or competitive advantage is alarmingly reduced. The chapters of this book are all linked back to this endeavor, i.e., how your investment in organizational and leadership practices can create an engaged, talented workforce that is committed to the organization's goals and, over time, builds loyal customers and value for the enterprise.

Look more closely at each pillar to understand how employees are affected by such practices throughout his or her employment life cycle.

Pillar One

Leadership Behaviors

Leadership behaviors directly impact how employees feel about working for a particular organization. As a leader, you create visions and establish values that resonate with your investors and customers as well as your employees. These visions and values create cohesion and commitment within the hearts and minds of your employees as they come to see their work as a fruitful contribution linked to a higher purpose. Even further, when the employment brand of an organization is attractive to the kinds of talent required to excel in the marketplace and drive toward the vision, employees are engaged from the very start of their careers.

Organizational Practices

Organizational practices are those that encourage or enable a desirable culture within the workplace. Practices that are most engaging to employees–that create loyalty and intention to stay and do excellent work–prompt positive answers to employee questions like these:

- Am I welcomed and valued here?
- Do I have good growth opportunities?
- Can I contribute by using my strengths?
- Do I like the people with whom I work?
- Do I get the support and resources I need to do a good job?
- Do I fit in? Am I proud to belong to this organization?

Your organizational practices will influence the culture of your workplace and your employees' entire cycle of employment. They include key work dimensions such as:

- **Hiring practices.** The type of employees you hire and the manner by which they are sourced and managed throughout the hiring process. These practices also include your employment brand, strategic staffing and forecasting, and, finally, the process of recruiting and selecting talent into the organization. The process continues as new employees are oriented and assimilated into the job and the company.

- **Performance management.** Objectives and goal setting processes followed by feedback. The approach you use to communicate with employees about how they are doing and what they need to do in order to attain high levels of sustained job performance is key. Your employees' feelings and beliefs will be more positive when these processes are seen as helpful, i.e., developmental and opportunity increasing, rather than punitive and opportunity limiting.

- **Training and development.** Programs and processes that provide employees with knowledge, skill enhancement and experiences to improve existing abilities and to prepare them for future responsibilities. The quality of professional growth opportunities through training, developmental experiences and coaching are major factors in why employees stay with an organization.

- **Providing career opportunities.** Knowing what experiences will provide desired challenge and growth for the employee while assisting the organization to meet its goals is an important element in engaging and retaining your top talent.

- **Involving employees in the way things are done.** Organizations that elicit employee feedback and participation in the creation of an environment that supports its vision and values find that employees are more likely to stay because they have become invested in successful outcomes.

- **Listening to your workforce.** Measuring and adjusting your leadership and organizational practices are needed to ensure that the organization's investments are the ones that will create value through employee engagement and retention into the future.

The investments you make in both leadership and the above practices will translate directly into the attitudes and behaviors of the organization's employees.

Pillar Two

Employee Attitudes & Behaviors

Various research studies (many of which are cited within the chapters of this book) have shown that strong, positive employee attitudes lead to commitment in the organization's future, which can be measured in the following three areas:

1. Strong belief in the organization's goals and objectives.
2. Willingness to exert considerable effort on behalf of the organization.
3. Strong desire to maintain membership in the organization.

Commitment, or lack thereof, is one of the most powerful employee attitudes that manifest in both positive and negative behaviors.

Figure 1.2

On the positive side, organizations with a more committed workforce experience:

- Higher levels of performance by employees;
- increased productivity from those who are committed to the mission;
- extra effort behaviors, i.e., going above and beyond what is expected;
- better safety records; and
- reduced shrinkage.

On the negative side, organizations with a less committed workforce experience:

- Higher turnover rates;
- aggressive behavior;
- higher intentions to leave;
- higher absenteeism; and
- increased tardiness.

Commitment is contagious and infects not only the other employees in the organization but the customers of these companies as well. A high level of employee commitment is a home run; companies with highly committed employees outperform similar companies on significant performance metrics. On the other hand, a less committed workforce may spell trouble.

Pillar Three

Customer Satisfaction

Customer commitment (attitude) leads to improved customer service (behavior) and, ultimately, customer satisfaction (outcome). In work done by Heskett, Sasser, Schlesinger, Maister and others called the Service-Profit Chain, studies tie employee satisfaction to customer satisfaction, leading to:

- loyalty
- repurchase practices
- reputation

With committed employees creating loyal customers who continue to repurchase and expand the company reputation in the market, it is easy to see how greater value is created. According to "Putting the Service-Profit Chain to Work," employees in customer-facing positions *are happiest when they are empowered to make things right for customers and when they have responsibilities that add depth to their work.*

Pillar Four

Value Creation

Increases in value can be actualized in a variety of ways:

- Customers paying on time or even in a shorter cycle, which increases cash flow.
- Customers willing to pay a higher price because of perceived higher value.
- Repeat business reducing the amount of administrative selling or marketing costs.
- Customers referring business that expands reputation and reduces selling costs again.
- High employee satisfaction, which reduces turnover and increases productivity making the profitability of the firm greater and contributing to higher market valuation.
- An organization with lower than competition employee turnover, greater sales growth and higher margins that has a greater return on assets, thus having a true competitive edge.

There are a number of examples that show how value is higher when your customers are both loyal and feel that they have received a high level of service, which creates a desire to purchase more or even allows your organization to charge a higher price.

Culture & Environment

Looking at the model in Figure 1-1, notice the arrows that point from each of the pillars. These arrows signify that leadership behaviors and organizational practices together create a specific, engaging culture and environment. Over time, the culture and environment impact employee attitudes and behaviors, which creates a customer culture and environment leading to customer loyalty, repurchase and reputation in the market. This becomes your brand.

Investment

Value creation requires investment in leadership and organizational practices and will occur over time. An initial investment will not show an immediate return on that investment but should pay off in positive ways over a reasonable time period. If the investments are made over the life of one employee, for example, here are some things you can expect:

- **Selection**–A candidate feels good about the company not only by what he has heard prior to applying for a job but because of how he was treated in the interview process. He is also impressed by the quality of the people with whom he will work if he is hired.

- **Performance planning and feedback**–Because the employee is clear about what is expected and learns how she is doing toward those expectations, she is able to see the impact that she is making and willingly gives extra effort in the hopes of improving the way the customer feels about doing business with the organization. In fact, she is more likely to talk her friends into seeking a job in the same company. When employees help their friends find work in the same company, it reduces the cost of recruitment, increases the level of talent in the organization and increases the level of engagement of these employees.

- **Training and development**–An employee has performed at a high level for the last 2 years, for example, and is now interested in exploring opportunities to grow, learn and provide value in other areas. Because of good training, opportunities to participate in company projects outside of his direct job, the employee has gained good experience and exposure to other areas. Instead of going outside the organization to find experienced talent, the organization promotes the internal candidate. And instead of seeking growth opportunities outside of the company, the employee feels good about internal opportunities and works harder to demonstrate that the promotion decision was a good one. This encourages greater loyalty and commitment to the organization along with a great deal of extra effort.

- **Career opportunities**–With the training mentioned above and the opportunities to get involved, more and varied opportunities within the organization continue to present themselves to the employee. Such opportunities create a hopeful, positive view of the future that feels more comfortable than taking a chance with another firm that has not demonstrated the same willingness to promote and invest in him or her. This reduces the level of turnover that impacts productivity, morale, culture and satisfaction.

- **Involvement**–When employees feel they have the ability to influence the process and quality of work life, select who works for the organization and change how people experience organizational life, it is exciting and engaging.

Summary

Employees who are engaged and involved are less likely to feel negative about the company and more likely to look for ways to continue to improve it, to support others in doing great work and to aid the organization in servicing its customers and realizing its goals. Engagement doesn't happen by accident. It takes dedicated leaders to sustain a high-quality culture, healthy relationships, barrier-eliminating processes and clarity of vision. People thrive when they work alongside people who show them respect and support, and when they are contributing to something they see as valuable and worthy. Attracting, engaging and retaining top talent does not happen overnight, but it can be accomplished over time and leads to fulfilled employees and competitive advantage.

Resources

"Putting the Service-Profit Chain to Work," *HBR OnPoint*, March 1994

The Value Profit Chain, Simon and Schuster, New York, ©2002.

Part One

Attract:
Defining Your
Employment Brand

1

Aligning Your External & Internal Brand

Employer, or internal, branding is the process of defining the relationship employees can expect to have with their employer and managing the perceptions around that relationship. Employer brands help companies respond to current and prospective employee expectations.

A company with an outstanding employer brand is one whose internal brand matches its external brand. This means that the value proposition the company defines is mirrored by the actions of employees at all levels on a consistent basis.

Internal branding is about building an image in the eyes and minds of the current workforce, and the prospective employment pool, that this organization is a good, if not excellent, place to work.

External brand is a product, service or concept that is publicly distinguished from other products, services or concepts so that it can be easily communicated and marketed. A brand name is the name of a distinctive product, service or concept. Branding is the process of creating and disseminating the brand name. Branding can be applied to the entire corporate identity as well as to individual product or service names.

An organization's external brand displays its products and services to its customers. The internal brand identifies and describes its relationship with its employees. The internal brand is a way for an organization to tell the employment world who they are and what can be expected.

A key to achieving a strong internal brand is to align the company's mission and values with its external brand. If companies expect employees to demonstrate natural brand behavior when dealing with customers, the link between external and internal messages has to be immediately visible.

At the heart of internal branding is the understanding of what it is like to work for a particular company and what drives employees' desire to keep working for that company. There is also a need to understand what would attract a future employee to the company. By focusing on the employer brand, companies can better understand the attributes most likely to attract new recruits to the organization, allowing them to alter the recruitment strategy accordingly. It also allows them to retain the top talent in whom they have already made a significant investment.

Examples of companies that have worked hard to align their external and internal brand are Starbucks in the retail sector and The Ritz-Carlton in the hospitality industry.

Starbucks spends virtually nothing on traditional marketing yet has created a culture in which staff know how to behave in a manner that supports the brand, in their attitudes to customers, each other, their presentations, etc. All of these say something about their brand and help fulfill the brand promise.

Howard Schultz, Starbucks chairman, is quoted as saying, "Ultimately, Starbucks can't flourish and win customers' hearts without the passionate devotion of our employees. In business, that passion comes from ownership, trust and loyalty. If you undermine any of those, employees will view their work as just another job…their passion and devotion is our number-one competitive advantage. Lose it, and we've lost the game." He went on to say, "When I looked back, I realized we fashioned a brand in a way no business school textbook could ever have prescribed. We built the brand first with our people, not with consumers—the opposite approach from that of the crackers and cereal companies. That's the secret power of the Starbucks brand: the personal attachment our partners feel and the connection they make with our customers."

Howard Schultz had a vision in the 90's to serve a great cup of coffee. Attached to this vision was a principle: to build a company with soul. This led to the development of practices that were unprecedented in the retail industry. For example, all employees working at least 20 hours a week get comprehensive health insurance and employee stock options. These practices led to strong employee loyalty, low turnover and strong commitment, even though salaries were lower than the competition.

The values of respect and caring are provided to each employee in a *Green Apron Book*, which exhorts employees to *be genuine and considerate*. In addition, the company works hard to treat coffee growers in developing countries with dignity while purchasing their products at above market prices.

The alignment of vision, values and action in the external and internal brand are clear and compelling in Starbucks' overall results.

The Ritz-Carlton carries one of the highest brand profiles in the hospitality industry. The company has worked to align the internal brand with this high profile external brand by its motto,

> *We are Ladies and Gentlemen serving Ladies and Gentlemen.*

It also publishes a credo:

> *The Ritz-Carlton is a place where the genuine care and comfort of our guests is our highest mission. We pledge to provide the finest personal service and facilities for our guests who will always enjoy a warm, relaxed, yet refined ambience. The*

Ritz-Carlton experience enlivens the senses, instills well-being, and fulfills even the unexpressed wishes and needs of our guests.

The Ritz-Carlton also publishes its service values, which begin with *I am proud to be Ritz-Carlton* and goes on to detail 12 items to which all employees must commit.

Starbucks and The Ritz-Carlton are two unique yet visible examples of aligning the external brand with the internal brand.

Organizations that seek to develop their employer brand are aiming to enhance their profile both internally and externally. This requires specific insight into what is driving perceptions of an organization. What underlies one employer brand will differ from another. To develop a strong employer brand, you must know what is specific and unique about your organization and the culture that creates the actual brand.

Developing a Strong Employer Brand

A strong employer brand elevates the company to a desired status where people want to work for you and look for ways to be considered for any open position that might get their foot in the door. A strong employer branding strategy provides:

- A common theme, so that current employees express similar views on their experiences with the company.
- Visibility for the organization and for its products and services.
- Encouragement to job seekers to apply for opportunities within the organization.
- Information about the company's work practices, career development, and culture and environment.
- Reinforcement for current employees as to the quality of the workforce and the value of employee contributions.

Building an employer brand strategy takes time and effort. It usually starts with using any and all product or service marketing opportunities to link employment benefits. Following are nine suggested steps for building your employment brand.

1. **Define your current employment brand.** Know where you stand right now with your employees and in the marketplace. In order to build an effective employment brand, know the strength of your present brand and how it relates to your present needs.

2. **Identify successful branding strategies in other organizations.** Be able to recognize successful branding strategies. Look at other organizations and identify what they have achieved through their branding efforts. You can learn a lot from organizations whose branding efforts have succeeded as well as those that have failed. Know what you must do to make your branding project successful, then develop a to-do list that will give your organization a reputation as a great place to work.

3. **Identify the target market (candidates) for the branding effort.** What types of candidates would you like to attract: college graduates, experienced professionals or both? What are their target profiles, and where will you find them? The answers to these questions will help you determine the methods by which you should advertise your brand.

4. **Know your competitors' branding strategies.** Look at your product competitors as well as your employment competitors. What messages do they project? How do those messages complement or detract from the messages your organization projects?

5. **Assess what your organization currently offers.** Examine your management practices, benefits and company culture. Identify what you do well and what you need to improve or enhance. Identify those areas in which you have the edge. For example, a larger organization can focus on career advancement, while a smaller organization can focus on employees' individual accomplishments.

6. **Create a talent forecast.** Define what your needs for talent will be over the next two or three years. What critical skills, experiences and capabilities will be required to handle your future business challenges?

7. **Develop a branding plan to build awareness.** Use the information you have gathered to build a detailed action plan. This should include those messages you would like to convey to candidates regarding:
   - company culture
   - current workforce
   - image as leader in industry or community
   - learning and growth
   - management style
   - long-term opportunities
   - employment image
   - quality products

8. **Get internal buy-in to the plan.** Your branding strategy will not succeed if your managers and employees don't agree to it. A strong employment brand is consistent both within and outside the organization.

9. **Monitor your progress.** Once you have implemented your branding plan, track its success through surveys, focus groups and exit interviews. Know how others view you as an employer, and know how their views are shaped by your plan.

Resources

Visit *www.drjohnsullivan.com* to find several articles on employment branding.

50 plus one Tips When Hiring & Firing Employees, (Encouragement Press ©2006.) Chapter 7: Attracting Candidates: Employment Branding offers more information on this topic.

2

Your Employees
Are Your Brand

In the branding world so much time and money is spent on and aimed at external audiences, but many in the communications and public relations fields feel that branding has internal implications as well. In fact, there is a belief, at least among specialized practitioners, that in many ways employees are the brand and should be treated as a priority.

Every company brand needs internal champions–its employees–who impact, mold and convey the brand values to various publics. Indeed, the employees could be the determining factor in the brand's success or failure.

Senior leaders are often passionate about their brands, but what about everyone else? There must be an environment where everyone from the top down understands and views employees as those who deliver on the brand promise every day in every way.

The following quote is from the Honeywell website and outlines how the company feels about the role its employees play in the brand:

> *Every Honeywell employee is a brand ambassador. With every customer contact and whenever we represent Honeywell, we have the opportunity either to strengthen the Honeywell brand, or to cause it to lose some of its luster and prestige. Generations of Honeywell employees have built our powerful brands with their hard work, spirit of innovation, passion for quality, and commitment to customers. I am counting on every Honeywell employee to continue that legacy as we strive to keep our brand promise and build a better world.*

Examples of how employees demonstrate their company's brand occur with regularity. One early morning experience at an airport's Delta Air Lines departure gate is a case in point. Most of the travelers were quietly reading newspapers, talking on cell phones or just staring off into space. Gate representatives were checking people in for the flight and making what seemed to be the usual announcements. One such announcement requested that Mr. Pitt and Mr. Clooney please check in at the departure desk. A few people slowly looked up as if questioning if they had heard right. Then another announcement was made asking for those who had not yet arrived at the airport to please check in at the front desk, which created a little more stir in the crowd. With an unintentional nod to the successful branding of Southwest Airlines, one man was overheard saying to a friend, "What does he think this is–Southwest?"

Southwest Airlines is well-known for hiring employees who are relaxed and like to have fun, and the Delta employee was viewed as demonstrating brand behaviors associated with Southwest, a great demonstration of how employees' behavior has an impact on the brand.

Brand Types

Branding theory classifies employees into four types:

1. Brand champions are storytellers who spread the brand idea.
2. Brand agnostics are interested but not committed.
3. Brand cynics are not involved with the brand idea.
4. Brand saboteurs work actively against the brand idea.

There is no doubt that every company needs and desires brand champions. To determine the kind of environment that helps create brand champions, consider the following questions:

- How well is the company's mission and vision communicated in the organization? (Read more about this in Chapter 7.)
- How well have employees understood and accepted this vision?
- How empowered do employees feel to act on the vision?

The following story illustrates this last point.

Ailsa Petchey, a flight attendant with Virgin Atlantic Airlines, was organizing a wedding and experiencing all the issues associated with that task. She felt it would be easier to have one place that would be able to organize all of the details, so she took the idea to Richard Branson, Virgin's CEO. The result of that conversation was a new business, Virgin Brides, a chain of one-stop shops that cater to brides and all they need to plan a successful event.

Could this happen in your company? Could an entry-level employee feel they could come to senior management with an idea that fit the brand and be rewarded for it?

Most people feel that branding is the work of the CEO or a brand management group alone, or that internal branding belongs solely to the human resource department. In truth, successful branding belongs to every one of a company's employees. Indeed, the message must be communicated throughout the organization, and even more importantly, it must be internalized by the culture and demonstrated through actual behavior.

Author and speaker Anders Gronstedt has outlined four "S's" that will transform your employees into proud, effective brand ambassadors.

1. Storytelling

Storytelling is an art that many organizations find helpful when teaching brand messages. In fact, there are companies that specialize in teaching the art of storytelling. Their messages about founders, family members, heroic events and the like are used to ingrain the brand message into the hearts and minds of employees.

At the Mayo Clinic, for example, there is great pride in telling the story of the Mayo family, who funded the clinic's first microscope by mortgaging their house–they felt so strongly that it was important to the care of their patients.

At Nordstrom, stories are told routinely about the ends to which an employee will go to satisfy a customer, thus demonstrating the brand message.

At American Hospital Supply Corporation (now part of Cardinal Healthcare), the company's early lore is full of stories about how a sales representative or a customer service representative went above and beyond to ensure that a hospital had a critical product it needed to perform life transforming, and sometimes lifesaving, medical procedures.

If you want to capture the imagination of the frontline employees, tell them a story. Companies that are successfully *living the brand* use the art of storytelling to energize their employees.

2. Simulating Employee–Customer Interaction

Simulations can take storytelling to a higher level. This process allows participants to actively engage in creating the story that illustrates the brand behaviors.

People learn best by doing, and simulations allow employees to use their knowledge again and again before having to do so with customers. It also allows participants to practice and solidify behaviors without fearing that they may have not represented the brand appropriately with key customers.

Put employees into the live action of a customer service simulation, letting them practice the tasks they will be expected to master in their daily job– before they start demonstrating brand behaviors with real customers.

3. Selecting Top Performers

A company's desire to have everyone live the brand starts with hiring the right people who have a predisposition to the valued behaviors. Once top performers have been hired, your job is to turn them into brand ambassadors. It is easier to do so if desired behaviors have already been in evidence during the interview and selection process.

Brand ambassador training begins before the new employee actually starts his or her job. New hires can read company histories and participate in simulation exercises so you can see how they will handle the varied situations they will be confronted with on the job.

Hire top performers by assessing their attitudes and observing their behavior in simulated customer interaction scenarios.

4. Surveying

Most employees have opinions about how products and services are viewed by others. Ask them what they think; articulating their opinions will help them understand the link between the brand and their views of the brand.

Internal surveys help strengthen the brand messages among your employees and provide valuable information that may impact the product or service for the customer. In the long run, this goes a long way toward improving delivery of the brand message.

Try shifting your focus and resources away from external consumer marketing research to study your own employees' opinions, ideas and behaviors. They are the ones you count on to deliver on the external marketing promises.

Summary

If you accept the premise that customers own the brand, then you will surely agree that your employees–who form an intrinsic part of the brand and are ultimately responsible for delivering on its promise–also own part of the brand. A credible brand, therefore, is based on both external market forces and the internal reality of employee culture and values.

Your employees are your brand. They deliver on the brand message every time they have an interaction with one another and with your clients and customers. Make sure they are delivering the brand you want.

Resources

"Living the Brand: How to Turn Frontline Employees into Brand Ambassadors," *Communications World*, September-October 2004.

The Employer Brand: Bringing the Best of Brand Management to People at Work, John Wiley & Sons, ©2005.

3

Your Website &
Your Brand

Branding can be accomplished through many channels, including direct mail, print advertising, radio, special events, internal communications and through your own corporate website.

While all of these media options play an important role, the most important is the website. Organizations with excellent recruiting websites have the greatest number of qualified candidates, the most satisfied hiring managers and the lowest costs per hire.

Firms like Lowe's and Federated Department Stores have developed exciting and engaging websites that attract so many candidates they have been able to move print advertising dollars into other recruiting activities.

Lowe's is the second largest home improvement retailer worldwide. Lowe's opens a new store every 3 days, recruits more than 60,000 employees a year and employs more than 210,000 employees in the continental United States.

The store positions, which generally require a high school degree and some retail experience, are not difficult to fill due largely to the company's success in building a strong customer brand. They have also focused an equal amount of attention on building a strong employment brand to ensure a steady flow of top candidates for its many jobs.

Lowe's consumers know the organization for its wide, well-lit aisles and bright, easy to see displays. "We want our recruiting tools to simulate our stores with a brighter electronic environment that will entice candidates to work for Lowe's," says Catherine Keown, Lowe's director of recruiting.

Almost 75 percent of all corporate-level candidates come in through the Lowe's website. Making this website match the brand was an important step in the recruiting process.

Another example of a strong web-brand situation is that of Federated Department Stores. FDS, Inc. is the nation's largest operator of department stores, located in all major regions of the United States. In early 2001, FDS developed a strategy to control recruitment costs, broaden the applicant pool, increase quality and reduce time to fill open positions. This strategy included extending the FDS consumer brand to its employment brand. Because FDS owned and operated both Macy's and Bloomingdale's it needed a way to align and balance recruitment to the market and the brand. Thus was born the concept of retailology.com.

The tool *www.retailology.com* is a recruiting website used to fill positions in all functions and at virtually all levels nationwide for both Macy's and Bloomingdale's. Retailology.com (and its affiliated brand-specific recruitment sites such as *www. macysjobs.com* and *www.bloomingdalesjobs.com*) has the richest search capability of any retailing recruiting website, allowing visitors to search for individual positions by location, department and/or title.

In 2005, retailology.com was named America's Best Corporate Careers website by Electronic Recruiting Exchange (ERE), a leading industry organization.

In particular, retailology.com was cited for its innovation in Interview Schedule Management. This technology improves the online experience for individuals interested in applying for positions. In the 10 weeks of Federated's 2005 holiday hiring period, for example, the company sent 91,000 automated invitations to interview for positions, resulting in 49,000 confirmed interviews. For holiday 2005, more than 20,000 employees were hired through the online system.

Retailology.com has been able to deliver a positive applicant experience, as well, while improving recruiter effectiveness and building brand differentiation.

These two examples demonstrate how a recruiting website can enhance a brand. Not all organizations may need or can afford to have such a high-level functioning recruitment website, however. The following outlines four different tiers of websites.

- **Tier 1: Basic** These websites are not interactive and have static content. There is no position or job profiler, i.e., the ability to complete a profile that would direct an applicant to the positions available. The basic tier usually does not contain added employment information beyond a static position description. Applicants are asked to mail or e-mail a résumé and no e-mail acknowledgement or response is generated by the website.

- **Tier 2: Information Oriented** These recruiting websites are still non-interactive but contain more information about the organization and the culture. They allow the applicant to cut and paste résumés or contain a basic profiler. This tier may auto acknowledge receipt of a résumé.

- **Tier 3: Marketing Oriented** This tier tends to be interactive with dynamic pages rather than static as found in the first two tiers. It contains a profiler function and may provide advanced screening. These sites will typically have features such as testing or self-assessment tools. In addition, Tier 3 sites will contain marketing and branding content that outline and underline the benefits of employment with the organization. Many of these sites also have audio and/or video streaming and provide a personal response to applicants using e-mail or voicemail within 48 hours of application.

• **Tier 4: Highly Interactive** This tier contains the best of the first three tiers plus highly interactive content. It usually contains extensive screening and/or testing tools with automated candidate disposition. It contains links to valuable information such as how to write a résumé or how to interview, etc. It also contains targeted marketing messages and personalized communications. Most Tier 4 sites now contain blogs and/or chat rooms for applicants.

Microsoft and IBM, two technology companies, have created very strong blogs and chat rooms for applicants as well as employees.

When a company is considering developing or enhancing a recruiting website, the following guidelines should be used.

1. **Make it easy to navigate.** Don't make it so potential employees have to work too hard. Make sure the homepage provides an obvious link to the career section of your website. If users find it too difficult to apply for a position on your site, they likely will choose not to.

2. **Make it interactive.** Return visits and time spent on the webpage increases with interactivity. An interactive website that does a good job of qualifying candidates provides a huge competitive advantage. The hiring decision makers review only pre-qualified candidates and don't waste time screening piles of résumés. Some sites allow candidates to enter their own profiles and sort those profiles to positions for which they qualify.

3. **Provide content over fluff.** Every candidate wants information, company philosophy, procedures for applying and an idea of what work life is like inside the company. The more worthwhile information you provide, the better match you will get between qualified candidates and your needs.

4. **Test useability and applicability.** Constantly improve and evolve the recruiting site to compete effectively with the changing talent marketplace. Benchmark against your competition for talent within multiple industries that may be after the same talent pool. It is also wise to survey your target market to find out if your branding efforts are appealing to the talent pool you are trying to reach.

Upon examination of the websites of a number of *Fortune's* "100 Best Companies to Work For" (June 22, 2007), there is one common theme that stands out: All of the companies make very positive statements about their concern for the people in their businesses. This concern for the people-branding theme is prevalent in the recruitment segment of their websites as is exemplified in the following statements from those sites.

Genentech is a company with a different approach-one where people are the purpose and strength behind its existence, the Google site says. *Enjoy what you do, where you do it, and the people you do it with.*

Whole Foods Market states, *Come grow with us. We recruit the best people we can to become part of our team.*

Network Applications states, *We offer a competitive compensation package, and we ensure that every employee is treated as they deserve to be, because, simply put, we want to keep the best talent right here.*

Of course any type of recognition, national or local, is also prevalent as is born out by these companies making reference to being chosen as one of the "100 Best Companies to Work For" on the careers section of their sites. Simply stated, if your company is recognized for a positive achievement, receives an award or is proud of an affiliation, include that in your website and get all the mileage you can out of it.

As a company you know what you want your company brand to convey. How you incorporate that into your recruitment site and employment brand can mean the difference between recruiting the kind of candidates that will carry on your company mission, values and reputation or losing out on those candidates.

Resources

Global Learning Resources, Inc. (*www.glresources.com*) hosts white papers and articles on web recruiting.

"Blogs: A New Frontier in Online Recruiting," *Workforce Management Magazine.*

"The 100 Best Companies to Work For," *Fortune* magazine, Jan. 22, 2007.

Creating a
Leadership Brand

There is much written about leadership and what makes for a good leader. It seems that there is a new book on the best-seller list regularly discussing the virtues of good leadership. So what then is a leadership brand? Some of the most recent work done in this area, by Dave Ulrich and Norm Smallwood, suggests that a leadership brand is "the identity of the leaders throughout an organization that bridges customer expectations and employee and organizational behavior."

In previous chapters we outlined an external brand as *a product, service or concept that is publicly distinguished from other products, services or concepts so that it can be easily communicated and marketed.* We defined employment brand as *the relationship employees can expect to have with the employer.* We also outlined that employees are your brand because they *impact, mold and convey the brand values to various publics.*

A leadership brand transcends individual leaders and becomes the institutionalization of the leadership process for that organization. The leadership brand connects the outside (external brand) with the inside (internal brand) and helps to manage the consistent delivery of the brand promise through the management of the talent and talent systems.

Leadership Brand Value

Those organizations that have developed a leadership brand have definitely reaped the rewards. The following organizations have a leadership brand that has helped them to boast a higher price/earnings (P/E) ratio than their competition in the industry:

- Boeing–aerospace: 26.2 (10-year average P/E) compared to General Dynamics 17.05
- Nordstrom–retail: 22 (5-year average P/E) compared to Federated 17.8
- GE–27.58: 10-year average compared to Siemens 18.96

The implication of this is that those organizations with branded leadership seem to increase customer and investor confidence in their ability to win in the marketplace.

It is a known fact that those organizations that have a strong employer brand find it easier to recruit good people and to retain them longer than those who do not.

How to Create Your Own Leadership Brand

Creating your own organizational leadership brand is a five-step process involving the following:

Figure 4.1

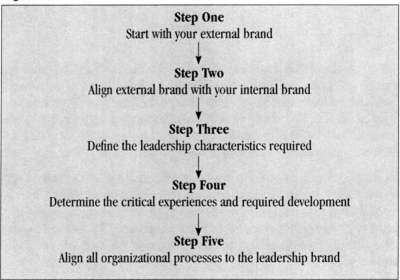

Step One
Start with your external brand

Step Two
Align external brand with your internal brand

Step Three
Define the leadership characteristics required

Step Four
Determine the critical experiences and required development

Step Five
Align all organizational processes to the leadership brand

Step One: Start with Your External Brand

This is a good time to look at your external brand and determine what it is saying about what you want to be known for in the marketplace. Do you have a statement or a message that is communicated consistently in all your external communication vehicles?

Recently a client-company went through this exercise, reviewing all of their external messaging, to realize that the brand message that was being developed and communicated to the outside markets did not match the view the new CEO had of what the target audience should be hearing. This prompted a realignment of the target audience, the messages that were being sent, and the desired outcomes of the newly crafted messages. Questions that were asked:

- Who is our target audience? Is there more than one?
- What is the message that we are trying to convey?
- Is the message consistent in each vehicle that we use?
- Will the message stand the test of time?

Step Two: Align External Brand with Your Internal Brand

In chapter one we outline how to align the external and internal brand. We highlighted that the external brand is a product, service or concept that is publicly distinguished from other products, services or concepts so that it can be easily communicated and marketed. The external brand displays its products and services to its customers. The internal brand identifies and describes its relationship with its employees.

The best way to achieve alignment between the two is to align the company's mission, vision and values with its external brand message. For example, if your brand message is that of a high level of customer support, your internal values need to include customer focus and support.

One of my favorite examples of a lack of alignment was with a new bank. The brand message that was being used was, *We are your local bank, we are here to service your needs.* As I was walking into the bank, I overheard a couple leaving the bank, the man saying to his wife, *They may think they are here to service our needs, but I don't think anyone has told that to the teller.* A clear mismatch between the desired brand message and the employees' behaviors was being observed.

A positive example of where real alignment was created is with Memorial Health Hospital in Savannah. At one point in time the hospital was struggling. It suffered from high turnover and lack of high occupancy in the hospital, and it ranked number three out of three in the local area. In looking at their brand they were not really distinguished from the other area hospitals and even their employees were not likely (as identified in a survey) to recommend the hospital to a friend or loved one. After spending time really looking into the brand message they wanted to convey, they looked first at the mission. They wanted it to be simple and straightforward.

The mission, which is now prominent on the website and in all external messaging, is as simple and straightforward as this: *We make people feel better.* This message is tied to the internal brand of being patient focused, highly collaborative and caring, and providing high-quality patient care, clinical insight and understanding.

There are clear links between the external brand and the internal brand. This has led to the hospital being selected as one of Fortune's top 100 companies for 3 consecutive years.

The message this sends is that of being clear about your external brand and aligning the internal brand to support the experience that you want each customer to expect.

Step Three: Define The Leadership Characteristics Required

When you have defined your external brand and your internal brand, you now have some of the information that will help you define the leadership characteristics that you require to manage the desired behaviors.

Start by asking a series of questions to some of your customers. Here are five sample questions to ask.

1. What is unique about this organization and the way they do business?
2. Where do you believe they struggle, if at all?
3. What have you come to expect the leaders to deliver in terms of value?
4. When you have observed a leader that has really impressed you, what is it that they are demonstrating?
5. When you have observed someone who has struggled or failed, what were some of the causes?

Analyzing the answers to these questions will start to give you a very clear picture of what a leader must demonstrate in order to manage to the customer's brand expectations.

Step Four: Determine the Critical Experiences & Required Development

Knowing what leadership characteristics are important to manage the brand behaviors leads you to the next step, which is how do we help develop these characteristics? There are three ways that this is accomplished.

1. Hire people who have or can demonstrate these characteristics. This is the most obvious and in some ways the easiest. What if you want to develop leaders from within?

2. Determine what key experiences leaders need to have in order to develop these characteristics. For example, one organization said they found that each of their leaders needed to have had a cross-functional experience early in their career. Another found that they needed to have worked in a high traffic customer-facing role, like a fast food restaurant or a customer service position.

3. Provide developmental opportunities within the organization in the form of specific assignments or specific education targeted to support the needed skills outlined.

The companies that are the best at doing this actually use all three of the above methods in determining the experiences and development required to ensure a successful grooming of the leadership brand.

Step Five: Align All Organizational Processes to the Leadership Brand

Step five is the most important step to ensure that all the processes used in the company actually support the leadership brand. The systems and processes that most support or guide the leadership brand include:

- **Selection**–the right people with the right characteristics are being hired.

- **Pay**–the pay practices are consistent with the talent market.

- **Performance Management**–the right goals are being encouraged and feedback is provided.

- **Promotion**–the right people are being promoted who match the characteristics and brand messages.

- **Development Planning**–the right development is available and the right individuals have access to it.

- **Succession Planning**–a process exists that allows a bench of talent to be groomed for the next level assignment.

Summary

Having a leadership brand will deliver a long-term payback that outlasts any individual leaders. It reinforces the product or service brand message by ensuring the necessary behaviors required by the internal employees to deliver on the brand promise.

Resources

"Building a Leadership Brand," *Harvard Business Review*, 2007.

5

Be a
Talent Magnet

The best way to win in the struggle for top talent is to make sure your company is a magnet for talent. You can learn a great deal about how to do this from the best companies to work for, based upon some of their practices.

The Great Place to Work Institute Inc., responsible for research on the characteristics of great workplaces as well as determining the "100 Best Companies To Work For" list published annually in *Fortune* magazine, suggests that one of the benefits of being a part of the 100 best is that the companies receive many more applications for employment than others in their industry. Having a reputation as a great place to work clearly is a draw for new talent while retaining talent longer in the organization.

Our own research and experience, along with the learning from the best, indicates the following practices can provide the foundation for becoming a talent magnet if not a best place to work.

Hire the Best

Good people are attracted to good people. In other words, having good talent matters. It makes no difference the type or size of your organization. Why are top sororities and fraternities able to stay on top? How do good sports teams encourage other athletes to want to join them? How do some companies seem to attract the highly sought after more than others? The answer is: By continuing to select top talent that adds to their reputation as a great organization. People want to be associated with the best. They want to be a part of something that will put them in good light in both the short run and the long run. One of the best ways to attract the best is to always hire the best. Companies get a reputation on college campuses based upon which candidates were made offers, which ones were accepted and which ones were rejected. When you have a reputation for hiring the best, you will attract the best.

Create the Right Buzz

Those products, services or organizations that seem to have a flair, or pizzazz, or buzz do much better than those without this quality. What we mean by the right buzz is the energy surrounding the organization, product, service or individual that attracts people toward it. Once the buzz is created, it brings people from all over to see what it is all about. A product buzz example would be the iPhone by Apple. There was so much buzz surrounding the introduction of this new phone that lines began to form 2 days before the product was to be sold in the store. This created positive buzz for the product and also the value of the company stock.

Negative buzz has the potential to shoot down the launch of a new product or even diminish the good an organization may have done. Negative buzz reduces the view someone may have of an organization and can adversely affect the value in the marketplace.

The right buzz has a positive viral marketing impact (the geometric multiplication of replications of your marketing message), which increases brand awareness. Having this positive buzz about your organization as a place to work draws people to you, making you a talent magnet.

Engage People Immediately

Great places to work are characterized by inclusive environments in which all employees are invited to participate in the cultural life of the organization. This means that people feel a part of the organization as quickly as possible. This should actually take place even before an individual is hired. Having people feel part of the company when they visit or apply for a job is not too soon to engage them in the culture. Make an attempt to have every person feel special and important. Treat each as an individual, with respect for their time and talents. When people feel this in the initial meeting they are more inclined to want to return.

Welcome new employees into the organization by making them feel special by using their name, introducing them to other employees and helping new hires get acclimated to the new environment. Help new members get to know the organization and the organization get to know them.

Provide Interesting & Meaningful Work

The lack of fulfilling work leads the list of reasons why people choose to leave employers. Meaningful work helps people have pride in both their own output and that of the organization at large. Today more than ever before, people are looking for work that they can feel good about. They want to tell their family and friends that what they do and what the company does provides a product or service with a purpose that goes beyond just the profit or earning contribution that is made. When you feel pride in your organization and the work that you do to support that mission, you are more likely to be committed and productive versus unhappy and looking elsewhere.

Reward, Recognize & Appreciate Good Performance

Research shows that recognition and appreciation is one of the strongest motivators of employee performance. Saying thank you goes a long way toward having someone feel that her efforts are appreciated. There are many ways, both formal and informal, that companies use to show appreciation. Here are a few to think about:

Formal
- Financial rewards (bonuses) for overachievement, company stock.
- Points for being on time, giving good service, good attendance, safety, etc., where you use your points to earn prizes.
- Employee of the month/quarter/year nominations that lead to days off, parking spaces, gifts and more.
- Incentive trips to desired locations for top performers.
- Service awards/banquets for tenure with the company.
- News articles in company publications.
- Travel upgrades for long hours and constant travel.
- Health club memberships.
- Participation in learning events.

Informal
- Personal notes, cards and letters of praise and appreciation;
- spontaneous celebration;
- open praise;
- bulletin board notice;
- public recognition;
- time off;
- spot awards of gift certificates;
- tickets to an event;
- company apparel; and
- participation in task group or company activity.

Continually Develop Employees

When employees have the opportunity to develop new skills, to grow personally and professionally, they usually feel a greater level of commitment to the organization that provided those opportunities. When this is done in a planned and well-executed manner, the entire organization is improved.

Using the organization to provide learning opportunities strengthens the actual learning more so than sending someone to a classroom experience. Creating opportunities for cross training, special assignments and action teams, engages employees and keeps them more interested.

Smart companies learn to do this in a way that builds talent for the future and creates the kind of workforce that makes it easier to recruit others who want to learn and grow and acquire new skills.

Respect & Value Diversity

Recognizing diversity of opinion, style and approach sets excellent organizations apart. Top employers know how to value and leverage differences in their people to create exceptional results.

Respect in the workplace takes the form of respecting each individual's time and expertise by being on time for meetings and letting them use their skills appropriately. Asking employees for input on how something might be accomplished rather than telling them how it should be done always shows respect for his or her abilities.

Respect outside the workplace is demonstrated by recognizing that people have a life beyond work and may require some flexibility to meet other commitments to family, civic organizations or charities.

Valuing diversity goes beyond race or gender. The workforce today is made up of different age groups and ways of thinking. It means that you are open to looking at different ways of thinking, working and learning. When people feel valued and respected they are not afraid to recommend others who are diverse to join the organization because they will have a chance to grow and prosper in this environment.

Summary

To be a talent magnet a company has to make sure it hires the kind of people that will attract others to the company and create the kind of positive buzz that will have people standing in line to be a part of the special magic that is in the air. Organizations must engage individuals from the very first opportunity and maintain it by providing interesting and meaningful work. Employees who are recognized and appreciated will perform better and longer than those who do not feel valued. Companies that develop people and provide career progression will attract more people than those who do not. Finally, valuing diversity and respecting people for who they are and what they bring will easily cause you to be a magnet for the best and the brightest. Keep that energy flowing.

Resources

www.greatplacetowork.com–The Great Place to Work˙ Institute publishes the list Best Small & Medium Companies to Work For in America.

1001 Ways to Reward Employees, Workman Publishing, New York, ©1994.

Part Two

Translating Business Strategy into Talent Needs

6

Creating a
Workforce Strategy

Workforce strategy is the planning process that integrates an organization's major goals, policies and actions into a cohesive whole. It is a process for analyzing an organization's competitive situation, developing the company's strategic business goals and devising a plan of action and allocation of resources (human, organizational and physical) that will increase the likelihood of achieving its strategy.

Workforce planning helps ensure that an organization has the right talent mix—by education, experience, capability and skill—to execute on its business strategy.

The need for strategic workforce planning has steadily increased with changing views of work, more individuals moving and changing positions more often, greater competition for highly talented employees and larger numbers of employees nearing retirement.

Workforce planning is not a one-time event. It is a continuous process that ensures an organization has the right talent in the right numbers, with the right skills, at the right time, in the right jobs to drive the achievement of the organization's goals.

The issues driving the need for workforce planning include the following:
- The workforce is aging.
- The workforce is diversifying.
- The work itself has shifted to a knowledge base,
- The workforce is shifting and changing in values and expectations.
- The competition for talent continues to escalate.
- Retirements are increasing, and thus a real brain drain of talent is anticipated.

Organizations that are unprepared face a very difficult challenge of attracting, engaging and retaining a workforce that is ready, willing and able to deal with new strategies, geography, technology and regulations.

Effective workforce planning provides many benefits to an organization. It provides:
- More effective and efficient use of talent in the workplace. This is so important to improving productivity and profitability.
- An effective staffing plan for dealing with retirements, promotions and anticipated expansions or contractions of product or business areas.

- A training and development plan for retention and new hires.
- A diversity and inclusion plan for anticipating talent pool availability or shortages for key areas of the business.

For workforce planning to succeed, it should answer questions regarding workforce characteristics today and into the future, and how organizational practices are supporting or developing these characteristics.

Gaining commitment for engaging in workforce planning is a critical step in an effective process. This can be done through some of the following techniques:

- **Gain support from senior leaders.** It is extremely important that senior leadership understands and buys into the value of workforce planning. Their support of the process can make or break its success.

- **Communicate the value of workforce planning to managers and employees.** Those individuals who need to be involved should understand the overall value to the organization and the individual employees in order to gain and maintain their support.

- **Involve key line managers in all steps of the process.** The line managers know the capabilities needed to be successful and can translate high-level business strategies into clear goals and expectations for the workforce.

- **Automate as much as possible.** It is helpful to have a common source of data and the ability to retrieve the data by different groups. The ease of data storage and retrieval makes acceptance more realistic.

- **Solicit continuous improvement feedback.** Once implementation has been completed, it is important to encourage feedback regarding those areas that can be improved for the future. This keeps the process fresh and maintains a continuous cycle of improvement.

The capability and comfort with completing workforce planning takes time to develop. Beginning slowly and getting all key parties on board is a good first step.

The Strategic Workforce Planning Model

Numerous models have been developed over time to conduct workforce planning. Essentially there are four critical phases to conducting this work.

Phase I: Direction Setting

Workforce planning is derived from the organization's strategic plan. The strategic direction of the organization outlines where the organization is today in the market and where it intends to go. It outlines plans for achieving its goals and requires a workforce plan that outlines the specific tasks and actions needed to ensure the organization has the resources to accomplish its goals.

A strategic plan charts the future with broad mission-related targets and milestones. A workforce plan translates strategic thinking into concrete action in terms of staffing, training, development and deployment. Phase I should answer these questions:

- What is the mission of the organization and will it change over the planning horizon?
- What are the key strategic drivers of the organization?
- What are the measurable goals to be achieved over the planning horizon?
- What are the future functional requirements of the workforce over the planning and budgeting horizon?

Figure 6.1

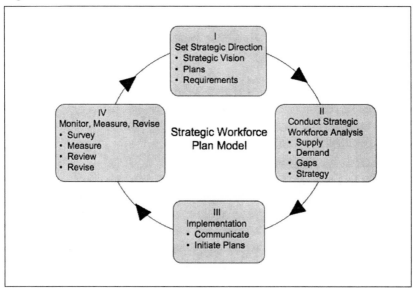

Phase II: Conduct a Workforce Analysis

Analyzing the workforce in light of the strategic elements outlined in phase I is a key element of the workforce planning process. This analysis usually includes information on how each function impacts the strategic drivers of the organization. The activity involves four steps.

Step 1: Supply Analysis

Supply analysis focuses on the specifics of an organization's existing workforce and projects future supply. A profile of the existing workforce helps to understand where the organization is in terms of the right number of people with the right skills. This type of analysis usually includes:

- number of employees and contracted workers
- skill assessment of employees and contractors
- workforce diversity (age, gender, race, etc.)
- turnover
- retirement eligibility statistics
- location
- trend data

Step 2: Demand Analysis

Demand analysis identifies the workforce needed to carry out the mission and strategy of the organization. In this step the focus is on both the number of employees needed and future skill requirements. This is completed by doing an environmental scan looking at trends and issues in the economic, social, technical, legal and regulatory areas. It is also good to view the status of the changing workforce and work patterns including demographics, outsourcing and occupational shifts.

The product of this step is a future workforce profile that outlines the number of workers and the skills needed to successfully complete the organization's strategic objectives.

Step 3: Gap Analysis

Gap analysis is the process of comparing the workforce supply projection in step 1 to the workforce demand forecast in step 2. The analysis should show where gaps exist in numbers or skills or where potential surplus may exist due to changes in technology, regulations, etc.

Step 4: Strategy Planning

The final step in the workforce analysis phase involves the development of strategies to address future gaps and surpluses. Strategies include programs and practices that might help to attract, retain, educate, develop and plan succession. Additional strategies might include looking at outsourcing certain tasks, contracting or eliminating certain operations going forward.

Phase III: Implement Strategic Workforce Plan

The workforce plan should have an implementation strategy aligned with the business strategy. There should be support from the leadership of the organization and the appropriate resources need to be allocated to perform the defined strategies. Timelines and performance measures also need to be detailed. Lastly, a good communication strategy must be implemented so that all involved will understand their role and expectations going forward.

Phase IV: Monitor, Measure & Revise

In this phase it is natural to assess what is working as planned and what is not working as desired. It allows for making needed adjustments to the plans and deals with any new organizational issues that affect the workforce.

There are many tools that can be used to help evaluate the success of the plans and actions. These tools include:

- employee surveys
- specific program evaluations
- turnover reports
- exit interview summaries
- customer surveys
- skills inventories
- performance review data analysis

Organizations that establish a regular workforce planning review process are able to assess what is working and what is not and make adjustments to the plans. New workforce and organizational issues can also be addressed when they occur.

Keys to Success

There is no doubt there is a need for a workforce strategy to deal with the rapid changes that take place in the business, community and talent pools. The keys to successful workforce strategy planning include:

- Keep it simple;
- secure top leadership commitment;
- involve key managers and employees;
- communicate value and progress; and
- monitor results and adjust as appropriate.

Resources

The Workforce Scorecard: Managing Human Capital to Execute Strategy, Harvard Business School Publishing, ©2005

Clarify & Communicate
Your Strategy to All Levels

Strategic success comes not simply from crafting a good, sound workforce strategy and implementation plan. Both are essential ingredients, but translating that strategy and plan into action requires communication and alignment with the course and direction, priorities and plans established. Executing strategy through the workforce requires a clear communication strategy as well. The following will outline first the steps involved and then the tools involved in communicating the strategy.

Step One

Identify the Various Publics or Audiences Impacted by the Strategy

In most companies, every employee plays some role in implementing a strategic vision. At different organizational levels, people need to understand what the strategy is, what they are expected to do and what they are not supposed to do. Often, employees fall into two or three groups that differ in a variety of attributes. Most management teams have little difficulty separating their audiences into a select number of groups.

Groups that differ in the type of work they do, the authority they have, their experience or level of sophistication will require different types of communication for best results.

One of the best examples of this idea was driven home in the early '90s when American Airlines was working on its vision alignment process. The desire on the part of the organization was, in part, to be the largest airline in the free world. Bob Crandall, the CEO at that time said, "This may have great meaning for those of us in corporate, but what does it mean to the baggage handler in Chicago? More work." He knew different communication strategies would be needed in order to get the message heard in a way that would get the right kind of buy-in.

In many businesses, success depends on the actions of other critical stakeholders. This might include boards or directors, bankers, investors, suppliers, etc. This is another group to be considered in the communication process.

When you complete this step, you will have identified a small number (two to four) of distinct audiences for which you will craft communications approaches.

Step Two

Detail Actions You Desire from Others

If people are going to do what you want, you will need to tell them. The two most common complaints of workers about their leaders are that they are not sure exactly what the leaders want from them and how well they are doing it.

Review the objectives and strategies you have developed and determine what you expect in terms of results and actions for each audience you outlined above. At the end of this step, you should know specifically each group's expected responsibilities and desired results.

Step Three

Decide What Information Each Group Needs

Different groups require different information to understand what they are supposed to do. Typically, managers must know the "what and why" of the firm's strategy to make the best decisions at various points in the future, since they deal with ambiguous situations. In contrast, more task-oriented workers need to know who, how and when, with emphasis on their specific tasks.

- **Mission Statements and Goals** contain the minimum, big picture information that all of the audiences will need to know.

- **Key Objectives** let your audience know the major initiatives you will be undertaking.

For audiences that need more specific information on who, what and when, you should have developed material on detailed action plans.

At the end of this step, you will have developed one of two levels of big picture information and you will have a set of specific, narrower, action-oriented information for each audience.

Step Four

Develop a Communication Approach for Each Audience

People have different communications styles and needs, and the message must be crafted to speak to each recipient of the information. The message can come from the CEO, the management team as a whole or the immediate manager, for example. The approach can be large group meetings, one-on-one presentations and almost everything in-between. For the audience you should answer the following:

- Who will present the message?
- What media will work the best to present the message?

Build in feedback mechanisms so that you can determine if the message has been understood completely.

Step Five

Reinforce the Message at Regular Intervals

Strategy is about change, and we all resist change at first. Saying something once is rarely enough to change behavior. Senior management has a clear responsibility to reinforce the communication of strategy constantly. There are a variety of tools that can be used to make sure that the strategy is being reinforced consistently. Not all of these tools need to be used but many of them are helpful with different audiences.

Communication Tools–Face-to-Face

All Employee Meetings

Gathering all employees to send a message that everyone hears at the same time is used by many organizations. This is often used when major events such as the following might be occurring:

- an acquisition or divestiture
- change in ownership
- change in key leadership
- change in strategy
- year-end results or new year objectives
- any other key message important to all

These meetings require good planning and orchestration in order to have the message be delivered in the best possible circumstances.

Not all organizations can afford this type of gathering due to the type of work or the global makeup of the organization.

All Employee Webcast

For organizations that are scattered or have multiple locations, an all-employee webcast can be used to deliver a message using technology that simulates all being together.

One company had two major locations, Chicago and New York, and an equal number of employees working out of each location. A year-end webcast was used to announce the recipients of the yearly awards and to set the stage for the next years' objectives. Each location was able to view what was happening at the other location.

Regional Meetings

For organizations that have regional sites, it may make more sense to do a traveling road show to present the key messages to each region in person. This choice may allow for tailoring of the message to fit the group or region.

Departmental Meetings

If different departments play a different role in the strategy, tailoring a series of meetings for different departments is something to consider.

Smaller Networking Meetings

Groups often gather at a conference or educational event. Scheduling time to network and discuss strategy, roles and expectations with the group at hand may be a preferred method of delivering information.

Communications Tools–Other Than Face-to-Face

Written Documents

Most strategic plans are written documents that include schedules, models and other supporting items. Most often there is an executive summary that can be used separately to provide the direction being taken without requiring all the back-up documents to make the case.

Newsletters

In-house newsletters can be a good vehicle for informing and reinforcing the core elements of the strategic message. These can be quite valuable as long as you are careful not to share confidential information that you do not want to get into the hands of a competitor.

Intranet

For organizations with a well-used Intranet, this can be a very good method of communicating the strategic intent and an ongoing method of highlighting the status and progress of the plan and various stages or schedules.

Voicemail Bulletins

Short and well-timed all-employee voicemail messages can also be a method of communicating various elements of the strategy. One CEO was quite famous for using voicemail to communicate key messages at least once a week. This is not the most effective way to reach your entire audience, yet it may be a good vehicle for a portion of your organization.

Two-Way Communications

It is important to build relationships with all key audiences. What channels are you going to use to get feedback, and how are you going to communicate what you did about what they told you? With any of these suggested communications channels, a feedback process should always be an element of the course of action so that a regular feedback loop is incorporated.

Summary

Ensuring success with your strategic plan and workforce strategy requires a sound communication strategy as well. Make sure you tailor your tools and activities to the level of time and human and financial resources available.

Resources

"Translating Vision Into Action: 8 Steps to Communicate Your Strategy," by Paul A.S. Minton, (*www.strategyletter.com.*)

8

Identify Mission Critical Positions

Successful implementation of any organization's strategy rests not solely on the right strategy but also on the recognition that some key positions will have more impact on the execution of that strategy than others. These positions we call mission critical. Some organizations may use the term pivotal positions. These positions are ones that you can clearly map to the specific execution of one or more of your strategic plan drivers.

The process of identifying these pivotal positions must rest within the organization and not be given to external markets or job evaluation processes. The identification of these positions is not about the level of the position or the title of the position but rather it is the specific role that it plays in the execution of the strategy.

For example, a group of human resource managers was asked to look at the Disney Theme Park organization and determine what position(s) they believed were most critical for executing the strategy. The following background information regarding the theme park business was provided to them:

- Walt Disney World in Florida contains four theme parks.
- It attracts more than 30 million visitors a year.
- It employs 50,000 people, the largest number of workers located at any one site in the United States.
- The theme parks are all based upon Disney movies, cartoons and characters.
- Employees are called cast members and undergo rigorous training.
- Employees are generally assigned jobs such as:
  - characters
  - shop merchants
  - maintenance engineers
  - creatives and animators
  - performers
  - food service
  - park sweepers and cleaners
  - executives

In using the list above there were good solid points of view in support of each role. This points out that every position plays a role in executing on the strategy, so how do you determine the pivotal or mission critical positions? If a strategic driver is to grow the amusement park business, which positions impact the execution of that strategy the most?

The Disney characters are important, of course, but a costume can be worn by various individuals somewhat interchangeably. The performers are also important, yet it is possible to shuffle the positions of the people who have the theatrical and voice talent while still maintaining a good show. In fact, many performers get their start at the park and then go on fairly frequently to other forms of entertainment not connected to Disney. The shop merchants are able to project an important image, too, but the actual merchandise has a stronger role in pulling in the customers than does the merchant. Food service and maintenance engineers are certainly important and, once again, are not the principal players in executing on the strategy. The creatives and animators may indeed be pivotal positions for the movie business but not so with the park business. The executives are certainly important for the development of the strategy but are not pivotal in the execution of that strategy. This leaves the sweepers and cleaners, those who are in plain view of the guests, answer questions and help guide the guests through the park and to events. They are visible and nonthreatening and know their way around the park.

Being able to identify the mission critical positions, the frontline sweepers and cleaners in this case, allows you to focus your efforts on the right selection, training and career track to meet the needs of the business.

Using this example, let's walk through how to identify these mission critical or pivotal positions in your organization.

Mission Critical Positions Are...

1. **Determined from key business objectives by function or business across the organization.** There is a need to break down the business strategy into key strategic drivers or objectives and then assess what functions have primary impact on driving that particular strategy. For example, if one of your business strategies is to introduce a new generation product each year for the next 3 years, you might see the research and development function as having primary impact on the development of these new product extensions. Depending upon the organization, the sales function may also be primary because of the role they play in introducing the product into the market.

2. **Disproportionately important to the organization's ability to execute some part of its strategy.** This means that the position within the function that is considered primary must have significantly more influence on the ability to execute that strategy than other positions. For example, it could mean that the sales representative has far more influence on the ability to execute than the sales trainers. Although the sales trainers are part of the sales function and have an important role in educating the sales reps regarding the new product, it is really in the hands of the frontline sales reps to make the sale.

3. **Indicated where there is a wide variability in quality of work (performance) by incumbents.** This means that there must be a number of incumbents in the position and that performance in the position is varied. There are those who execute in a superior manner, and there are those who seem unable to create the same level of results. For example, some sales reps consistently produce 110 percent of quota while others produce at 85 percent or less. This suggests that there are great gains to be made by bringing everyone up to the highest levels.

4. **Areas where competitors are likely not performing well.** If the competition seems unable to execute because of internal issues or market circumstances, this may be a perfect area for you to shine. Let's keep our example and suggest that the competition works through distributors rather than employing its own direct sales force. This is a weakness of the competition and thus something that can be considered a great opportunity to exploit–making the sales rep position a competitive advantage and thus a mission critical or pivotal position.

Mission Critical Positions Are Not...

1. **Determined by job level or compensation.** Many times a mistake is made in thinking that because positions closer to the top of the organization are more mission critical to the organization. This is not necessarily the case. It is an important position, and the market may suggest that it needs to be paid well, but it is not the same as a critical execution position.

2. **Determined by how hard the position is to fill.** There are some jobs that are extremely important to the success of an organization and are often hard to fill. This does not make them a critical execution position, just a critically important position. A position cannot be presumed to be a critical execution position just by virtue of being hard to fill or unique in qualifications.

3. **In functions that do not have primary ownership in executing some portion of the strategy.** If a function in an organization does not have primary impact on the execution of a strategy, you will not find a critical execution position; these positions cannot reside in supportive roles. For example, a sales trainer in a corporate training function who has an important role in training the sales organization on a new product may have a critical role but does not reside in the function that has the primary impact on execution even though he or she may support those who do.

4. **Determined by the individual in the position.** The key to critical execution positions is the positions themselves, not the incumbents. You do want to make sure that you put your best people into the most critical roles, but it is not the person who determines the criticality of the position but the role that the position plays in the execution of the strategy. Some individuals have the ability to raise the visibility of any role they assume;

keeping and using them in the right roles is important. The strategy and the position should dictate the type of incumbent necessary to execute effectively.

Summary

Mission critical positions are jobs that have significant influence on the execution of the firm's strategy and are critical to the firm's competitive advantage. In fact, mission critical positions have a disproportionate role in the company's success. In smaller organizations this may not be as important to determine, but as competition significantly impacts the market it becomes more and more important to assess where the most critical positions are in your organization for the best execution of your strategy. Once this is done you can measure the quality of the talent in those positions, the training and development that is spent on those positions and the performance ratios of incumbents in those positions. Identifying the right critical execution positions will impact your ability to compete in the marketplace at a level above the rest.

Resources

The Workforce Scorecard, Harvard Business School Press, ©2005.

Execution: The Discipline of Getting Things Done, Crown Business, ©2002.

9

Build a
Staffing Plan

A staffing plan can be defined as predicting and preparing for changes in the organization's workforce. This includes retirements, changes in job responsibilities and required skill sets. A strategic staffing plan is built to meet organizational goals. This process attempts to ensure that the demand for talent, which can change at any particular time in the planning horizon, will be met with the appropriate resources.

A strategic staffing plan is the process of identifying and addressing the staffing implications of business plans. This effort typically includes:

- Defining the number (staffing levels) and types (capabilities) of employees required in the future to implement business plans and strategies (demand);
- identifying resources that are currently available;
- projecting the supply of talent to meet defined future needs (supply);
- identifying the gaps between the forecasted demand and anticipated supply; and
- developing and implementing staffing plans and actions needed to close talent gaps and eliminate surpluses.

Successful execution of a strategic staffing process occurs not in how the above steps are defined but in how they are developed and implemented.

Defining the Number & Types of Employees Required

Usually strategic staffing plans are developed to provide input for both short- and longer-term expected needs. Managers often find it hard to predict the future as it relates to specific staffing needs, but asking them to think about long-term implications of the business strategy on staffing needs in the short run is a better way to think about the needs. Most managers can recognize the implications of business changes on the staffing requirements from the present position.

For example, a new product will be introduced in 2 years requiring an additional 25 sales representatives. How would needs like this be filled? Positions could be filled from outside hires, internal promotions from inside sales reps or use of temporary or contingent staff. To select the option or combination of options that will work best, the manager needs to look to the future to determine what will be happening that will suggest the best approach. Will another product be launched or will the product be integrated into the current sales organization? The answers to these longer-term questions will inform the choices that are made for the middle or near term.

The types of employees or the specific capabilities required are also a little difficult to determine if you do not look at it through the strategic business planning lens. Using the last example, assume that the 25 new sales reps required need experience selling pharmaceutical products in the cardiovascular area and none with that experience presently exist in the organization. You know that 25 sales reps are needed, and now you know they must have specialized knowledge and experience in a new area. This information will clearly change the sourcing strategy, i.e., knowing and understanding that the strategic plan calls for a significant increase in number along with a unique set of capabilities. This now reduces the probability of promoting from within.

Several different techniques can be used in demand forecasting, and two of the most common mathematical ones include:

- **Statistical projections**–using correlations and regression analysis to convert anticipated outputs to talent requirements. For example, the number of sales related to the number of sales reps required, or the number of production items related to the number of production employees, etc.
- **Experience curve projections**–as the number of units of production doubles, the number of direct labor hours it takes to produce a unit decreases by a constant percentage. Once the learning percentage is established, it is relatively easy to determine the number of direct labor hours needed, which then equates to the number of direct labor employees required.

A third technique, which is different from the above models, is the Delphi technique. This is subjective in nature. The objective is to predict future situations by integrating the independent opinions of experts. This method is helpful in generating good insights into future requirements, and talent implications, of the particular business.

Identifying Resources That Are Currently Available

A starting point in staffing planning is detailing the resources already in place. This activity is conducted by determining both the number and type of resources already in the system. The chart shown on the next page (Figure 9.1) is a general template of how to start with present talent by category and build expected changes over a 3-year period. This can be done by function, location, unit, etc., and then rolled up to the company level.

Strategic Human Resource Planning Guide

3 Year Talent Forecast Roll-up–Total Organization

Figure 9.1

	Executives	Managers & Supervisors	Professionals	Sales	Technicians	Administrative	Skilled Crafts	Unskilled Operatives	Totals
Beginning Year 1									
New Positions 2008									
Year 1 Turnover									
Internal Promotions									
Replacements									
End Year 1									
New Positions Year 2									
Year 2 Turnover									
Internal Promotions									
Replacements									
End Year 2									
New Positions Year 3									
Year 3 Turnover									
Internal Promotions									
Replacements									
End Year 3									
New Positions Year 4									
Year 4 Turnover									
Internal Promotions									
Replacements									
End Year 4									

Part of current resources is developing an attrition forecast. Your organization will want to specify assumptions based on factors specific to your company to forecast an attrition rate. These factors include estimates of the number of employees who will separate, i.e., resign, transfer, be dismissed or retire.

A general attrition rate is a calculation. For example:

$$\frac{\text{number of resignations} + \text{number of transfers} + \text{number of retirements}}{\text{the total number of employees}} = \text{attrition rate percentage.}$$

Projecting the Supply of Talent to Meet Defined Future Needs

The U.S. Bureau of Labor Statistics (BLS) collects a vast amount of data that can help you conduct supply analysis. BLS data include employment projections, occupational outlooks, demographic profiles and much more.

Identifying the Gaps between Forecasted Demand & Anticipated Supply

Gap analysis is the process of comparing information from the supply and demand analysis to identify the differences, or gaps, between the supply of and the demand for human capital. Gap analysis identifies situations when demand exceeds supply, such as when critical work demand, number of personnel or current/future competencies will not meet future needs. It also identifies situations when future supply exceeds demand, such as when critical work demands, number of personnel or competencies exceed needs.

Issues Facing Companies Today as They Relate to Building a Staffing Plan

In studies conducted by Towers Perrin (Global Workforce Study, 2005) and Development Dimensions International (with Monster, May 2007), a number of issues were identified that make staffing planning difficult.

- **Competition for talent** More than 30 million managers and leaders will retire within the next 5 years and far fewer than that are being added to the workforce. Companies are competing vigorously for the remaining talent.

- **Emerging markets** Most global companies are finding the need to move into the Eastern markets, and too many organizations are chasing a limited supply of talent in these markets as well. Companies feel compelled to place U.S. talent into these regions until they are able to find or grow local talent, putting a further strain on limited talent in the United States.

- **Silo thinking** Given competition, many organizations find it necessary to reduce headcount and focus talent on very narrow areas of expertise rather than involve more employees in broader systems thinking. This creates a more narrow and limited level of expertise in the workforce.

- **Decreasing numbers of skilled talent** As baby boomers begin to retire, the emerging Generation X workforce is not large enough to make up the difference. There are simply fewer people available, and those who are available oftentimes do not have the skill sets required for the business of today or tomorrow.

- **Talent as a competitive advantage** Successful companies have begun to understand that having and keeping good talent is a competitive advantage. This makes the work of recruiting away good talent more difficult for those who need them most, and it makes the work of keeping them engaged within the present organization a real priority.
- **Employees and occupational mobility** Employees find that they are more willing to follow their occupation and less committed to a certain organization. This has been true for quite some time as it relates to technology positions. The talent wants to follow a certain program or process and may be easily willing to leave an organization to follow the next generation system.

Summary

Strategic staffing planning creates a longer-term context within which more effective short-term staffing decisions can be made. Integrate staffing planning into the overall business planning process. Create strategies and plans to deal with specific issues, and update staffing plans whenever significant changes in strategies or plans are being considered. Keep these plans updated based upon what happens both internally and externally in the market. Finally, let these plans drive the kind of development that is needed to secure the right talent to support the needs of the business plan.

Resources

www.bls.gov–U.S. Department of Labor.

www.hrps.org–Human Resource Planning Society.

10

Outline Useful & Strategic Position Descriptions

Position descriptions have been used in business for more than 90 years. Today almost every business maintains some formal descriptions for the various jobs within the organization. Such descriptions are accepted because they have proved useful in recruitment and selection of new workers, appraisal, wage and salary administration, training and many other secondary activities.

A position description is a formal document that summarizes the important functions of a specific job. It can also be used to sell the organization or the specific job to potential qualified candidates. Since jobs can be similar from one company to another, one objective should be to show candidates how your organization differs from the competitor's.

More recently, organizations have begun to look at these descriptions as having a more strategic use as well. We will outline a few ways to develop and utilize these position descriptions in a useful and strategic manner.

Successful position descriptions contain the following critical blocks of information:
- description of the organization (overview)
- candidate profile
- job components
    - title
    - date position documented
    - dimensions
    - working conditions
    - relationship to other jobs
    - supervisor title
    - position summary/basic function
    - essential duties and responsibilities
    - physical demands

Description of the Organization (Overview)

The overview describes who you are as an organization and what you do. It outlines the location, size and other contextual items. It should include a description of both the larger organizational unit (e.g., company, university, community agency) and the unit where the job is located (e.g., division, function, department, joint venture).

This is a good opportunity to include the organization's mission, purpose, vision and values, and why it is meaningful to work for this organization. It helps to provide the context within which someone might be working in this position–for example, because of significant growth or a recent merger etc. –and then how this position fits into the larger context.

This introduction can set your position description apart from those that only include the job components. It helps to sell the company as well as the job and positions the job in a more strategic context.

Tip
Part of the objective of the position description is to help sell your organization to qualified candidates. Make this section stand out.

Candidate Profile

The candidate profile identifies the qualities of a successful candidate in terms of the skills, type of work experience, educational background and experience desired. These qualities are typically tied back to the overview by defining specific challenges that might be faced and thus the skills and experience required to deal with those challenges.

As it relates to previous job experience, describe the type, amount and level of experience that is considered necessary and desirable. Differentiate between desired and required.

Tip
Given the dynamic nature of today's work world, experience requirements typically should not exceed 5 to 6 years.

Job Components

While position descriptions may detail many different aspects of the job, the nine functional areas, or components, are primary to any description.

1. Title

Position title should be at the head of the job component section. When positions are known by various titles, the most commonly known title should be used in the description. A list of common job titles is contained in the *Dictionary of Occupational Titles*, which is published by the U.S. Department of Labor.

Tip
Avoid inflating titles or using titles that may not convey the nature and level of the work.

2. Supervisor Title

Knowing the title of this job's supervisor helps to explain the level of the position to potential candidates. The supervisor title should also include the division, location or function; for example, vice president of marketing, ABC Division.

3. Date Position Documented

The date on the position description indicates when last it was reviewed and edited for organizational use. If the date is quite old, this might send a signal that it has not been updated to the issues of today. If the date is more recent, it appears that it is up-to-date and encompasses the present-day situation.

4. Position Summary/Basic Function

The purpose of this section is to provide an overview of the job. It is a summary of four or five sentences that briefly describe the duties, education and training, work environment, etc. This section describes:

- What the incumbent does, including physical and mental actions.
- How the incumbent does it, including the tools used, job knowledge applications and decisions to be made.
- Why the incumbent does it, meaning the expected result or product.

5. Dimensions

The dimensions define the scope of the incumbent's authority and accountability. This includes the number of direct and indirect reports, the sales volume or production amount, the inventory or budget controlled, etc. This section sometimes includes an organizational chart that shows supervisor, peers to the incumbent and direct reports.

6. Essential Duties & Responsibilities

Essential duties and responsibilities are those fundamental job-related duties that are necessary to the position. A job function may be considered essential for a variety of reasons, including:

- The reason the job exists is to perform the function.
- There are a limited number of employees available among whom performance of the job function can be distributed.
- The function may be highly specialized requiring specific expertise or ability.

Limiting the number of essential duties and responsibilities to around eight is recommended so it does not look like a listing of anything and everything that might be asked for in the job over time. Also, listing the responsibilities in descending order of importance helps to demonstrate some level of weighting to the duties.

Identify the level of knowledge, skill and/or abilities (KSAs) required to perform the essential job duties and responsibilities competently. When possible, incorporate the appropriate adjectives to indicate the required level of each KSA.

Suggested levels are:

- **Basic**–knowledge sufficient to perform recurring assignments with a reasonable degree of independence under normal supervision and after a customary orientation period.
- **Intermediate**–knowledge sufficient to coordinate, interpret, critique and/or synthesize the work of others and to make a meaningful contribution to such work.
- **Advanced**–knowledge sufficient to qualify as an expert, an internal consultant, or a resource to other qualified specialists in other departments.

7. Working Conditions

This section describes the environment in which the work is to be performed. It includes items such as travel requirements, on-call requirements, variable shifts, multiple locations, home office, fieldwork, etc.

8. Physical Demands

The physical requirements of the job must also be reflected in the position description for ADA (Americans with Disabilities Act) considerations. Examples of physical requirements may include lifting, standing or sitting for extended periods, carrying, pushing or pulling, noise level variances or specific vision requirements. The time spent or reasons dealing with the physical demands should be noted as well.

9. Relationship to Other Jobs

If the job is in an established career path or promotional sequence, then it is important to indicate the relationship between the job being analyzed and other jobs.

Detailing other positions that the incumbent has a strong relationship to and interacts with on a regular and necessary basis should be defined. There may be important reasons why some peer positions have impact on the performance of the incumbent; for example, a business development director my need to work closely with the in-house attorney, R&D and marketing since all are affected by an acquisition or joint venture the business development incumbent is responsible for transacting.

Benefits of Strategic Position Descriptions

Position descriptions have always helped to define the daily work of a job, but they continue to grow in value when used in a strategic manner as well. Their benefits include the following:

- They define jobs for performance planning, promotion, career planning and disability accommodation purposes.
- They provide a standard format that allows for consistent application.
- They give employees written definitions of their jobs.
- They provide reliable sources for comparing salary surveys.
- They help organizations move swiftly to increase or replace staff due to increased business or turnover.

- They help sell a prospective candidate on the company and the position.
- They provide context for the position within the organization while still providing key accountability detail.

Summary

While many see position descriptions as a simple laundry list of job responsibilities and/or a requirement for determining exempt or non-exempt status, others have begun to see the value of expanding on the information and using them as a strategic tool to engage potential employees and provide a greater context for the position in the organization.

Resources

www.occupationalinfo.org–U.S. Department of Labor Dictionary of Occupational Titles (DOT).

www.dol.gov/oco, Occupational Outlook Handbook.

Part Three

Identify Talent Requirements for Key Roles

11

Identify & Integrate Career & Culture Fit Criteria

Selection criteria identify and define the particular knowledge, attributes, qualifications and experience an individual needs to successfully carry out a position. They provide a way for potential candidates to assess their own abilities against the organization's requirements, and in the end, they match the right person to the position and organization. In order to define these criteria it is important to recognize that there are two types of selection criteria. One important type is the functional criteria, which defines the specific requirements to be successful in the position. However, there is an additional set that looks at the requirements to be successful in not just one position but in the organization over time. This set we call career and culture fit criteria.

The Difference in Criteria

Most selection criteria focus on what it takes to be successful in a target job. For instance, what it takes to be successful as a customer service representative. A profile is usually built to define and screen candidates to be successful in that position. However, there is also a need to determine what it takes for an individual to be successful in the organization. If you only select for job fit and not organization fit, you can end up with someone who is a great performer in narrow circumstances but does not demonstrate the ability to be successful outside the parameters of the position. A customer service rep who is great with customers and handling their issues but does not get along with anyone else in the department is an example of good functional skill set fit but poor organizational fit. Customers might think he is the best of all the reps, yet everyone internally finds him difficult to interact with on a regular basis. Organizations are typically much better at defining each position's functional criteria and less rigorous at defining cultural aspects the individual must be able to demonstrate in order to be successful in the short run in his specific position and in the long run in the organization.

Steps in Defining the Career & Culture Fit of the Organization

1. **Understanding the business and strategy of the organization.** When hiring employees, especially for leadership positions, understanding the business strategy, the business drivers will suggest certain types of criteria that will likely be required. For example, if your organization is young and growing there is likely a lack of good process and defined methodology. Employees are usually asked to build the process while they are using it, meaning there are fewer concrete expectations and a lot of change occurring regularly. Contrast that with a stable company with a long history and established processes that might be only a modest growth company. The culture and expectation of an employee in this situation is far different. It is likely that the same person would not be as successful or happy in both organizations.

2. **Surveying successful employees.** Knowing what made for success for those incumbents who have already demonstrated success to the organization is the next key step. There are two ways of doing this:

   a. One method uses an interview technique. An interview protocol is developed that is then used to interview a number of successful employees from the organization. Once a good sample (depending on the organization size) has been interviewed, key themes are then identified and defined.

   b. A second method is to create an online survey that can be sent to a number of successful employees who can be analyzed to determine common themes.

   The importance of this step is to isolate those items that appear to have a positive effect on the success of these individuals. This is only a preliminary list and will be used in a later step.

3. **Surveying unsuccessful employees.** The next important step is to determine what may have contributed to a lack of success in the organization. This step can also be done in two different ways:

   a. One way is to interview individuals who have not been successful using an interview protocol. Sometimes this exists in exit interviews that have already been conducted. If not, conducting a series of these interviews with recent departures from the organization can also provide themes.

   b. A second approach also includes using an online survey to reach a larger pool of ex-employees to determine if important themes can be isolated and used in conjunction with successful employees' data.

   This set of data provides a different window to view what it takes to be successful in a certain organization. This data combined with that learned in Step 2 can now be consolidated and used in the next step.

4. **Analyze and prioritize themes.** Taking the data from the interviewing and surveying done in the prior steps and turning it into usable information is the next step in this process. This requires a good sample size and coding of each response. When there is a high number of matching responses or common codes, these become key themes.

5. Reviewing output with senior management (confirmation). Once the data has been analyzed by the third party and defined, it is important to share these findings with a senior management team. The team of individuals who have been responsible for developing talent and building a management team will have a perspective of what has been presented. They may be able to shed additional light on the data and suggest that the strategic direction of the organization will require different skill sets than those that may have led to success in the past. They may also be able to confirm the findings.

Using a method of group prioritization, the team can then determine the prioritization of the items that have the most impact on successful employees. This process is easily accomplished by taking the number of items presented and dividing that number by 3. For example, 15 items divided by 3 is 5. Each person is given 5 votes to spread over the 15 items. The process will yield the highest priorities for the group.

6. Defining behaviors to support criteria. Once the priorities have been established, their supporting behaviors need to be added to the top criteria. This should be done by first reviewing what was stated in the interviews and then by adding those behaviors known to have a direct link to the criteria. Let's take one criterion as an example. Tough-mindedness: boldness to make difficult decisions for the good of the organization, to stand up for what one thinks is right and not to shrink from confrontations with others when necessary. The definition should be one that both explains the criterion as it was meant by the interviews and what is professionally accepted by psychologists and behaviorists.

7. Integrate criteria into the organization. Once the criteria is identified, agreed upon and defined, they now have to be integrated into more than just the interview guide. In order for the criteria to really have meaning they must find a way into all the key processes within the organization. This usually means that they are used in the following:

- **Performance reviews**–giving feedback to employees regarding how they demonstrate these criteria in their work.

- **Succession planning**–assessing the level of demonstrated behavior seen in succession candidates.

- **Development planning**–determining how the criteria can be developed to a greater degree within the organization.

- **360-degree feedback**–a customized feedback tool to provide specific feedback regarding the demonstration of these criteria.

Summary

Every organization is unique in its culture and in the way it expect its employees to behave. In order to make sure that you hire the right individuals, you need to define what it is about the organization that a candidate should be able to demonstrate. This goes beyond what specific skills sets an individual needs to demonstrate to do the specific job; it means that everyone who is successful in the organization must be demonstrating certain attributes that allow them to be successful in the long run and in more than one specific role. Determining what those attributes or criteria are and then defining the supporting behaviors will provide a key tool for assessing behavior of external candidates, internal candidates for promotion and developing talent for the long run of the organization.

Resources

"The Effective Interview: Eight Practices For Hiring The Best," SH&A (*www. staubin.net*).

12

Forecast Changes in Market & Business

The concept of forecasting is both an art and a science. The type of forecasting discussed in this chapter have to do with the changes in the market or business that might affect the skills, talent requirements and numbers to successfully compete in the future. Organizations will go through the strategic planning process by defining the organization's mission and goals, its external opportunities and threats, and its internal strengths and weaknesses. By taking this information and applying it to the talents and skills required based upon the SWOT analysis–Strengths, Weaknesses, Opportunities and Threats–you will be able to forecast the talent implications. Another type of analysis can also be used to measure a business's market and potential according to external factors; Political, Economic, Social and Technological (PEST).

Completing a SWOT analysis can be done in various ways. It measures a business unit, i.e., a new idea or product, and a PEST analysis measures the market. The following will provide some direction through this process. To begin a basic SWOT analysis, create a four-cell grid or four lists, one for each SWOT component:

1. Strengths

Think about what your company does well. What makes you stand out from your competitors? What advantages do you have over other businesses? Think about these areas:

- capabilities
- financial reserves
- quality
- competitive advantages
- location/geography
- culture
- people/talent
- price/value
- bench strength

2. Weaknesses

List the areas that are a struggle. What do your customers complain about? Ask yourself these questions:

- Gaps in capabilities?
- Business continuity?
- Resources?
- Reputation in the market?
- Reliability?
- Systems?
- Financial position?
- Talent?
- Morale?

3. Opportunities

These are external to the company where you try to uncover areas where your strengths are not being fully utilized. Are there emerging trends that fit with your company's strengths? Is there a product or service area you could do well in but are not yet competing? These are questions to ask:

- Market changes?
- Social trends?
- New markets?

- Competitors' weak spots?
- Global influences?
- Product extensions?

Threats

Look both inside and outside your organization for anything that could damage your business.

Internally
- Financial challenges?
- Product or business development issues?
- Talent or culture issues?

Externally
- Competitors becoming stronger?
- Emerging trends that highlight one of your weaknesses?
- Political?
- Social?
- Environmental?
- Market demand changes?

Simple Rules for Conducting a SWOT

When preparing for or conducting a SWOT:

- Be realistic about the strengths and weaknesses of your organization when conducting a SWOT analysis.
- The SWOT analysis should distinguish between where your organization is today and where it could be in the future.
- Be specific, avoid generalities or gray areas.
- Always compare yourself to the competition and the market. Examine where you might be better or worse than the competition.
- A SWOT is subjective, so try to use as much data as possible.

Once the SWOT is completed it highlights what is good and not so good about the business and directs you on where improvement should be made. When it comes to the strengths that have been identified, you will want to maintain, build and leverage these. As it relates to the opportunities identified, you will need to prioritize and focus on the most optimum. Where weaknesses are identified, you will want to shore up or consider exiting this area. For those areas of threat, you will want to determine how you might counteract them before they can cause a problem.

In order to better understand how to work with a SWOT, the following will provide two examples of a simple SWOT using information that is readily available.

1. Sample SWOT–Wal-Mart Stores, Inc.

Wal-Mart is the largest retailer in the world. The company consists of five retail businesses: discount stores, super centers, neighborhood markets, Sam's Club and international. It employs more than 1.6 million people worldwide.

The following is an example of a simple SWOT for Wal-Mart. These data were generated from *www.walmartfacts.com* and is not intended to be a complete SWOT, only an example.

Strengths
- Wal-Mart is a powerful retail brand. It has a reputation of value for your money, convenience and a wide range of products all in one store.
- Wal-Mart has grown substantially over the years both domestically and through acqusition globally. For example, it purchased the United Kingdom-based retailer ASDA.
- The company has a core competence in information technology to support its international logistics system, and IT also supports its efficient procurement.
- A focused strategy is in place for human resource management and development. Talent is key to Wal-Mart's business, and it invests time and resources into the training and retention of its people.

Weaknesses
- Wal-Mart is the world's largest grocery retailer, and control of its empire, despite its IT advantages, could leave it weak in some areas due to the huge span of control.
- Since Wal-Mart sells products across so many sectors (clothing, food, electronics, etc.) it may not have the flexibility of some of its more focused competitors.
- The company is global but has a presence in few other countries.

Opportunities
- It has the opportunity to take over, merge with or form strategic alliances with other global retailers, focusing on specific markets such as Europe or the greater China region.
- The stores are only in a few countries and opportunity exists to expand in large consumer markets like India and China.
- New locations and store types are moving from large super centers to local malls.
- Continued strategy for the opening of large super centers.

Threats
- Being number one means that you are the target of competition, locally and globally.
- Being a global retailer exposes you to political and social problems in countries where you operate.
- Intense price competition is a threat.

The SWOT leads to an outline of key action steps that need to be taken, which can be enhanced by looking into the different stages of evolution that an organization must traverse over time.

2. Market Forecast Example

A different example exists at a significant market level with United States farm groups. A considerable threat for these organizations has come in the form of increased scrutiny of illegal and undocumented workers. Changes in both legislation and enforcement of immigration laws have significantly impacted the pool of workers for agricultural groups in the United States.

Past workers who may have crossed the border each year are finding it harder to accomplish this task. Those undocumented workers living in the United States are under greater scrutiny and as such not reporting for work they had previously done. This has caused a significant gap in the number of farm and dairy workers available and willing to help produce the country's agricultural products. This former one-time threat has become a reality for many, causing agricultural industry leaders to look elsewhere to find labor to harvest their crops. Some of the strategies developed to deal with changes in the labor market include:

- Increased investment in mechanical harvesting decreasing the need for labor.
- Work with the U.S. Government to develop a more farm friendly guest worker program.
- Work with Central American countries to provide guest workers where they need jobs and the United States needs the labor.

Completing a SWOT would have identified the threat as a focus on immigration and the possibility of lost crops due to unharvested products. That threat turned to a weakness for those organizations that did not develop alternative strategies. For those who made the investments in increased mechanical harvesting, no business interruption occurred. For those who waited, it became a competitive disadvantage.

Summary

Being able to forecast changes in the market and business will lead to insights regarding potential issues and opportunities to be faced in the future. The insights gained from engaging in this forecasting exercise can then be used to create plans of action to deal with the issues before they can have a detrimental effect on the functioning of the business.

There are various ways and means to complete this exercise, and the SWOT is the most basic and widely used method to provide input to the business, marketing and human resource planning for the organization.

Resources

www.businessballs.com provides free SWOT analysis templates and examples.

www.walmartfacts.com provides information about Wal-Mart.

13

Update Functional Skill Requirements

Every individual who performs a job will alter that job in a way that fits his or her skill set, personality and experience. When that position opens due to a promotion, transfer or termination, updating the job's requirements is a valuable exercise. Given that the position has been impacted by the previous incumbent, analyzing the open job will provide good insight before interviewing candidates.

Analyzing the position with an eye for updating the functional skill requirements means that you need to look both to the past and to the future to ensure that you have the correct requirements to meet the objectives of the company through this position. This does not have to be a long and involved process if you know where to look. You do not need to review all of these sources before every interview, but you should do an extensive job once and then periodically update your understanding of the functional requirements.

Sources from the Past

Looking back to see what made for success in the position is a great way to begin your analysis. There are numerous places to begin your research and some of the most relevant are detailed below.

The Position Description

The first place to start is with the position description. This document is often created by the human resource department or the position supervisor when a position is new. Reviewing what is in writing is a good way to start collecting existing information about the functional criteria. However, it is important to realize that the position description often has many uses beyond detailing the job requirements. It is used to provide input for compensation purposes as well as job evaluation and is, therefore, often an incomplete picture of the full range of qualities, skills and knowledge needed to be successful in the position. It is the best place to start, just remember it is not enough to complete your analysis.

There are some good questions that can be asked in order to determine if the current needs of the business are being considered. They include the following:

- What results must be achieved in this position?
- What level of experience is required to achieve these results?
- What level of education is required to achieve these results?
- What qualifications are required and/or nice to have?

Performance Reviews

Performance reviews of incumbents or former incumbents of the job are another source of information that will help make known the job requirements and expectations. Look for patterns of qualities that make for success and those to avoid in future hires.

Work Plans

Work plans are documents created by departments that detail the expected work products for the fiscal year to support the business strategy. Many departments break these work plans down by position and at times by individual. These plans detail the desired output by quarter and a summation by year-end. If there are multiple years to review, it may provide a good picture of what plans were in place and what expectations were defined for each position and person. This information coupled with the performance information can provide a very comprehensive picture of the position.

Position Incumbents

Although documentation like position descriptions, performance reviews and work plans can be very useful, you will likely find that individuals are even more essential for the type of information about functional requirements you are seeking. It is quite useful to talk to the people who are actually doing the job today or who have done it in the recent past. It is in these interviews where you will find more subtle but important pieces of information. Obtaining what these individuals find to be successful and not so successful elements of the knowledge, skills and abilities required in performing the job will round out the information you gleaned from the written documents discussed earlier.

Position Subordinates

If the position has subordinates, it is useful to pull the subordinate group together and ask them what they feel are the critical elements that make for success in the job. Almost everyone has an idea of what worked and what did not with prior incumbents and what expectations they have for the supervisor. You may find some valuable information when you pose questions to this group. This position not only has to deliver on the business expectations but also on the human expectations. You will be rewarded with a more complete picture from the past and now into the future.

Sources for the Future

Now that you have evaluated the sources of information from the past, it is important to look to the future to see if expectations for the job may be different for anyone filling the position today given the direction of the business, organization, function or department. The following are places to learn more about future expectations and requirements.

Business Plans–Strategic & Operating

Business plans outline the steps required to carry out the activities critical to achieving the stated goals of the company or department. The plan usually includes sections on the strategic positioning of the company, product or service offerings, potential product extensions, and milestones to be reached and key functions to reach those milestones. This information may suggest more of the same from the past or it might suggest new or different skill set requirements based upon changing strategy. The future expectations of the function are a key resource for defining skills, knowledge, experience and abilities needed in the position.

Interviews with Position Customers

Whether an inside customer or an external customer, your customers know what expectations they have and know the qualities related to providing superior performance. Customers also have business plans and future expectations and may provide some key insights regarding success of the next incumbent. Interviewing these customers, although not necessary every time a position opens, can be especially helpful on a semi-regular basis. Gaining information is one outcome, but building rapport by asking for your customers' feedback can be a real side benefit.

Organizing Job Information

Gathering information in the manner described above is the first step in a two-part process. The second part involves analyzing and organizing the information into a format that will be helpful in the selection process.

Analyzing the information allows you to look for patterns that emerge from each of the individuals and documents involved. Using the following headings, you can list the information culled from your work.

- **Knowledge**–work experience or specific education requirements, such as experience as a product manager and an MBA.
- **Skills**–an art, a trade, a technique or dexterity that has been developed or acquired.
- **Ability**–a natural or acquired skill or talent.
- **Behavior**–the manner in which the candidate needs to behave in order to be effective in the position and company.
- **Environmental Issues**–the fit with the unique environment outlined by the analysis.

Knowledge, skills and abilities are the easier items to define; they are what most position descriptions capture and what most interviewers think of first when it comes to job requirements. The other areas are more difficult to define since they tend to be more subjective in nature. However, once defined with specific behavioral attributes they become as objective as the first three above.

Once all of this data is outlined, it is now possible to prioritize those criteria that are the most critical aspects of performing the job. If items are easily learned, they should not be considered critical. The list should not be exhaustive. No more than eight to ten are recommended. The more specific the criteria, the easier the selection decision will be.

Summary

Updating functional skills requirements is a good exercise before attempting to fill any open position. If you make an effort to think through the knowledge, skills, abilities, behaviors and environmental issues surrounding the position, you will have the framework in which to place any information you collect from candidates making it easier to produce the best decisions regarding fit for the job.

Resources

"The Effective Interview: Eight Practices for Hiring the Best," White paper, which can be found on the website: *www.staubin.net.*

Part Four

Recruiting & Selecting Talent

14

Use Your Brand to Recruit Talent

Previous chapters have outlined the importance of building an employer brand that creates demand in the talent market. This chapter will further define the employer brand as the organization's image as an exceptional place to work in the minds of current employees as well as potential candidates, clients, customers and stakeholders. Your employer brand is the value proposition your organization conveys to your employees and the external labor market. Now it is time to use that brand to attract the talent you would like to your company. Great organizations create such a strong brand that it draws the talent to them rather than having to spend significant time and money on selling the organization to the talent market. Many benefits in the recruiting world are provided by a strong employment brand.

Recruiting Power

With a strong employer brand, you are not limited by the size of your recruiting budget. In fact, your entire workforce becomes recruiters for you. This is one of the biggest side benefits to having a strong employer brand. Your own employees are so pleased to work for the organization they cannot resist telling anyone who is interested about the benefits of working for the company. Employee referral programs help encourage current employees to refer outside talent, although even without this encouragement employees will openly encourage others if their company has a great employer brand.

A good example of employees selling their own company can be seen in a blog by a Yahoo! employee, Matt Martone, who discusses what it is like to work for Yahoo!. Yahoo!, of course, was ranked one of the "Top 100 Companies to Work For" by *Fortune* magazine. Job blogs are becoming commonplace among those branded best for employment. You really cannot pay for this kind of employment advertising. When employees themselves send the good news, it has far more impact than a recruiting brochure or even a good website. In a study conducted by McKinsey in 2004, almost 50 percent of companies surveyed said they allocated resources for internal branding. The survey found that employees rated factors such as *fun place to work, for people like me, training opportunities* and *innovative company* to be more important than *high salary* when it comes to winning over a potential recruit. These items all tend to be more believable when they come from current employees and are consistent with the brand.

Recruitment Strength

Using your employment brand when it is strong will decrease the amount of time spent trying to sell potential employees because they already know it is a great company to work for based upon brand attributes. This brings more people to your door lowering your recruitment costs and bolsters your recruitment strength, which is a true competitive advantage. Employees who are enamored by their own work experience are going to spread the word far more quickly and loudly than those whose experience is just viewed as satisfactory. If your employees are not telling really good stories, you are likely not in a position of strength in the talent market and your brand may not hold up. If your employees are telling positive stories, congratulations, because the benefit will be seen in a steady flow of interested candidates.

Employees Are Your Brand

We actually dedicated an entire chapter to this idea, and it is important to reinforce the message here. Using your brand also means using your branded employees. They become the brand ambassadors and attract talent to them as well as to the company. Potential recruits experience the brand through your employees and are attracted to the mission, vision and demonstrated values. The brand comes alive.

Having employees who demonstrate your brand does not just happen by accident. It occurs when appropriate time and attention is paid to holding managers accountable for delivering on the brand attributes. It takes focus on strengthening the culture through actions and organizational practices that consistently demonstrate desired brand attributes.

There is a potential downside to using your employees as brand ambassadors, however. Employees who may not demonstrate all the aspects of the brand or are inconsistent with the brand may actually confuse the brand message or attract individuals who will not engender the desired brand attributes. The brand can then become tarnished or confused making it harder to sell your message to the talent pool you desire.

When using your employees as brand ambassadors, make sure you pick those who naturally demonstrate your brand. Also, create an ongoing program of communication, coaching and development to support the brand attributes.

Good Talent Gets Good Talent

When you have top talent and a top employer brand, you tend to attract top talent. For example, GE has developed an employment brand of grooming excellent managers. Brad Smart, in his book *Top Grading*, outlines how GE routinely evaluates the internal talent as A, B and C talent. Those who are A are expected to demonstrate certain performance and potential. Those who are B are expected to attain an A rating with development and coaching. Those who are rated C are expected to improve or be asked to leave. The idea is that A-level players will attract A players. When an organization is able to attract a higher quality talent pool, it is able to be even more selective than those organizations having difficulty finding the numbers or quality level desired. This positive cycle continues to fill the pipeline, making everyone's life much easier. Recruiters find it easier to attract high-level talent, managers can be very selective with the talent they hire and the management process becomes much easier, given the level of talent and desire to succeed in the environment. Such results are possible when you have a strong employer brand.

Inside Out vs. Outside In

In order to use your brand to recruit talent you need to start on the inside, which means that your brand cannot just be a clever or glitzy advertising campaign developed by your marketing department. It must start with making sure that what you are selling outside is actually being delivered inside. An employment brand that fails to provide employees with the value it has promised them will fail in its efforts to build a positive and productive internal brand. It is also important for the company to align its content, communication and service delivery so that your employees' experience in each one of these elements will reflect the brand attributes. Employees will send a message–which is not always clearly evident–if the brand promise is not being delivered. Employees just begin to cool in their enthusiasm for the organization and may stop selling the benefits of working for the company. In order to make sure this is not happening, here are a six suggestions.

1. Survey your employees to see how their attitudes map to the brand attributes.
2. Run employee focus groups to learn how they talk about the organization.
3. Survey recruits to see how they feel about the organization and the employer brand.
4. Track sites that target specific companies or market employees.
5. Request feedback on sites such as Electronic Watercooler at Vault.com where individuals are encouraged to share information about employers.
6. Survey your customers to see if your employees are conveying your company's positive brand image.

The internal brand is not created just to attract new talent. When existing employees are satisfied with their employment situation, their loyalty to the organization and the internal brand increases, which in turn helps attract high quality talent from outside, reduce turnover and increase employee commitment.

Summary

When you have a good employer brand, you will dramatically increase your ability to recruit the talent you need. This occurs because it is easier to attract talent, and your existing employees will help seal the deal. Having a strong employer brand will ultimately reduce your cost of hiring, lower turnover, and increase employee productivity. This also has a direct benefit on reducing operational expense and increasing profitability.

Resources

www.jobsearchmarketing.com for recruitment blog.

Top Grading, Penquin Books, ©2005.

"Employment Brand Management Helps Attract Top Talent", Peter D. Weddle, 2006, *www.careerJournal.com.*

www.shrm.org for various employment branding articles.

15

Define the Selection Process

Does the way you present yourself and the organization in the interview and selection process really make much of a difference to candidates if you have the job they are interested in pursuing? In May 2007, Development Dimensions International (DDI) and Monster® surveyed 4,000 job seekers, 1,250 hiring managers and 628 staffing directors to find out how an organization's hiring process affects a candidate's decision regarding accepting a position with that organization. The study revealed that negative impressions during the interview process lead to negative perceptions of the organization. The research showed that organizations are making many mistakes with the interview and selection process that impact its ability to attract and hire the talent it wants. So what can you do to make sure that your interview process meets the standards that will show off your organization as a great place to work? The following practices will provide a good basis for elevating your process into a competitive advantage.

Have a Positive, Defined Approach for Every Candidate

There are three elements to the interview and selection process. They include:

1. **Recruiting**–the process of finding candidates for a job or function.

2. **Selecting**–the act of carefully choosing an individual or group of individuals from among a pool of possible candidates.

3. **Hiring**–the process of landing those you have selected by getting them to accept the offer of employment.

Defining what each of these processes do, who is responsible and what roles each person involved must play is the first step of making sure you are putting your best foot forward. When candidates feel they are part of a well-oiled machine, they feel more valued and cared for than when things seem to be disorganized and last minute.

Existing employees need to understand what role they play and how they can support the process in a positive, appealing yet factual manner.

Be Clear about Roles & Responsibilities by Providing Training & Education

In the study conducted by DDI and Monster, the majority of job candidates surveyed said that their impression of the interviewer was a top factor in their decision to accept or reject the job. This says a great deal about the need to educate everyone who will be involved in the interviewing process. This can start with defining roles and responsibilities in such a way as to make expectations clear. The sample flow chart below outlines the roles of the hiring manager and the

Figure 15.1

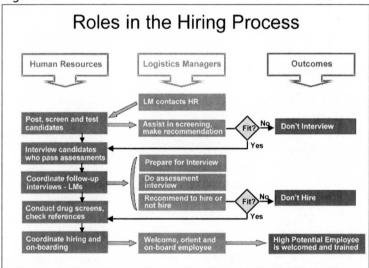

human resource manager. Each process should fit the level of the position and the environment of the business. The hiring manager should be involved in making some important decisions, which include:

- Who will participate on the interview team?
  We recommend there should be three.
- Who else will have a role? For example, who will give
  the candidate a tour or take them to lunch?
- How should the interviews be focused for each interviewer?

Provide training to anyone on the interview team, and educate those who have other contact with the candidate. In the end, the candidate should feel good about experience even if they do not get the job for which they were interviewing.

Be Realistic about the Job Requirements

Hiring managers may feel so desperate to fill a position that they begin to oversell what the job entails to make it more attractive to a good candidate. The problem with this is that it might cause early turnover when the candidate feels the hiring manager was not really honest with them.

New employees who have realistic and aligned expectations will perform better and stay longer than those who have unrealistic ideas about what is expected of them on the job and in the long run.

Schedule Appropriate Time for the Process

Managers who are trying to fill staff positions may find a real conflict between their daily work schedule and the time it takes to fill those positions. If there are three people on a hiring team, someone to give a tour and someone to take the candidate to lunch, it can be a very full day.

However, if the appropriate time is not devoted to the interview and selection process, the candidate, might feel less important than an experience where proper time and attention was given. The following are general guidelines for interview time:

- Hourly employees: 30-40 minutes
- Entry level non-exempt: 45-60 minutes
- Entry to mid-level exempt employees: 60-75 minutes
- Senior level employees: 90 minutes or more

If the interview time has been lengthy, try to schedule some debriefing time to the agenda at the end of the day. We suggest a short discussion while the information is fresh for the interviewer and while the candidate is still feeling good about the experience.

Manage the Candidate Based upon the Schedule

One way to impress a candidate is to show that you are prepared and know how to execute on a plan. Prepare a schedule for the candidate that details the flow of the day for them. Each person on the schedule should be aware of where the candidate has been and where they go next. Managing a schedule efficiently will impress the candidate and develop the kind of rigor that is admired by those who want to work for the best.

This also means that when the time comes for the debrief session, it is attended to with the same concern for meeting the schedule as were the interviews. Even if this means you need to be called into the session, it should still be an important aspect of the selection process.

Interview Based on Agreed upon Selection Criteria

Chapters 11 and 13 outlined how to define the criteria for selection purposes. It is important legally and from a good business standpoint to use these criteria as the focus of the interview and not to go off into other areas. Since these criteria have been defined and supported through behavioral examples, prepare an evaluation form that includes all the criteria to focus attention toward those elements during the interview itself. Preparing questions in advance on this form keeps the interview moving in the right direction.

Use the form during the interview to note areas where the candidate shows strength and where he or she may be lacking, then use it as a tool during the debrief process to have a good discussion that is criteria based and observation focused.

Follow Up with Candidates in a Timely Manner

Given the speed with which information travels today, move swiftly with good candidates to let them know you want them to become part of your organization. Repeated or multiple interviews or waiting until everyone gets back from business trips or vacations, etc., is a good way to lose the individual you most want to hire.

Following up quickly, whether you intend to hire or not, allows a candidate to stop any further interviews or to work harder at setting up additional interviews. Either way, a quick follow-up shows respect for the candidate's time and creates a good impression.

Integrate Interview Data into the On-boarding Plan

Once the hiring decision has been made, use the rich assessment data from the interviews that were conducted to integrate the new hire into the organization. Customizing the new hire orientation and assimilation plan can shorten their time to productively, making them more comfortable and the organization more successful.

Summary

What does your process tell a candidate about your organization? Are you putting your best foot forward so that candidates want to work for your organization and are so excited about how they have been received that they cannot wait to send the word to all the people they know?

By following the strategies outlined here, you will present a good image of your company and an appealing look at the environment within which potential employees may expect to work.

Resources

A complete article on the survey conducted can be found in *T+D* magazine, May 2007.

Additional information can be found in Chapters 11,13,14 and 18.

16

Use Your Employees to Help Select Talent

The main purpose of this chapter is to explore how to develop a pool of viable job candidates by using your employees to help select that talent. While the term recruiting usually brings to mind employment agencies and classified ads, current employees are often your best source of potential employees.

Promote from Within

Filling open positions with inside candidates has several benefits. For one, employees see that competence is rewarded so morale and performance may be enhanced. Inside candidates are also already committed to the company goals and thus are less likely to leave the organization.

Promotion from within can also boost employee loyalty and facilitate a long-term perspective when making managerial decisions. It may also be safer to promote employees from within, since you already have an accurate assessment of the person's skills, and, finally, inside candidates may require less orientation, assimilation and training than outside candidates.

Promotion from within requires using tools such as job posting, internal candidate slating and/or skill banks. Job posting facilitates the promotion of qualified inside candidates, and skill banks list current employees and their specific skills. This chapter explores each of these areas further.

Job Posting

Job posting is a process whereby employees make their desires known for a new opportunity under a defined system. The company posts a job, which is open for all to see, and job bids are taken from those who are interested in that opportunity. A good posting system posts the job for a long enough period of time for all qualified employees to see it and bid if they are interested, and it provides feedback to those who have placed bids. The benefits of a job posting system are:

- It is visible for everyone to be aware of open positions if interested.
- Hidden talent is often uncovered.
- Recruitment costs are often reduced when jobs are filled internally.

The potential downsides include:

- The process can cause unwanted competition among employees for limited advancement opportunities.
- It can be time consuming to interview all interested candidates.
- Employee morale can be decreased for those who are not selected.

Skill Banks or Skill Inventories

Many organizations that like to promote from within create skill banks or inventories where employee résumés are built to record progress in terms of experiences, skill development and capability. These skill banks might include items such as overseas assignments, language skills, degrees, courses taken, etc. These inventories or banks are used when creating internal candidate slates for management positions that are vacant and not part of the job posting process.

The problems encountered with skill inventories have to do with maintaining and updating them, which can be time consuming. If they are not kept up-to-date, good potential candidates may be missed. Having employees update their own information is helpful, but information must be verified to ensure its validity. People are sometimes willing to stretch the truth in order to increase their chances of promotion. We have seen this many times over the past few years in high profile coaching and executive positions.

Employee Referral Programs

Referrals from current employees are another valuable source for finding job applicants. In some organizations, employees may receive a cash bonus when they refer a candidate who proves to be successful on the job for a given period of time. In order to ensure that there are adequate returns on bonuses for employee referrals, it is essential that a good performance appraisal system is in place to measure the performance of the referred new hire. A good applicant tracking system to ensure that new hire performance is maintained over time is a good idea as well.

Even companies with a good employee referral program should look for ways to increase participation. Here are some ideas to consider:

- **Pay referral bonuses.** Distribute part of a referral bonus when the candidate is hired, then after a defined period of time, usually 90 days, distribute the remainder of the fee. This can be a great incentive for newer entrants into the workplace who have large networks of school or business associates who may also be in the search process. There are two precautions to consider: First, making too many small payouts dilutes the effect of the bonus—it should have impact and visibility. Second, some companies have tried paying over a year to make sure the employee stays, which can be viewed as a real disincentive.

- **Ensure retention of referrers.** A study on employee referral networks by Emilio J. Castilla of Massachusetts Institute of Technology (MIT) Sloan School of Management showed that employees who bring friends and associates into the organization can just as easily take them elsewhere if the referrer's view of the company changes. Castilla's study was based on a call center where about one-third of the applicants were developed from employee referrals. He concluded that managers need to be aware that the social web of engagement can be damaged if the referral source becomes unhappy with the organization.

- **Encourage every employee to be a talent scout**. Provide business cards that clearly show a web address for anyone interested in learning more about opportunities with the organization. Remind employees that good talent comes from good talent and, therefore, to always be on the lookout and ready to refer.

- **Host an information session.** Have employees invite friends and family to a gathering where the company discusses plans and future opportunities and welcomes interested parties to leave résumés or contact information for follow-up.

- **Host a contest.** Take a period of time, say 90 days, and give everyone who refers a legitimate candidate a chance to win a prize. Add additional incentives for those who are given offers and those who accept. If the prizes are significant enough, there is no telling how many referrals you might get. The benefit of this is twofold: It is a cost effective way to accumulate referrals and your employees become excited and engaged in bringing in top talent.

- **Incorporate employee referrals into the job.** Establish active networking as one element of performance discussions and reward employees for the volume of activity here as well.

Build a Talent Pool from Your New Hires

New hires often are some of the best individuals to ask about other potential candidates. Once an individual has agreed to join an organization, an attachment has been completed that allows the new hire to share a potential new opportunity with others they have worked with in the past. This is the best time to ask about referrals for people who might be the right talent for open positions.

Peer Interviews

A technique that is becoming popular in companies today is that of peer-to-peer interviewing, where employees meet one-on-one with potential peers. IBM and Motorola are examples of two large organizations that use this type of interviewing. It is more common in smaller or team-based organizations; morale and productivity improve significantly when employees have a say in who they will work with as part of a team.

Whole Foods Market, a rapidly growing grocery chain, uses teams to accept or veto new hires for their departments. This process enables the transfer of knowledge and improves retention since the team takes responsibility for the success of the new hires.

Be aware that there are a couple of downsides to peer interviewing, which include:

- **Competitive employees.** If an employee is threatened by a potential peer, he or she may be less likely to want them on the team since they may perceive that they are more skilled or experienced and thus able to progress faster.

- **Inappropriate questions.** Team members must be trained to conduct appropriate interviews so they do not ask questions or share information that should be kept confidential.

Organizations that use peer-to-peer interviewing may find they are able to secure a more complete picture of the candidate before they are hired. They are quick to add, however, that proper training and preparation are necessary for the process to succeed and that management should maintain the right to make the final decision.

Summary

Employees are one of your best sources for selecting additional talent. They know what it takes to be successful in the organization and can help sell the company and the opportunity. It is one of the best ways to attract and retain one of your most important resources–your talent.

Resources

Monster has a series of articles that deal with interviewing and recruiting talent.

There are many vendors today for skill inventories that connect to succession planning and development software.

17

Prepare for the Interview

Preparation may be one of the most important yet most forgotten elements of a successful interview. Indeed, preparation and planning pave the way for focused, well managed and successful interactions.

Aspects of appropriate preparation include the following:

- more productive use of interview time
- functional and job related criteria are identified and agreed upon in advance
- increased chances of hiring the best candidates

Problems encountered when planning is not done:

- lack of control over time and topic
- reliance on inappropriate questions or topics
- disagreements with other interviewers at the evaluation stage regarding selection criteria

Interview Criteria

Planning begins with having a clear set of criteria for the ideal candidate. There are two sets of criteria to be defined: The first is job specific or functional, i.e., the basic skills required to perform the essential daily functions of the job. A number of different tools can be used to determine the job specific criteria. These have been discussed in detail in Chapter 13.

The second set of criteria involves the career and culture fit criteria, i.e., those that have some impact on the present assignment but are more critical for assuming higher levels of responsibility and/or cultural alignment and compatibility.

Career and culture fit criteria are usually organization-wide and define the elements that make for a good citizen in that specific organization. Because all organizations are not alike even if they are in the same industry, these criteria define expectations for a specific company. For example, team players may be valued more in one organization than in another that places high value on independent risk takers. This set of criteria is usually a list of no more than eight items. Chapter 11, Identify &

Integrate Career & Culture Fit Criteria provides direction on how to identify career and culture fit criteria.

Once you are armed with both organizational and job specific criteria, you have the basis of a roadmap in your search for the ideal candidate. Having a set of criteria and a defined process clearly provides a strong guide going into an interview and raises the predictability of both short- and long-term candidate success.

Analyzing the Environment

It is important to analyze the different aspects of both the social and the physical environments a new hire will be entering. The social environment speaks to the activities and opportunities for social interaction, or expectations for social interaction, within the workplace. The physical environment speaks to the actual physical location of the individual's job.

Social Environment

Consider an organization that prides itself on being a team oriented, fun-loving company that attempts to recruit employees to participate on company sports teams so they can build a history of great competition and fun stories. Now consider a new employee who has a family, is going to school and is involved in the community, so he only wants to do his job, do it well and leave at the end of the workday to meet his other commitments. The organization works hard to recruit him to get involved and be a team player, then begins to think he might not really be committed to the organization because he chooses to decline all invitations. The new hire wonders why he should be expected to participate in after-hours activities that have nothing to do with his job and that prevent him from meeting his personal obligations and commitments. This scenario is an example of a mismatch between the employee and the company social environment.

An opposite situation may also occur. Consider a college recruit who is considering joining an organization where her skills and experience make her a perfect fit for the position. She is also hoping to get involved in activities and events that might provide a social network outside of work since she is moving to a new city full of strangers. The company is one where many of its employees travel a great deal or work part-time from home making it difficult to create company sponsored activities that involve others. Once again, there is a disconnect between the existing social environment and the expectation of the new hire.

Although these examples may seem unusual, the fact remains that there is a need to recognize in advance the type of social environment that exists in your company so you can consider it during the interviewing process.

Physical Environment

To some the physical location of their workspace has a significant impact on how they view the opportunity; to others it has little or no impact. Therefore, knowing the physical environment and making sure there is a match is another important step in the process. If you are planning to hire someone who will be working in a cubicle in the basement of a building with no windows and they have been working in a corner office in a high-rise building, discuss this in the interview to avoid any potential discontent if the individual is hired.

Preparing the Interview Environment

When it comes to where an interview should be conducted, professional and private should be the rule. A private office free from interruptions is ideal, but if a private office is not available, the next best location is a conference room. Be sure to schedule the conference room in advance for at least 30 minutes longer than what you expect to need so you do not have to disrupt your interview to move to another location if the interview runs long. In addition, post a note on the door that an interview is in session so no one attempts to enter the room while the interview is being conducted.

Interviewing in a public place is not recommended, yet circumstances may make it your only option. If this is the case due to the need to interview people around the country, for example, following are some suggested ways to plan ahead.

- Many hotels now have interview rooms or office suites just for this purpose; check to see if one is available.
- If you only have a short time and are interviewing at an airport, many airline clubs have rooms to rent for this purpose.
- If you are stuck using a restaurant, try meeting at off-peak hours and request a more secluded table or booth away from the traffic pattern.

Everything You Need to Do to Be Prepared

The most important preparation items have already been outlined: determining the criteria to be used, recognizing the physical and social environment for the job and arranging for private and professional space in which to conduct the interview. There are still a few more things to consider in your preparations.

- Have the candidate's résumé or application at hand. Even if you have reviewed it in advance it is helpful to have it with you in the interview.
- As the hiring manager, determine who else should be a member of the interview team; three is an ideal number. If the candidate has already been through some screening process in advance, there is no need for more than three on an interview team. (See more about this in Chapter 15, *Define the Selection Process.*)
- As the hiring manager, determine if there are other roles you need to fill, such as greeter, chaperone, lunch or tour guide, etc.
- Schedule debrief time for the end of the day with the other interviewers so that a good discussion can take place while the interviews are fresh in everyone's mind.

- Provide an interview evaluation form that everyone is expected to complete.
- Have a copy of the interview schedule so you know who the candidate has seen before you and who they will see after you.

Summary

Appropriate preparation and planning contribute to more productive use of the interview time and increase the chance of hiring the best candidates. Advance planning also provides a set of tools and an agreed upon process with defined roles that, when conducted properly, aid the interview team and present the company in the best light.

Resources

"The Effective Interview: Eight Practices for Hiring the Best," white paper found on website *www.staubin.net.*

18

Use the Eight Practices for Hiring the Best

Selecting the right people who fit the organizational culture and who have the right skill set for today and into tomorrow is a serious endeavor. It is important that you pay attention to this work and recognize the impact each interview will have on how the organization is viewed. This chapter outlines eight concrete practices for hiring the best talent for your organization.

Practice One: Planning the Interview

Preparation and planning pave the way for a focused, well managed and successful interaction. The previous chapter outlined the elements involved in properly planning the interview.

Practice Two: Creating the Right Environment

Just as planning is so important for facilitating a good outcome, so, too, is creating the right environment that will encourage free flow of information and behavior observation. Key elements of the process–the setting, approach and all other interview components–will help create the optimal environment for a successful interview.

The interview components make up an important element of setting the stage; include all five of the following interview components to establish and sustain an optimal environment. They include:

1. **The opening**–where you set the stage.

2. **The gathering of information**–where you look to find behavioral examples of the desired criteria.

3. **The continued building of rapport**–where you sustain a friendly and positive approach while digging beneath the surface to find the information you need.

4. **Note taking**–where you record observations of the demonstrated behaviors.

5. **Closing**–where you set the stage for the next steps with the candidate.

Each component has a role in how you set and maintain an environment that is friendly yet professional.

Practice Three: Maintaining Professionalism

The best interviewers are professional at all times. They ask appropriate questions and follow legal guidelines to avoid any appearance of discrimination in the hiring process. Questions should relate only to the established criteria and should avoid forbidden interview areas such as:

- age
- marital status
- religion
- disability
- ethnic heritage
- family relationships
- political opinions
- arrests or court records

Practice Four: Navigating the Discussion

The best interviewers control the direction and flow of every interview, guiding it so they can gather the information necessary to uncover the real person and make the best hiring decisions. They do this by consistently using the interview components outlined below.

Opening

The opening to the main part of the interview (after the initial greeting and small talk) should set the agenda and parameters of the interview. The interviewer describes the:

- purpose
- content areas to be covered
- candidate questions
- length of the interview
- note taking

Gathering Information

The majority of the interview consists of the interviewer asking questions and the candidate doing the majority of the talking (generally 80 percent or more). The best interviewers use effective questioning strategies to guide the interview in appropriate directions. Different types of questions used in an interview are:

- **Open-Ended questions**–These are broad questions designed to get the candidate talking about a topic. These questions ask for the candidate to use thinking and interpretation skills.

- **Probes**–These questions are the most frequently asked questions during an interview. They are intended to elicit more information and/or greater depth in the response. Experienced interviewers use probes to dig beneath the surface, explore critical choice points and discover likes and dislikes.

- **Redirection**–This question type is used to change the topic of discussion because the candidate gets off track or is no longer providing helpful information on a topic.

- **Reflection and paraphrase**–With this technique, interviewers summarize what the candidate just said in order to prompt the candidate to elaborate or clarify their statements.

All questions should relate to actual experiences rather than hypothetical or scenario-based situations. In research conducted by Pulakos and Schmitt (Experienced-based and Situational Interview Questions: Studies of Validity. Personnel Psychology, 1995), experienced-based interview questions resulted in higher levels of validity than situational questions.

Building & Managing Rapport

Rapport is the level of comfort and emotional affinity between the candidate and the interviewer. A low level of rapport increases the guardedness of the candidate. Experienced interviewers know that by reducing the guardedness of candidates they will get the most open, real information.

Closing

Experienced interviewers also save some time at the end of the interview to close in a consistent manner, similar to how one is expected to open an interview. Close the interview by doing the following:

- Tell the candidate you have completed your questions;
- ask the candidate if there is additional information they would like to share;
- ask the candidate for any remaining questions they have about the position or organization;
- explain next steps; and
- thank the candidate for his or her time and interest.

Practice Five: Recognizing Your Own Biases

It is probably not a stretch to say that everyone has some sort of bias when it comes to evaluating applicants. These biases tend to subtly sway interviewers in favor of one candidate over another for reasons that may be unrelated to on-the-job potential. Some of the more commonly encountered biases are:

- **Halo effect**–The tendency to generalize about a person based on only one characteristic.

- **First impression**–The tendency to evaluate a person very early in the interview rather than on patterns of behavior observed over the course of an interview.

- **Similar-to-me effect**–The tendency to evaluate those who are similar to ourselves higher or more positively than someone who is dissimilar.

- **Negative or positive leniency**–The tendency to be too hard or too easy in evaluating behaviors.

- **Contrast effect**–The tendency to evaluate one candidate relative to other candidates rather than according to preset criteria.

Bias and error by interviewers is a key reason for interviewing failure. Without some scientific tools and training, interviewers will often make hiring decisions based on gut feel and intuition. Feelings and intuition should only be used to probe deeper to uncover more accurate data.

Practice Six: Building Pattern Maps

The notes that experienced interviewers take consist of patterns of behavior observed in the candidate, not just what the candidate says. That is why these notes are better referred to as pattern maps. As behaviors are observed, the interviewer keeps a record of each occurrence; a pattern truly exists when five instances of a particular behavior are observed. These patterns will almost certainly show up later in on-the-job behavior.

Practice Seven: Observing Behavior

To observe patterns of behavior (at least five) in a candidate, you need to set a relaxed, friendly environment and manage the level of rapport between the candidate and the interviewer. Practice observing beyond the words a candidate speaks to the music the candidate displays; the music cannot be rehearsed like the words.

For example, look for facial expressions, nervousness, examples of courage, interpersonal warmth, level and depth of articulation and word choice, and other nonverbal behaviors that represent the music the candidate will display should he or she join the organization. These behaviors also give insights into the level of honesty and openness the candidate has for certain topics.

Practice Eight: Deciding on Fit

The best hiring organizations use core teams of interviewers to assess candidates from multiple perspectives. Additional research conducted by Pulakos, Schmitt, Whitney and Smith ("Individual Differences in Interviewer Ratings: The Impact of Standardization, Consensus Discussion, and Sampling Error of a Structured Interview," *Personnel Psychology*, 1996), indicated that the validity of consensus ratings was significantly higher than other approaches.

Summary

Choosing the right talent can add significantly to the bottom-line success of an organization or, if a mistake is made, cost the company millions.

There are few responsibilities that impact the business more than who you hire. You have a responsibility to make sure you hire the right people because they will affect the business, the work life of others and the customers.

Resources

"The Effective Interview: Eight Practices for Hiring the Best," white paper found on website *www.staubin.net.*

19

Make the Right Selection Decisions

Cost & Impact of the Decision

One of the main reasons for focusing on making the right hiring decision is because of the significant implications, both financial and nonfinancial, attached to this decision. Three different entities are most affected by the right decision: the organization, the new hire and the hiring manager.

The Organization

Research into the cost to an organization for a miss-hire suggests that at least one to three times the employee's yearly salary is a starting cost. This number can easily increase if the person is in a critical position and/or if it is a difficult position to fill. Many sales organizations, for example, fear that even one lost customer due to a miss-hire could cost years of work and untold lost revenue for the company. In such a case, the cost to the company could soar as high as 7 to 10 times the sales representative's annual salary. The elements that should be considered in any turnover include:

Predeparture Costs
- tenure of employee
- job complexity
- lost productivity
- department morale
- level of expertise
- reduced customer satisfaction
- lost sales
- exit interview

Replacement Costs
- recruitment costs (ads, agencies, etc.)
- selection costs

New-Hire Costs
- orientation
- technology
- manager's time
- reduced customer satisfaction
- training
- inexperience errors
- coworkers' time
- lost productivity

The New Hire

The new hire also has an investment in the success or failure of the position. There is usually a financial as well as a personal investment by anyone who changes jobs.

When it does not work out, the individual has to deal with personal career issues as well as family and social issues. The more investment made, the harder it is to deal with the fallout, especially if relocation issues are involved.

No one feels good when a hiring decision is not a good one. But the new hire must redo the process of finding the right position, which can take a very personal toll that is hard to calculate.

The Hiring Manager

The hiring manager has much to be thankful for when a good hiring decision is made and much to regret when a poor hiring decision occurs. With a good hire, the manager finds that he or she can be more productive, and the work environment gains a positive energy boost. When a poor decision is made, the manager's job becomes much more difficult. Usually the manager has to spend more time educating, training or problem solving while also dealing with morale issues in the group.

How to Make the Right Decision

Once the interviewing is over, it is time to make a decision. Many interviewers make an educated guess based upon an accumulation of impressions and data. This is not always a bad approach but could be improved by using steps to organize and interpret the information you have gathered about the candidate. Research on the process of decision making after an interview suggests that organizing the information before arriving at a decision results in a more accurate assessment. Here are ways to do this.

Fundamental Questions to Answer

As discussed earlier, planning is done to provide a road map for conducting the interview. This process included developing a set of criteria that comprises aspects of the specific job, aspects of the environment and aspects of the organizational culture that would be important. During the interview you ask questions that will help elicit information related to these criteria, which means your task is to answer these questions in the end.

- Can the candidate perform the open position?
- Will the candidate demonstrate the desired behaviors that support the cultural norms?
- Will the candidate be a good fit given the uniqueness of the company's environment?

During the interview you are expected to take notes that relate to answering these questions. Since your notes will most likely be in chronological order, they will need to be reviewed and put into an organized candidate evaluation sheet.

Note Taking

Note taking is a skill, and it takes practice. Notes should be taken discreetly. If they are too detailed, consisting of the words of a candidate rather than the music of their behaviors, it is more difficult to assess the candidate against the job's specific and career/culture fit hiring criteria.

Since note taking is a skill requiring practice, encourage working with a format that is most comfortable for the interviewer to keep track of observations. A sheet of paper that has the criteria on the left with a place for notes on the right is one approach that helps to log information easily.

This practice will help when reviewing and redistributing your notes to the final evaluation sheet. Completing this final evaluation sheet allows the interviewer to take a few minutes to reflect on the notes, determine actual patterns that emerged and use these patterns to support the decision to hire or not to hire.

Decision Principles for Hiring the Best

Avoid Influences of First Impression & Other Biases

As mentioned in the previous chapter, we all have some sort of bias when it comes to evaluating applicants. These biases can subtly or overtly sway us to favor one candidate over another for reasons that may be unrelated directly to their ability to do the job.

Bias on the part of interviewers is believed to lead the list of items that contribute to miss-hires. Recognizing which, if any, of these biases an interviewer might be prone to repeating is a healthy step. Once the bias is identified, it is easier to guard against.

Discuss Observations with Other Interviewers without Regard to Hierarchy

Interviewing is a skill, and, as with any skill, practice will hone the process. This means the skill may reside at any level in the organization. When an interview team is selected, and all members are appropriately trained, no one individual simply because of title should be viewed as having better observations than any other. There are some hiring teams who set a rule that any one member who, with good reason, feels a candidate should not be hired has equal ability to stop that candidate from moving forward.

The more open and equitable the conversation regarding the candidate, the more learning takes place and the more comfortable each member feels in their role.

Emphasize Behavior Patterns when Discussing Candidates

The purpose behind an effective interview is to gather enough information about the candidate to determine his or her fit for the job and the company. The job of the interviewer is to elicit behavior that will support or detract from the agreed upon criteria. One statement or one observation cannot be considered a pattern of behavior. The interviewer's job is to elicit enough behavior to be able to see a pattern. A pattern is considered five examples, which means that taking one statement and blowing it out of proportion is not focusing on behavior patterns. Many times mixed patterns emerge; then the focus should be on those patterns that can be identified.

Make Final Decision Based on the Candidate's Fit with Predetermined Criteria

Once all the information is in and shared, the final decision must be made on the candidate's best fit with the job today, and the career and culture fit for the future. It is often easier to find someone who can do the job today than it is to find someone who can do the job today and also be a good fit for the needs of the company for the future.

Summary

Making the right hiring decision is one of the most important activities that any manager performs. The benefits of making the right decision are great, and the best way to be assured that the right decision is made is to engage in the right planning: Ask questions that will help determine the right fit for today and tomorrow, and take notes that can be shared with the other members of the hiring team.

Resources

"The Effective Interview: Eight Practices for Hiring the Best," white paper found on website *www.staubin.net.*

Part Five

Engage:
On-Boarding New Hires

20

Day-One Hints to Capture the Hearts & Imagination of New Talent

First impressions are very important when it comes to winning over new employees. Impressions are often formed early in the hiring process and then confirmed or disproved during the earliest stages of employment, including orientation and on-boarding. In fact, from the very beginning of the selection process applicants should go away from each interaction feeling good about the organization and wanting to work for the company even if they may not be the right fit for the available position. Those very first impressions can aid in setting positive expectations for any potential new hire.

The terms *orientation* and *on-boarding* are often used interchangeably, but as a rule, new employee orientation is defined as the process of receiving factual information about pay, benefits, company policies and procedures, and completing necessary paperwork along with understanding the new organization and the role of the new hire. New employee orientation is an essential part of the first day on the job and having competent, knowledgeable employees to conduct new employee orientations is critical to cementing that first impression. Unfortunately, too many organizations become overwhelmed by the paperwork and neglect the fundamentals of the day-one process. A better approach is to put the focus on welcoming and integrating new hires on day-one, which will lay the groundwork for improved performance and retention.

Engaging the Heart Hints

An effective orientation program makes the new hire feel comfortable and introduces the company culture. The goal is to engage the new hire in the culture from day-one. In fact, The Ritz-Carlton, a two-time Malcolm Baldrige Award winner, is so engaging in its day-one activities that employees are encouraged to have their cars valet parked, have lunch in the dining room and take a tour of the property. "The first day on the job has nothing to do with filling out forms and everything to do with who we are and how new employees are going to contribute," says Kathleen Smith, senior vice president of human resources for The Ritz-Carlton. The following are tips to help you engage your employees on day-one.

1. **Make the new hire feel welcome even prior to day-one.** Because there is so much paperwork for any new hire, try to make it available either online or in a package before they begin work, and let her know you will review it with her on day-one. Give her information about the organization and the job along with a *welcome to the organization* letter. In this letter, let her know what she will experience on her first day and week and what is expected of her in this process.

2. **Connect new hires to the big picture.** The more new hires understand about the mission, vision, goals and uniqueness of your organization, the more engaged and committed they will be from day-one. If the basis of your orientation is rules and paperwork, they will not engage as quickly or as deeply. Programs that do not have the vision and values of the organization front and center are not able to take advantage of one of the most valuable assets a new hire brings to the organization: energy and enthusiasm with a desire to make a difference. Imagine a new maintenance employee at The Ritz-Carlton being directed to use valet parking and to lunch in the dining room; she is already getting a feel for the company's expectations of employees.

3. **Engage new hires.** Engaging employees by connecting them to the big picture is one step, but you should also include how the new hire will help implement that big picture. This step is even more important for Generation Y new hires, who place a high priority on work that matters and on being able to make a difference in their work. How you engage people with the work they will be doing will make a huge difference in how they choose to do the work and how they talk about the work to others. After day-one they should be excited to start working and not just antsy to get out of the orientation room.

4. **Begin by storytelling.** Great companies have great stories: Starbucks is one example where its desire to build a company with soul led to providing comprehensive health insurance and stock options for employees working at least 20 hours. Every company has a story or a series of stories that touch the heart or capture the imagination of employees. Make sure that your stories are told again and again, and that new ones are added regularly. These stories, expecially when told by the employees themselves, demonstrate how employees make a difference. This has many advantages:

   • It makes for a more interesting and engaging message.
   • It communicates to current employees their importance to the organization.
   • It demonstrates leadership at all levels of the organization.

5. **Focus day-one activities on the new employee.** Too often companies act as if day-one is all about getting the information it needs and sharing information they think the new employee needs. Take a good look at your day-one process as if you were the new employee. Ask newer employees what they feel worked for them and what they might have liked to see. Constantly look at ways to make this program feel fresh and focused on the new employee.

6. Engage the family. It is very important to on-board the family as well as the new employee; this begins before day-one and continues far beyond day-one. Southwest Airlines, for example, conducts employee and family benefits fairs so employees' spouses and partners can see and understand the benefits that are available to them. Southwest believes that it is harder for employees to leave the company if the family, too, is tied into the benefits, culture and mission of the organization. If you have products that might be of interest to families, send some home with the employee on day-one. If you have a company store, give a gift certificate for store merchandise to the family as well as the employee.

The Manager's Role

Surveys show that the employee-manager relationship is one of the most significant in an employee's work life. In fact, most employee turnover and, conversely, most retention is ultimately a result of that relationship. This emphasizes then the importance of the manager in the initial assimilation of new employees.

An employee's direct supervisor manages career progression, educational opportunities and project assignments. So a manager who takes time to discuss issues with a new employee, who shows concern over that person's assimilation and who knows what the employee can do and wants to do will make wiser decisions and build loyalty over time.

Indeed, the manager should be an integral part of the day-one on-boarding process. In some firms, managers attend a session designed to provide the employee with an initial set of goals—perhaps for the first 30 to 60 days. Others include the manager in team-building exercises or have a luncheon during which the manager sits with the new employee. At the executive level, the senior executive can invite new hires to dinner at his or her home or set up a special quarterly dinner and reception for new executives. The key is to make sure the manager has a real role in both the formal process of on-boarding as well as the informal one that happens every day. Suggested activities include:

- Meet new employees on day-one.
- Introduce them to the facilitator of day-one activities.
- Outline the day's activities.
- Introduce them to the department and their workspace.
- Review their position description and initial expectations.
- Set out a 30-, 60-, and 90-day plan.
- Outline the mission, vision and values even if it was done earlier.
- Provide a "buddy" who helps with the socialization process.

Summary

An effective day-one program can:

- Help a new employee become engaged;
- encourage company loyalty;
- build and strengthen relationships within the organization; and
- save time and speed productivity and performance.

To gauge the success of your company's day-one activities, conduct feedback sessions that measure employees' positive and negative experiences through interviews, focus groups or surveys. Continue to build a positive day-one experience that inspires new employees to feel that they are valued and in a place that allows them to use their special talents.

Resources

There are numerous articles at ere.net that discuss orientation and on-boarding programs.

There are many new organizations that offer online tools to aid with on-boarding just search for on-boarding tools on the Internet.

21

On-Boarding &
Technology

The previous chapter described on-boarding as the process by which companies enable new employees to connect to their new jobs, the hiring manager, their team and the company's values and culture. The on-boarding process is one of integration, assimilation and socialization for the new hire as he or she becomes part of the larger organization. The whole objective of the on-boarding process is to speed up the learning curve of the new hire so that he or she is able to contribute to the company's success as quickly as possible. The key concept here is speed, and many companies have found that technology is an integral part of winning the race to on-board their newly found talent and help them become productive members of the organization.

James Brodie, in his article "Getting Managers on Board" (*HR Magazine*), tells us, "Many businesses have found that automation processes for employee on-boarding–especially for management level employees–can improve employee retention, reduce turnover, and increase compliance with internal policies and regulatory requirements."

As companies become convinced that the key metric in their on-boarding process is time to productivity for the new hire, they are investing the time and money in on-boarding software and Internet-based portals to provide pertinent information that was previously distributed in handbooks, manuals and other paper or e-mail files. Most companies are phasing out the slow and costly paper file systems of on-boarding employees and converting to Intranet or web-based portals. For companies with the resources (i.e., the in-house staff) to put all of their on-boarding software and forms online, the transition can be done as quickly as management appropriates the resources to develop their Intranet. For companies that do not have or do not choose to use in-house resources to devote to their on-boarding software, there are numerous reputable talent management software companies that can provide solutions and services at your call.

Software Companies to Explore

This is an appropriate time to examine some of those software companies to explore what they have to offer.

Cornerstone OnDemand, Inc. (*www.cornerstoneondemand.com*) is an integrated talent management firm that provides a comprehensive suite of talent management solutions for learning, performance, succession and compliance management, as well as robust reporting and analytics. Randstad North America's CLO, Vince Eugenio, praises Cornerstone for enabling Randstad to implement a sophisticated on-boarding process that includes 16 weeks of job shadowing, training, performance reviews and knowledge tests. Derek Moscato, in his article "Using Technology to Get Employees on Board" (*HR Magazine*, April 2005), goes on to say, "In addition to creating reports on a new hire's progress that go to the individual manager of the new employee, the (Cornerstone) software provides data on four or five key indicators that each new hire uses to rate the on-boarding process." As you can see, Randstad not only went online and away from its previous paper-based strategy but carried the on-boarding process much further with Cornerstone's expertise and software.

Vurv (*www.vurv.com*), formerly Recruitmax, is a software company with a product called Vurv Recruit, which automates manual processes such as pre-hire provisioning, benefits enrollment, interactive new hire orientation and mentor/training assignments. Key features of Vurv Recruit include document and form management, electronic signature, multiple workflow, dependent tasks, non-HR workbench and seamless candidate/employee portal integration.

Enwisen (*www.enwisen.com*) promotes its on-boarding software as one that engages new employees and speeds them to productivity. AnswerSource OnBoarding from Enwisen helps companies manage the three main components of the on-boarding process: task management, forms management and socialization. AnswerSource OnBoarding incorporates knowledgebase content, forms and workflow into an easily used tour framework that helps engage new hires with a personalized on-boarding experience, speed time to productivity, improve new hire retention, build your brand as an employer of choice, capture and route new hire data, and reduce legal exposure with consistent policies and electronic acknowledgments.

Silk Road technology's (*www.silkroadtech.com*) completely web-based, hosted on-boarding and life events solution, RedCarpet, helps both employees and HR professionals effectively manage change for all critical employee transitions by providing the following:

- Completely customized portals for socialization and efficient delivery of relevant information.
- Robust task management so you can have a defined process to see where all employees are.
- Electronic forms capable of eliminating errors and speed time to completion.
- Reduced administrative burden of paperwork and managing tasks.
- Consistency and accountability of processes.
- Easy administrative features and user management, giving you the power to dictate who can create, contribute and even view each task or record.

Peopleclick OnBoarding (*www.peopleclick.com*) tells us on its website that on-boarding is a critical business process that, when conducted effectively, can make the difference between an engaged employee who decides to stay with your company or a detached employee who chooses to leave. You need to create an experience for new hires that gets them up and running quickly.

Traditional on-boarding solutions accomplish part of this process by facilitating the collection of forms and managing tasks. These solutions help companies ensure compliance, increase recruiter productivity, accelerate time-to-productivity and monitor assets. But you need to address the most important first months for a new employee or internal transfer–the time that they require the most assistance with integration into the organization–to help them understand the culture and the company's goals and objectives while engaging them as essential to the organization's success. Peopleclick Onboarding is an inclusive on-boarding solution with a strategic approach that:

- Accelerates time to performance;
- increases internal mobility;
- improves retention;
- establishes your employee value proposition;
- enhances your brand; and
- builds alignment.

Kenexa (*www.kenexa.com*) offers a flexible on-boarding system that is configurable to your company's process. It accommodates multiple on-boarding processes with varying workflows and assists in the distribution of new employee orientation packs specific to job level and department or division. Kenexa integrates provisioning tools with forms management and culturalization tools that help employers complete important tasks involved in the on-boarding process, drastically improving efficiency of previously decentralized manual processes. Kenexa's on-boarding service comprises three key components:

1. **Discovery and design**–Kenexa Client Services works with HR project teams to assess on-boarding requirements and designs a system, including notifications and government and corporate forms, to meet specific needs.

2. **Implementation**–Once the design is complete, Kenexa's on-boarding experts configure each system and set up appropriate wizards and internal and external notifications, and form packets to make employees productive as quickly as possible.

3. **Adoption**–Kenexa Client Services provides user and administrator training to help its clients maximize the benefits of the on-boarding system and utilize all of the available features that ensure successful on-boarding of new employees.

Other notable talent management software providers include HRLogix, Root Learning, Knowledge Management Systems (KMS) and Deploy Solutions. It is up to you to decide whether these providers' software packages meet the needs of your on-boarding program. Some vendors offer customizable, stand-alone solutions to the on-boarding process, but most offer their services and products as part of a suite of products that complement and build upon each other.

Involve IT

It is critical to get your company's IT department involved in the process early on whether you decide to create your own online on-boarding program, use a web-based program or work with a vendor of your choice. Whatever solution you employ, develop metrics to make sure you are fully reaping the rewards of the technology involved.

The Human Element

Even the most sophisticated electronic on-boarding technology cannot provide the same experience as face-to-face encounters with the hiring manager, peers or the company CEO. Technology most assuredly has its place in the on-boarding process, and the technology a company chooses to employ can enhance the company's brand and contribute to the new hire gaining that all-important positive day-one impression. New hires feel welcome when they can come into work on the first day with technical and legal forms already completed online and some basic information about the company's history and culture. But what really enhances the employee's tenuous new bond with the company is the human relationships that will form during the first few months and the first year. To feel truly welcome, the new employee will need to learn the unwritten elements of the job, i.e., the people aspects of the company culture. Look to chapters 20 and 22 to read more about the human side of on-boarding.

Resources

www.shrm.org–Society for Human Resource Management.

www.hr.com–Human resources community for knowledge, expertise and resources.

22

New Hire Follow-Up– the First Year

The previous two chapters talked about the importance and methods of on-boarding a new employee to reap the benefits of retention, employee engagement and productivity. While success of the initial on-boarding process is essential, follow-up with the new employee is just as critical. The lines of communication between the new hire and his or her manager will more than likely determine whether the new hire remains past the first year.

Many companies devote considerable time and energy on the recruitment and selection process to bring the right people into the organization. As outlined in earlier chapters, this is important; however, the process should not stop once the offer has been accepted. An additional process to assimilate the employee into the new job, department and company is key to reducing potential performance problems and turnover.

Objectives of a New Employee Assimilation Process

1. Improve new hire retention to reduce the costs of turnover, especially costs attributable to new hires who leave the organization in the first year.
2. Shorten time to productivity and proficiency.

Meeting these objectives requires companies to positively impact the new hire's first impressions; integrate them through socialization efforts; increase the speed of acclimation, assimilation, engagement and productivity; and gain feedback on the new hire experience.

Characteristics of a Solid Process

- **High touch**–Although a solid plan is necessary, what ultimately makes a difference is how quickly you can engage personally with your new hires. Having them feel a part of the organization quickly is desired, but capturing their heart and not just their head is the ultimate goal.

- **Scalable**–Making the process work for any number of new hires is important. You do not want to develop a process that only works for high volume, and then some of your best hires feel that they are waiting around for the others to arrive.

- **Individualized**–A program must be capable of being customized to the person and the situation. Making everyone go through the same process may not be as effective as making sure all the elements have been incorporated for each individual.

Suggested Components

- **Assimilation team**–Assimilation should not be just an HR function or just the role of the manager. A team approach will garner a much better product in the end. The team should include:

  –**The HR department representative:** the role of this individual is to provide a bridge from the outside to the inside and to be a liaison between the new hire and the organization.

  –**The manager:** the manager has a responsibility to make sure that the new employee is filling the designed role and is able to move quickly to proficiency.

  –**The buddy or mentor:** this person helps to ease the strain of entering a new organization where the new hire may not know anyone or be familiar with the culture or ways of doing things in the new environment.

- **Resources**–The resources to do the job and to make an impact must be available and ready to use as soon as the new hire walks through the door. A new employee who knows what these are and begins to use them immediately will assimilate and move toward productivity much more quickly than one who does not.

- **Business expectations**–Outline for the new hire the most important elements of the business in terms of the mission, vision and values, strategies and expectations. This includes the level of professionalism and community role that define the organization.

Assimilating the New Employee

A solid orientation program will make the new employee feel more at ease with the organization and what is expected, however, attention is often placed on paperwork rather than on what will engage the employee for the long run.

There are a number of key strategies companies can employ to improve their rates of new employee retention during and beyond that critical first year. The approach may need to be adjusted based upon your company's size and complexity. The following steps provide suggested guidelines for a successful process.

Provide a Good Welcome

As a part of the initial orientation, make sure the new hire has a ready workspace, which means that keys, employee badges or entry codes are provided right away. It means a telephone, computer or other necessary equipment to perform the job are available and working. There is an immense feeling of belonging when new employees step into their workspace and it has been properly prepared for them.

Provide an Assimilation Checklist to the Manager

The manager is one of the principal members of the assimilation team and should be accutely aware of his or her role and what is expected of him or her. This can be done through the use of a manager checklist. One of the most common faults of an assimilation program is a hiring manager who is not present and available on the first day with a plan of action for the first 30 days. A successful plan should include some of the following items:

- **Pre-hire**–notify coworkers, send a welcome letter, assign a department buddy (someone who can help break the ice), prepare an organization chart, telephone and acronym lists, emergency plan and facility amenities.

- **Day-One**–meet the new employee, introduce employee to coworkers and a buddy, conduct a tour, provide organization overview, outline job responsibilities, ensure that workspace is available and ready.

- **Week-One**–review the new hire's role and responsibility in detail and establish a 30- to 60-day deadline for goals, share organization goals and function or department goals, check in with buddy, have lunch with new employee as appropriate, check with employee at end of week on status and to answer questions.

- **Month-One**–make sure policies are reviewed, discuss performance goals, check with buddy, check in with employee.

Individualize the Assimilation Process

Companies that hire a small number of people may tend to want to wait until there is more than one new employee before providing some of the assimilation components. Customizing the process for each individual will be more productive and more motivating for the individual, however, than waiting for a class to be filled.

Create an Organized Socialization Process

Management must do its best to make sure the new hire understands and buys into the company mission, vision and culture. Opportunities for the new hire to form relationships within the company and its customer base must constantly be nurtured and encouraged by everyone involved with the new hire from the CEO on down. If an individual does not feel part of the culture by the end of year-one, he or she is not likely to last.

Conduct a 30-Day Follow-Up Interview

This is a perfect time for the HR function to check in with the new hire and pose questions that will help determine if the manager is following the outlined plan and determine if the employee is engaged in work that she believed she would be doing when hired. This is also a good time to review policies, benefits and cultural norms, and to reinforce the company's position on ethics, harassment, corporate citizenship, etc. So much happens in the first week or two that reinforcing key messages at the 30-day mark will help reinforce the important messages and learn if there is anything that can be corrected quickly before it becomes a problem. For the new employee, being able to suggest areas that are not quite what was expected can keep her from getting upset and deciding to leave. Such communication also provides an opportunity to determine what the positive items are that will increase motivation and assimilation.

Six-Month Survey

Conducting a simple 6-month follow-up survey with each new hire that assesses the effectiveness of the process in terms of job duties, manager expectations and communication, mission, culture buddy, etc. will signal potential problems and possible changes to the process. This is the time to see if anything might be misaligned, for example:

- performance expectations
- disengaged manager
- lack of accountability
- internal networks
- lack of feedback or coaching

One-Year Celebration

The end of the first year is a time to celebrate and recalibrate. At this point it is easy to assess if the assimilation program has had the desired effect and to set the stage for the next year with the organization.

Summary

The bottom line is that it is expensive to attract, hire and develop employees; it is even more costly to have to replace them within the first year. An effective new hire assimilation strategy can ensure better retention and thus more productive use of resources.

Resources

www.asrt.com, "The Top 20 Ways to Improve Employee Retention."

Fortune magazine, "The 100 Best Companies To Work For," January 22, 2007.

23

Involve Supervisors, Buddies & Mentors

It is no surprise that one of the downsides of hiring new people is that they are not immediately productive. It can take a long time to impart all of the information required to see consistent performance that is sustained at the highest level. Even those individuals who may know the products, markets and skills required to do the job do not always know the local environment, steps, processes and internal requirements to quickly contribute to the highest degree.

One way to increase productivity of new hires is to involve supervisors even before the employee starts work, assign a buddy from the department who can help shepherd them through the first few days and weeks, and provide a mentor who can continue to help guide their development beyond what the immediate supervisor can do. Each of these roles can help a new hire feel welcomed and engaged with the new job. When a new hire feels welcomed, he or she will:

- Be able to develop good relationships with fellow employees that strengthen ties to the department and the organization;
- readily provide support and assistance when it is needed for other team members; and
- more easily integrate into the work life, thereby accelerating the time from hire to full productivity at work.

The following will detail the roles that each supervisor, buddy and mentor can play and some of the best practices that organizations use to welcome and assimilate new employees.

Supervisors

Studies have shown for years that the supervisor is the most important influence on how an employee feels about the organization and the work they perform. For this reason the hiring manager needs to connect with the new hire in a deeper manner than just a provider of direction. The manager should engage the new hire early in the assimilation process in four critical topics of conversation, which include:

- **Roles and Relationships**–The supervisor should outline the role the new hire has in the organization and how that role interacts with other key organizational roles. This includes: What are the primary relationships that exist and how can they be built and maintained over the next few months?

- **Mission, Vision and Values**–The new hire will be more committed if his or her supervisor explains what the organization stands for and what the company is trying to achieve. He also wants to understand what he can do to achieve that mission in a way that fits the values of the company.

- **Passion**–Supervisors should get to know what the new hire is passionate about and what challenges him so they can help channel and support those items on the job.

- **Direction**–Supervisors should learn what is important for the long term for the new hire so they can keep him excited to learn and grow in the direction he would like to move, thus keeping him engaged and committed to the organization over time.

Besides these conversations, there are a few other things a supervisor can do to help welcome and engage the new hire:

- Send a welcome letter to the home of the new hire before he starts work.
- Send a welcome e-mail to introduce new employees to others in their department or company at large.
- Start each meeting by introducing the new employee and welcoming him to the company.
- Assign a buddy to help guide the new employee's first few weeks on the job.
- Assign a mentor to take over and help guide the new hire in his long-term career with the company.

Buddy Program

One technique for quickly bringing a new employee up to speed is to assign that person to a buddy, someone who will mentor the new employee through the first few days and weeks on the job. This helps to reduce the time he may be struggling to find simple answers while not wanting to bother people who seem quite occupied.

A buddy acts as a guide, explaining how things are done and where things are. New hires need to know how to use the phone system and where the bathrooms, cafeteria or break rooms are located. It is also nice to have the buddy take the new person along to lunch and introduce him to others, maybe even scheduling a series of lunches to help ease him into the social aspect of the job.

After 4 to 6 weeks, you may choose to end the buddy relationship. This can be done in a formal manner by officially thanking the buddy for his service and having the new hire share what the buddy meant to him in this early stage.

Potential Buddy Problems

Even a well-developed buddy program can run into some snags. Following are some of the more common issues that can arise:

- **Poor buddy assignment**–Some people like the idea of being a buddy better than the actual assignment that goes along with it. In addition, the buddy may feel that it is his job to act as a second supervisor, which is also not appropriate. Make sure the buddy is fully trained and ready to handle the assignment the way it is designed; this could be a good test for a future supervisory assignment.

- **The buddy does the work**–The buddy may feel it is faster to do the work in the first few weeks than to help the new hire begin to figure it out. In this case, the work may get done faster but the new hire does not get the intended learning experience.

- **The experience gets interrupted**–The buddy is called away to do another assignment, which renders him unavailable to the new hire. This can cause stress for both parties making the relationship a burden on both rather than a helpful tool for both.

Creating a buddy system for new hires is a great idea that requires an appropriate amount of planning and execution in order for it to truly be effective. When organized properly, however, it can dramatically reduce the time a new hire requires to be productive and engaged.

Assign a Mentor

Once a new employee has been oriented and provided a buddy for a period of time and begins to feel adjusted to the new job, organization and ways of doing things, it is helpful to assign a mentor. The mentor is usually someone outside the department who has enough tenure and position to be able to help guide the new hire's career. This allows the manager to direct the performance of the employee and have help in guiding the employee's career with the company. This is not meant to reduce the job of a supervisor but to enhance it.

A well-planned mentoring program can enhance your culture and help retain your talent. Successful implementation of a mentoring program for new hires requires a good design and a pool of well-trained mentors. Mentor programs are effective when you focus on the following:

- **Select appropriate employees to be mentors**–Just because someone volunteers to be a mentor does not mean he will be the best at this role. Develop a good process for selecting mentors and make it a professionally rewarding role.

- **Train mentors before assigning them**–Do not pick good people and then allow them to do it in their own way. Every mentor should understand the philosophy, tools and rules that accompany the role.

- **Make it formal and flexible**–The program should have a set of responsibilities and processes to follow, but too much bureaucracy can weigh the program down and not allow for natural events to occur. Mentoring meetings should happen on a regular schedule with agendas tailored to the needs and desires of the new hire.

Summary

There is no doubt that involving supervisors, buddies and mentors will reduce the new hire's time to productivity while supporting the company's goal of employee retention. With the right approach any organization can benefit from this investment in new hire assimilation.

Resources

Great Places to Work Institute *(www.greatplacetowork.com)* has research and papers on welcoming employees.

www.humancapitalinstitute.org has information about ways to on-board new hires.

Love 'em or Lose 'em, Berrett-Koehler, ©2007, discusses how supervisors, buddies and mentors impact retention.

24

Assimilate New Leaders

Assimilating a new leader, whether new to the organization or just new to the team, is an important and truly productive effort. The new leader assimilation process uses techniques that compress the period whereby a new leader and the people who work for him or her explore each other's operating styles and approaches and become acquainted with their respective expectations.

Without a process like the one outlined here, it may take weeks or months to meet with each person and learn about them and their expectations while important bits and pieces of information slip through the cracks.

The objectives of a new leader assimilation process include the following:

- To brief the new leader regarding the team and the business at an accelerated pace.
- To reduce the level of preliminary apprehensions and concerns that may exist on the part of either the new leaders or the new staff.
- To provide both a climate and a forum for early two-way flow of information concerning such vital points as personal style, needs of the organization and problem areas that might need to be addressed.
- To begin to build the new team quickly in order to maintain existing momentum and to solidify the team spirit and identity.
- To provide a forum for the new leader to communicate with and align the team around his or her ideas and philosophies.

Mutual Benefits

The new leader assimilation process provides benefits for the new leader, the team, the facilitator and the organization at large. The benefits for each of these groups are outlined below.

The New Leader

- The process organizes and plans the new position orientation.
- The air is cleared right from the beginning of the manager-employee relationship.

- The process establishes the leader as a real person, rather than the boss or director of the work and unit.
- It demonstrates the leader's willingness to listen to the concerns and ideas of the people on the team and in the organization.
- The process provides multiple inputs to the leader on key questions that need to be addressed in the new job.
- It allows the opportunity to meet with all of his or her people promptly, rather than dealing with the delays that result when discussions occur one at a time. It does not replace the need to have one-on-one conversations but does get information out on the table that make subsequent one-on-one conversations focused and more productive.

Members of the New Leader's Staff

- The process provides each member of the staff the opportunity to promptly meet with the new leader in an open and engaging manner.
- The process provides staff members with inputs on the new manager as a leader, including operating style, personal priorities and team expectations.
- The process allows them to pose questions to the leader on potentially sensitive matters, that under normal circumstances they may hesitate to present to a new leader.
- The process makes it possible to meet the new leader in a more general context, rather than the structured contact normally experienced in work assignments and decision making.
- The process brings the group together as a team with the common objective of getting acquainted with the new leader and making sure that she knows how the team likes to function as a group.

The Facilitator

- The process provides a forum for assuring the continuity of professional management.
- It allows the facilitator to establish a relationship whereby he or she may expedite a flow of open communication between the team and the leader.
- The process makes the facilitator an active part of the new leader's staff by helping identify team and business priorities, concerns and plans of action.
- The process establishes the facilitator as an independent party where she becomes a consultant to the new leader on talent and team issues, opportunities and objectives.
- It allows the facilitator to become more acquainted with both the leader and the staff, and to be better positioned to function as a consultant with the operation on other matters.

The Organization

- The process provides a consistent methodology for assimilating all new leaders–from inside promotions to outside hires–into the organization.
- It sets up an expectation that the team should work quickly to establish the important processes and priorities that will accomplish the stated goal of the team.

- It provides the framework for open dialogue and communication throughout the organization.
- It compresses the time to productivity for a new leader. Rather than a process taking weeks or more, this process reduces that timeline, which adds to the productivity of the group and the organization.

Steps to Implementing the Process

The process begins with the facilitator meeting separately with the new leader and the team. The facilitator can be an internal human resource member or process coach, or an external facilitator who manages the process with the agreement of the leader and the organization.

The benefit of using an internal facilitator is her knowledge of the organization and the people involved. The benefit of an external facilitator is the outside, third-party perspective they can bring. The process also allows for an internal human resource member to participate, but employees cannot be both a participant in the process and a facilitator of the process.

Here are the suggested steps in implementing this new leader assimilation:

1. **Preparation**–The facilitator meets with the new leader and outlines the process in terms of the objectives, benefits and steps. This meeting is recommended even in advance of the new leader officially starting her job. If the leader, once briefed, is interested in using this process as a part of her orientation, then the facilitator meets with the new staff to gain their acceptance of this aspect of the process.

2. **Pre-work**–Once all parties have agreed to the process, the facilitator provides the new staff with a list of questions that will be discussed with the group. A date and location (preferably off-site or in a quiet conference room) for the meeting should be communicated as well.

3. **Team questions**–The list of questions provided to the new staff can vary depending upon the circumstances. Core questions such as those that follow should be limited to no more than 10.
   - What do you know about the new leader?
   - What don't you know but would like to know?
   - What do you want most from the new leader?
   - What do you want the new leader to know about how the team operates today?
   - What things are working well for the team?
   - What major obstacles exist for the team in trying to achieve the team's goals?
   - What should the new leader know about the business that she might not already be aware of?

4. **Leader questions** At the same time, the facilitator outlines four questions to the new leader for independent, advance consideration. These questions include:
   - What do you know about the team?
   - What do you not know about the team?
   - How do you like to operate?
   - What concerns do you have?

5. **Team meeting** The facilitator begins the initial group discussion with the team minus the leader, encouraging the group to be candid and open. Each team question is then placed on a flip chart, and all participants are encouraged to provide input to one question at a time before moving on to the next. At this point the team takes a break while the facilitator completes the next step with the new leader.

6. **New leader meeting** The facilitator now walks the new leader through the team's responses to the questions on the flip charts. The new leader can ask the facilitator questions for clarification purposes and take notes regarding how she might want to respond.

7. **Full team meeting** After the facilitator has briefed the new leader, the entire team now meets to discuss the questions discussed by the team. At this point the leader can go through and respond to everything item by item or identify key themes that can be addressed with the group. This is usually the place where the new leader can provide additional input regarding the items that she was asked to think about prior to the meeting.

Summary

This new leader assimilation process has proven to be successful in meeting its objectives in a variety of situations. It is a goal-oriented process that reaps many benefits for the new leader, the staff and the organization.

Resources

SHRM white paper, "Executive Assimilation" by William G. Bliss, Nov. 2004 *www.shrm.org.*

Part Six

The ABC's of Engagement

25

Act with Virtue

Most of us try hard to follow advice from our youth to *play nice* and get along with others. Many leaders might wonder whether there is business value in investing time and resources to build a *nice* organization where good values are woven into the fabric of everyday work life. But this chapter takes the stance that positive business outcomes occur when an organization lives by its values, and when employees are proud of the inherent and visible goodness of their organization.

Virtues are the best of the human condition. Indeed, some would say virtue is the most ennobling of behavior and outcomes, the highest aspirations of human beings. Plato and Aristotle described virtuousness as the desires and actions that produce personal and social good (*Positive Organizational Scholarship*, page 48). In a chapter on virtues and organizations from the book *Positive Organizational Scholarship*, Park and Peterson state that "organizational-level virtues are characteristics of organizations that contribute to the fulfillment of its members."

What Are Organizational Virtues?

Virtues are values in action. Virtuous people are those who act in consistent ways based on their value system. Most organizations also talk about their values. So, organizational virtues are work behaviors based on organizational values. Organizational virtues, such as those listed below, are organizational values in action.

- **Purpose**–a shared vision of the moral goals of the organization reinforced by remembrances and celebrations.

- **Safety**–protection against threat, danger and exploitation.

- **Fairness**–equitable rules governing reward and punishment and the means to consistently enforce them.

- **Humanity**–mutual care and concern.

- **Dignity**–the treatment of all people in the organization as individuals regardless of their position.

- **Compassion**–a sympathetic consciousness of another's distress together with a desire to alleviate it.

- **Integrity**–moral soundness, honesty, and freedom from corrupting influence or motives.

- **Forgiveness**–the act of excusing a mistake or offense.

- **Trust**–the intention to accept vulnerability based on the positive expectations of the intentions or behavior of another.

- **Optimism**–a disposition to expect the best in all things; to expect that all things will turn out well.

Making Virtues Tangible

In practical terms, virtues can be made more tangible by taking the following organization level actions:

- Posting stories that demonstrate values in action on the organization's internet site and/or intranet.
- Creating the disciplines of sharing examples and stories of values in all leader communiqués.
- Holding periodic celebrations of important organizational anniversaries.
- Creating programs that support community volunteering and involvement.
- Announcing and praising good business decisions based on principles and values.
- Consistently managing and leading in ways that uphold human dignity; for example, treating people as trusted individuals by giving them the autonomy to be innovative.

While this chapter has thus far focused on organization-level virtues, virtuous actions happen at the individual level as well. In fact, stories that gain the most traction in the verbal history of an organization are about actions that go beyond the expected routines and are seen as unexpectedly virtuous. For example, many people will pass along a positive story about a manager who went out of his or her way to help an employee undergoing a personal trauma, especially when the two parties had not been on the best of terms prior to the virtuous act. Or, they may pass along their positive impressions about a colleague who invests personal time in helping those less fortunate in the community, especially when these contributions occur while work demands are high.

How Does Virtue Benefit an Organization?

Is there evidence that virtuous behavior pays off? The answer is Yes. Here are some findings from recent organizational research as presented in *Positive Organizational Scholarship*.

The Virtue of...	...Is found to be associated with...
Forgiveness	Broader, richer social relationships, higher job satisfaction, greater feelings of empowerment, less physical illness, less depression and anxiety.
Optimism, Hope	Better performance, more perseverance, better moods at work, better social relationships, higher physical health levels, self-efficacy, and flexibility in thinking.
Compassion	Higher levels of helping behaviors, moral reasoning, stronger interpersonal relationships, less depression, reduced moodiness, less mental illness.
Integrity	High self-esteem, productive interpersonal relationships, productive teamwork, effective decision-making, participation, positive climate in organization.

Additional Benefits to Organizations of Virtuous Actions

Organizations that successfully establish a virtuous organization through a history of virtuous leadership and member behavior accrue two primary benefits: the amplifying effect and the buffering effect.

The Amplifying Effect of Virtuousness

Virtuous actions beget additional virtuous actions, and this contagious cycle of behavior naturally catches hold in an organization. As described in the book *Positive Organizational Scholarship,* virtuousness provides an amplifying effect in organizations because of these associated outcomes:

- **Positive emotions** (compassion, optimism, joy, etc.). For example, altruistic behavior in one person increases the altruistic behaviors in others. This is the so-called *pay it forward* effect.
- **Social capital** (values and understandings that facilitate cooperation within and among groups). Virtues such as empathy and caregiving build high-quality relationships in which people feel free to exchange more and better information, desire to strengthen relationships and exchange more valued resources.
- **Pro-social behavior** (individuals behaving in ways that benefit other people). Observing or experiencing an act of virtuousness unlocks a person's natural tendency to help others.

The Buffering Effect of Virtuousness

Virtuousness has been shown to buffer the organization from negative outcomes due to trauma. Typically, when organizations are driven to downsize, common effects include destruction of relationships; loss of trust; reduced loyalty, teamwork and information sharing; and increased deception, rigidity, conflict and vindictiveness.

However, organizations where virtuousness is high have greater levels of:

- resiliency
- solidarity
- a sense of collective efficacy ("We can influence our own future.")
- mental and physical health
- positive social capital (collaboration)
- organizational strength

According to Kim S. Cameron in *Positive Organizational Scholarship*, organizational leaders can strengthen these buffering effects of virtuousness during organizational trauma through leadership practices such as:

- open communication channels
- support of empowered, cohesive work groups
- reward and recognition systems
- facilitative, healthy physical architecture
- clear statements of value and vision
- opportunities for interpersonal interaction

The Bottom (& Top) Line

To summarize, demonstrations of virtue by organizational leaders serve as a source of identity and pride for employees. Virtuous actions create an upward spiral of positive emotions, having an amplifying effect and creating positive social capital. Positive emotions and social capital are the currency that creates great performance through collaboration, healthy colleague and customer relationships, and desire to contribute even beyond what is expected. A solid foundation of virtuousness can buffer an organization from the negative impact of trauma from events such as downsizing or other high-impact organizational changes.

Below are six principles for treating people right and creating virtuous cycles, adapted from "Leading a Virtuous-Spiral Organization" by Edward E. Lawler.

1. Examine the value proposition within your employment brand.

- How clear does your value proposition for potential employees describe the values of the organization that can attract and retain the right people?
- To what extent does this value proposition authentically align with the existing culture and leadership behaviors?

2. Refresh and clarify your hiring practices.

- Have you ensured that the differentiating criteria for hiring are consistently used?
- Are your hiring criteria and tools aligned with corporate values?

3. Build values and virtues into the training and development process.

- To what extent does training reinforce values and virtuous behavior?

- Are growth opportunities fairly apportioned to employees?
- What could be done to align training and development practices with organizational values?

4. Examine work design features.

- How might work design be enhanced to make work more meaningful?
- How does the organizational structure provide people with healthy feedback, support for growth, and fulfill the need for responsibility and authority?

5. Create virtuous reward systems.

- Are virtuous behaviors recognized and rewarded?
- Are nonvirtuous behaviors recognized and rewarded? That is, do those who exhibit behaviors that run contrary to espoused values get promoted, or are they denied promotion?

6. Promote virtuous leadership.

- Does the organization hire, develop and promote leaders who can create commitment, trust, success and a motivating work environment?
- To what extent do your leaders communicate openly, honestly and virtuously?

The best organizations put processes, structures and expectations in place to ensure that virtuous cycles are reinforced. Leaders in these organizations act on values that support virtuous actions and cycles that, in turn, enhance human capital so the organization excels even while (and perhaps due to the fact that) employees' needs for fulfilling, meaningful work are being met.

Resources

"Exploring the Relationship Between Organizational Virtuousness and Performance," *The American Behavioral Scientist*, Feb. 2004.

Positive Organizational Scholarship: Foundations of a New Discipline, Berrett-Koehler Publishers, Inc., ©2003.

"Ethical Character and Virtue of Organizations: An Empirical Assessment and Strategic Implications," *Journal of Business Ethics*,(2005) Vol. 57.

"Leading a Virtuous-Spiral Organization," *Leader to Leader*, Spring 2004.

www.valuesinaction.com

26

Be Trustworthy & Build Trust

"Trust is the lubrication that makes it possible for organizations to work."

–Warren G. Bennis

"Trust each other again and again. When the trust level gets high enough, people transcend apparent limits, discovering new and awesome abilities for which they were previously unaware."

–David Armistead

These quotes from business leaders ring true and are supported by research on the links between trust in an organization and organizational performance.

In a study reported by the *American Society for Quality* ("The Trust Imperative" by Hacker, Willard and Couturier), a high correlation was found between trust and profitability: "In divisions that outperformed others, 84 percent of survey respondents said they had high levels of trust, as compared to lower-performing divisions in which only 27 percent believed trust was high."

In an article titled "Trust and Efficiency," Ralph Chami and Connel Fullenkamp observed, "when employees who work together trust each other, they exert more effort in their jobs and expend less effort monitoring each other. This leads to increased productivity, lower costs, and greater satisfaction for workers as well as shareholders. ... It is in every corporation's interest to consider developing a culture of trust as a way of improving performance." (From the Social Science Research Network Electronic Paper Collection.)

Research into the extent that employees and customers trust corporations show some disturbing trends. For example:

> "There are also declining levels of trust within organizations, with employees questioning whether their employers are being honest with them. The vast majority (84 percent) of Americans think that the people who run their companies are trying to do what is best for themselves rather than the company." (Excerpt from an Accenture white paper referencing the World Economic Forum.)

Clearly, those employers who have lost the trust of their employees run a severe risk of high disengagement levels and loss of talent, along with the negative financial ramifications caused by lower productivity and loss of customer trust.

It is complicated. Trust is a powerful dynamic and notoriously hard to quantify and act upon. It seems that when you do everything else right to engage employees, trust is alive and well across the organization. But one slip-up can damage trust levels beyond repair.

A Definition & Some Frameworks

A definition of interpersonal trust that we find useful is: "A psychological state comprising the intention to accept vulnerability based upon positive expectations of the intentions or behavior of another." (Lewicki, Tomlinson)

A Trust Equation

A quick way to erode trust is by acting in ways that are self-oriented. In Trust in Business: The Core Concepts, (an article at trustedadvisor.com) Charles H. Green depicts the trust equation as follows.

$$T = \frac{C + R + I}{S}$$

The level of trustworthiness (T) assigned to another is the sum of credibility (C), reliability (R) and intimacy (I) divided by the level of self-oriented (S) behavior.

Quite simply, the trust level will go up if the numerator increases or denominator decreases; it will go down when the numerator decreases or denominator increases. With only one factor in the denominator, an increase here (more self-oriented behavior) results in much more rapid erosion of trust.

Tips for Growing Person-to-Person Trust

Using these concepts as a foundation, here are some tips that a leader can follow to build and sustain trust with his or her employees.

- Get to know your people, their preferences, motivations, interests and aspirations. Hold monthly information conversations to check in with them.
- Be careful to make promises and commitments that you can keep. If you cannot keep a promise you have made to a colleague, apologize, and then tell the person what happened and how you plan to follow up.
- Be consistent and predictable. Do what you can to show that your word has meaning.
- To be seen as someone who has the ability and the credibility to be a trustworthy person, you must be seen as someone who trusts.
- Avoid giving assignments with so many details, constraints and checkpoints that you are seen as a micromanager with the inability to trust a person's sense of responsibility and initiative.

"A person who trusts no one can't be trusted."

–Jerome Blattner

- Avoid hiring people who may support or create a climate of distrust. In your hiring criteria, define what integrity or character means in behavioral terms.
- After hiring employees, trust them from the start. Coach for lapses in judgment, but continue to trust.

"Don't employ someone you suspect, nor suspect someone you employ."

–Chinese proverb

- Be benevolent–show concern and care for others. This type of behavior begets similar behavior in the organization, so it has a reinforcing, contagious effect.

"People love to be nice, but you must give them the chance."

–Pierre-Auguste Renoir

- Communicate clearly, with openness, honesty and transparency. Be truly sincere in what you say. Avoid spinning the truth.

"The highest compact we can make with our fellow is– 'Let there be truth between us two forevermore.'"

–Ralph Waldo Emerson

- Create that deep sense of trust and safety among your people by holding confidences, asking for feedback, being open to ideas and concerns of others, being responsive to important needs of your people and being interested in their lives beyond work.
- Avoid self-oriented behavior. Empathy is the lubrication of trust. When you act without empathy, you rapidly erode trust.
- Foster a mature and trusting environment by showing appreciation for trust-building behaviors and coaching away from self-oriented behaviors in others.

Rebuilding Trust after a Violation

When you suspect that you have done something (however unintentional it may have been) to erode the trust level with another person, here are some things you might do at a person-to-person level. The following are from Trust and Trust Building by Lewicki and Tomlinson (visit *www.beyondintractability.org/essay/trust_building*):

- Take immediate action after the violation.
- Provide an apology and give a thorough account of what happened.
- Be sincere.
- Be cognizant of the day-to-day history of the relationship.
- Provide restitution/penance.
- Restate and renegotiate expectations for the future.

Teaming Requires Interpersonal Trust

A quick review of recent writings on teams and teamwork in organizations reveals that researchers clearly believe that trust is an essential element of team excellence.

- LaFasto and Larson, in *When Teams Work Best: 6,000 Team Members and Leaders Tell What It Takes to Succeed*, identify trust as being essential to the required collaboration between team members. They explain that this is especially true at the executive team level where the main task confronting top teams is open, collaborative, executable decision making.
- Robbins and Finley, in *The New Why Teams Don't Work: What Goes Wrong and How to Make It Right*, list lack of team trust as one of 14 reasons why teams fail and devote a whole chapter to *trust hell*.
- Patrick M. Lencioni, in *The Five Dysfunctions of a Team: A Leadership Fable*, identified dysfunction number one as absence of trust.

So what do teams do to achieve trust? To increase trust and create teaming excellence, a combination of some or all of the following steps has been found to be effective.

- Get agreement and commitment from the team leader around the importance of having an excellent, trust-based team.
- Prepare the team for the trust-building process.
- Gather information (interviews, online surveys, team feedback, etc.).
- Educate the team on the dimensions of excellent teams.
- Practice open communication, using team and individual feedback.
- Identify and explore the behavior or communication style preferences of each team member.
- Establish a set of team operating principles.
- Coach individual team members to resolve trust issues.
- Establish a process to reassess the level of team trust.

What an Organization Can Do to Enhance Trust in the Organization

Here are some ways that leaders can approach building or rebuilding trust in their organizations:

- Mitigate the negative impact of organizational change efforts through open, honest, proactive and frequent communication.
- Maximize team-building investments.
- Revamp or jettison policies and ways of doing business that impede the goal of regaining trust. Consider practices such as:
    - performance appraisals and development plans
    - selection and promotion processes
    - recognition, rewards and incentives
    - leadership communication
- Conduct interviews with employees about trust in the organization.

Above all, when seeking to enhance trust across the organization, the leadership team must keep one motto in mind:

We do what we say we will do.

Investing in trust-building programs at the person-to-person, team and organizational levels is well worth the effort–returning on the investment by several orders of magnitude. Such efforts build an engaged, loyal workforce while contributing directly to corporate well being.

Resources

"Trust and Efficiency, Social Science Research Network Electronic Paper Collection. (October 1999 – July 2001 version) Chami, R., and Fullenkamp, C.

Positive Organizational Scholarship: Foundations of a New Discipline. Berrett-Koehler Publishers, Inc., ©2003.

"Trust and Trust Building," "Beyond Intractability." Conflict Research Consortium, University of Colorado, Boulder. Posted: December 2003. *http://www.beyondintractability.org/essay/trust_building.*

Conflict Cooperation and Justice, Josie-Bass Inc. ©1995.

Trust and Mistrust, John Wiley & Sons Ltd. ©2003. Ward, A., and Smith, J.

"The Value of Building Trust in the Workplace," May 2003 *www.badergroup.com.*

The Trust Imperative, American Society of Quality. ©2002.

"The High Cost of Lost Trust," *Harvard Business Review*, 2002.

27

Create an
Engaging Culture

"Corporate culture is a tough opponent to go up against, and winners and losers approach it in totally different ways."

–Daryl R. Conner

"The thing I learned at IBM is that culture is everything."

–Louis V. Gerstner, Jr., former CEO of IBM

Employees who perceive that their organization aligns with their own values, provides meaningful work and treats its members with respect and fairness will stay longer and work harder to contribute.

Initiatives that focus on transforming an organization's culture are in vogue these days. This is no doubt due to immense pressures such as globalization, transparent pricing, competitive open markets, technological advances, government regulation, speed to innovate and competition for best talent. Frequently it is clear that for organizations to meet the demands of a turbulent business environment, the culture also must change or the organizational will lose.

What Does It Mean to Change a Culture? What Is Culture?

In *Managing at the Speed of Change: How Resilient Managers Succeed and Prosper While Others Fail*, Daryl Conner says "Organizational culture reflects the interrelationship of shared behaviors, beliefs and assumptions that are acquired over time by members of an organization." Edgar Schein defines the culture of a group as "a pattern of shared basic assumptions that the group learned as it solved its problems of external adaptation and internal integration, that has worked well enough to be considered valid, and therefore to be taught to new members as the correct way to perceive, think, and feel in relation to these problems."

It is when these shared beliefs and perceptions of the group turn into employee disengagement that the culture needs adjustment.

The culture of an organization is difficult to transform; many a leader with good intentions to bring about improved business outcomes has been foiled by the persistent stasis of an organizational culture. It is not unlike sailing. You can point the sailboat in the direction you need it to go with constant pressure on the tiller, but as soon as you release it, the boat resumes its course of least resistance by running in the direction the wind is blowing.

Given the focus of this book, a critical consideration is the extent to which an organization's culture inhibits or enhances the attraction, engagement and retention of talent. Ironically, it is often the case that when the leadership team attempts to steer the culture of the organization in a new direction, their actions disengage the workforce, at least over the short term.

Consider the following example of one organization that acquired another, younger organization, where the founding owners of the acquired organization were still in the key leadership positions. One of the cultural norms of this entrepreneurial enterprise was to pass all decisions by the founders. As the acquiring organization initiated much-needed process efficiencies, some members of the acquired organization saw this as an insult to or lack of trust in their top leadership team. As in many mergers and acquisitions, there was a resulting loss of talent with very real business impact over the short term. The organization is doing well now and was greatly benefited by leadership attention and support, including an all-employee listening campaign.

Researchers have attempted to describe the types of organizational cultures that are most common. In an article from Northwestern University's Forum for People Performance Management and Measurement website (*www.performanceforum.org*), four types of cultures are described. Are any of these familiar to you?

1. **Competitive Culture.** Members typically are rewarded for taking charge and being in control. In such organizations, winning is often highly valued and members are rewarded for outperforming each other. A competitive culture encourages decisiveness, rewards achievement and creates an environment of high expectations. On the other hand, an overly competitive culture can inhibit effectiveness by reducing cooperation and promoting unrealistic standards.

2. **Passive Culture.** Conflicts are avoided and members feel as if they must agree with, gain the approval of and be liked by others. Such organizations tend to be conservative, traditional and bureaucratically controlled. This type of work environment can limit organizational effectiveness by minimizing expression of ideas, suppressing innovation and stifling flexibility.

3. **Aggressive Culture.** Aggressive norms minimize influence at lower levels by emphasizing adherence to directives and authority. Aggressive norms promote such behaviors as procrastination, inflexibly following rules and procedures, and waiting for direction from superiors before acting.

4. **Cooperative Culture.** Members are encouraged to set goals, take initiative and work together to attain objectives. Cooperative cultures value and respect individuals and support distribution of decision-making authority along with the confidence and trust that authority will not be abused. Cooperative norms encourage behaviors such as goal attainment, enjoying one's work and maintaining one's personal integrity and standards. (Adapted from "Linking Organizational Characteristics to Employee Attitudes and Behavior – A Look at the Downstream Effects on Market Response & Financial Performance." *http://www.performanceforum.org/ Research.5.0.html)*

Clearly, the cooperative culture style would be more engaging to a larger percentage of the workforce than the other three types.

Organizational culture change efforts will not succeed if the leadership team underestimates the impact of culture. In addition, the leadership at the top must act consistently with repeated messages and explicit support of processes that align behavior. Leaders must practice what they preach, i.e., preaching often and practicing well. Finally, there must be a critical mass of these cultural change champions at visible levels of the organization, which John Kotter calls "the guiding coalition." Without it, the status quo wins.

Below is a description of cultural outcomes that lead to an engaged workforce and ideas for affecting change in the organizational culture.

Desired Culture Outcomes	Ideas for Changing Your Organization's Culture
"We listen and act on employee input."	Conduct a *Leaders are Listening* program. Announce and carry out a program to give all employees a chance to make their thoughts and ideas known. This must be championed and carried out by the top leader(s).
"We are proud to represent this organization."	Involve employees in key business activities. The more you can offer ways for employees to contribute to the success of the organization, the more employees take pride in membership. What might you do to involve employees in unorthodox ways? • Use a cross-section of employees to build important, visible programs such as an on-boarding process for new employees. • Use multiple levels of team members to interview and provide input into new hire selection. • Prepare to give monetary rewards and support for good business ideas from any employee at any level.

"We have bosses who care about us."	Develop a great supervisor program. For most employees, the culture of the organization resides in the style of their direct supervisor. Create clear guidelines to ensure every supervisor knows how to provide high-quality people management.
"We let people know what is going on."	Communicate until it hurts. John Kotter in *Leading Change: Why Transformation Efforts Fail* observes that organizational leaders underestimate the need to communicate by a factor of ten.
"We invest in developing our people."	Optimize training and mentoring activities. Employees who have access to training and valued growth experiences will be more engaged than employees with no access to these things. Do not underestimate the positive impact of having top leaders be active teachers and mentors.
"We promote fairly and inclusively."	Closely examine your promotion and job assignment processes. First, no supervisor should be promoted to greater levels of leader responsibility if there is credible information that the person's behavior disengages employees. Also, talented employees react negatively to any hint of favoritism, bias or exclusivity in the promotion process.
"We enjoy each other's company."	Throw a party or two. Successful organizations hold one or more social events for their employees during the year. These can accomplish goals beyond socializing, such as contributing to the community, recognizing extraordinary contributions, and celebrating successes.
"We say 'Thank You.'"	Create access to informal recognition resources. People like to be thanked and appreciated. (For more ideas see Chapter 46: Recognize & Appreciate.)
"We want our people to have full lives."	Support balance. Consider creating a program for paid time-off to contribute to clubs, community group or volunteer work. Build options for flexible work hours. Develop programs to allow people to work from home offices.
"We don't want to burn anyone out."	Check staffing levels, and act on insufficiencies. Take seriously any credible data that there are segments of the workforce working unreasonable hours to make up for staffing shortages, especially over long periods of time. Organizations that let this happen run the risk of sending the message to their most talented employees that we expect you to do more with less, and it will only get worse. Make visible your actions to bring in more talent to share the workload.

| "Our leaders help to clarify what is most valued here." | Create and reinforce the discipline of leading the culture. Edgar Schein in *Organizational Culture and Leadership: A Dynamic View* outlines specific disciplines that leaders can employ to drive a clearer organizational culture. Employees can align their priorities and behavior around:
• What leaders pay attention to, measure and control.
• Leader reactions to critical incidents and crises.
• Deliberate role modeling, teaching and coaching.
• Criteria for allocation of rewards, resources and status.
• Organization design and structure.
• Stories about important events and people.
• Formal statements of organizational philosophy and creeds. |

Resources

The Heart of Change, Harvard Business School Press, ©2002.

"The Road to an Engaged Workforce, Executive Summary of Research," *www.performanceforum.org/research.5.0.html*. (Research sponsored by Northwestern University related to performance improvement, engagement and culture change.)

Corporate Culture and Performance, Simon & Schuster, ©2002.

"Leading Change: Why Transformation Efforts Fail," Harvard Business School Publishing Corporation.

Managing at the Speed of Change: How Resilient Managers Succeed and Prosper Where Others Fail. Random House, ©2006.

Organizational Culture and Leadership: A Dynamic View, Jossey-Bass, ©1992.

Part Seven

Communication & Involvement

28

Get Feedback Right

"A pinch of praise is worth an ounce of scorn. A dash of
encouragement is more helpful than a dipper of pessimism. A
cup of kindness is better than a cupboard of criticism."

–William Arthur Ward

"I love criticism just so long as it's unqualified praise."

–Noel Coward

What's the Link?

The concept of giving and receiving feedback is fairly simple to grasp, but the
dynamics of organizational feedback are quite complicated. No one really likes to
get bad news, and positive feedback in the form of praise is nice but only if it is
sincere and authentic. If you want to improve yourself, it is difficult to do unless
you get some input from others. For instance, it is virtually impossible to improve
complex performance like building a consistent golf swing, playing a musical
instrument or building stellar presentation skills without feedback from someone
with experience in those areas. But how does the concept of feedback link to our
topic of engaging and retaining employees?

It would be easy to simply state that you need to have a feedback-rich climate in
your organization. But it is not as simple as that.

Feedback is a double-edged sword. First, there is the dynamic between positive
and negative feedback. When the two are given at the same time, it can weaken
the impact of both. Also, people vary on the extent to which they tolerate or need
feedback. Some want feedback all the time and are appreciative, and some would
prefer to just go about doing their job with little or no positive or constructive
feedback. And, regardless of their preference, both types of employees can perform
poorly or well. Even when organizations build state-of-the-art feedback processes,
increased employee engagement is not ensured. Often, formal feedback processes
(such as annual performance appraisals) are seen as arduous, backward looking and
a drain on psychological energy.

A New Point-of-View

This chapter will not focus on organization-based feedback loops such as scorecards, employee satisfaction survey feedback or advice on improving your performance management process (even though these tools and processes can add great value to organizational decision making).

This chapter will provide some useful reminders and new ideas on feedback to leaders and supervisors in order to impact the engagement and retention of employees. The more you can build these approaches into your feedback practices, the more likely your employees' commitment and loyalty will be positively affected.

Tips on Feedback Practices That Engage Employees

Most employees do believe feedback is important. It is a logical growth activity, but it is not always psychologically safe or pleasant. So, to build an engaging feedback climate, first examine where the tone and approach to feedback may create drag on employee engagement. Then add practices that nurture a climate of engagement.

What to Reassess or Weed out

- **Weakness-based feedback tactics.** Does your performance appraisal process result in new goals that are designed to fix the weaknesses of even top performers?

- **The process of performance appraisals.** To what extent does your annual or calendar-based performance appraisal system become overly labor intensive for key leaders and supervisors? In what ways could you replace less valuable performance appraisal practices with more valuable features?

- **Gotcha vs. thank you.** To what extent do your best performers perceive that the climate of your organization is thankless versus thankful?

- **Leadership apathy or complacency about upward feedback.** Do key leaders support or disregard upward feedback? Receiving feedback at the top is an excellent way to model the importance of feedback for growth and guidance.

What to Nurture

The best supervisors and leaders realize that feedback helps people know where they stand, what they do well and where they need to adjust or grow. Here are some tips to nurture a climate of engaging feedback.

- **Talk about strengths.** As the chapter on strengths-based development suggests, the greatest opportunity to help people flourish in their work lives is to help them develop their strengths. So, first notice and provide feedback on what your employees do well. Imagine the positive outcomes of employee conversations that revolve around what they do well, why those strengths are important for the company and ideas on how to tap into those strengths as part of an employee's job. Identifying your employees' strengths and interests is a good first step. *In Love 'em or Lose 'em: Getting Good People to Stay,* Beverly Kaye and Sharon Jordan-Evans suggest that you "open up a dialogue that gives you and your employees an opportunity to become more aware of who they are both professionally and personally. To get them talking, ask questions that help them to think more deeply about their unique skills, interests and values."

• **Support collaborative performance feedback based on clear standards and expectations.** One quick way to create disconnection between yourself and an employee is to provide feedback that is a surprise, i.e., feedback based on performance dimensions that were not identified as an expectation. As an employee begins in a new role, it is always best to clearly discuss key standards and performance expectations and to allow the employee to clarify what these expectations mean. When it is time to debrief with an employee on performance, invite him or her to do a self-assessment while you also consider the feedback you have on their performance. As you might expect, employees are often bigger critics of their own performance than the supervisor might be. This provides an opportunity for the supervisor to agree or disagree with negative performance dimensions and to appreciate positive performance.

• **Be more positive than negative.** An oft-repeated complaint in organizations is that employees hear only the bad news, never the good news. Best organizations ensure that managers provide good news as well as the bad. Research on negative feedback suggests that, on average, people remain receptive to negative reports of their performance only if it is balanced with four positive observations. Use this guideline to keep people receptive to feedback: balance each idea for improvement with four positive observations.

• **Be very clear about expectations to get to the next level.** Employees may disengage their loyalty to the organization if there is too much mystery, favoritism or inequity in the promotion process. Be clear with employees on the process and criteria around promotions for each career path.

• **Be mature when giving feedback.** Maturity is the personal ability to use courage and consideration when interacting with another. Courage is the confidence to state your observations, interests and needs. Consideration is the intent to understand and empathize with the perceptions, interests and needs of the other person. When giving feedback, best supervisors are both self-oriented and other-oriented.

Feed*forward* vs. Feed*back*

An essential problem with feedback is that it often focuses on the past, yet the value of feedback is in what will happen from this moment on. In his article titled "Try FeedForward Instead of Feedback," Marshall Goldsmith describes the process of feedforward and some of the benefits of using this approach.

The Process of Feed*Forward*

- Pick one behavior you would like to change. Change in this behavior should make a significant, positive difference in your work or personal life.
- Describe the behavior to a group or a supervisor.
- Ask for feed*forward*–two suggestions for the future that might help you achieve a positive change. No information is discussed regarding the past.
- Listen attentively to the suggestions and take notes. Avoid comments, replies or judgments while listening.
- Thank the other person(s) for her suggestions.
- If doing this in a group, ask the other person(s) to pick a behavior they would like to change and repeat the process. You now become a feed*forward* idea provider.

People who have used this process to get input into behavior changes and growth were asked why this exercise is seen as fun and helpful as opposed to painful, embarrassing or uncomfortable. According to Goldsmith, "Their answers provide a great explanation of why feed*forward* can be more useful than feedback as a developmental tool." Some of the helpful aspects of the feed*forward* approach follow.

- We can change the future. We cannot change the past.
- It can be more productive to help people be right than prove them wrong.
- Feed*forward* is especially suited to successful people.
- It can come from anyone who knows about the task; it does not require personal experience with the individual.
- People do not take feed*forward* as personally as feedback.
- Feedback can reinforce personal stereotyping and negative self-fulfilling prophecies.
- Face it. Many of us hate getting negative feedback, and we do not like to give it.
- Feed*forward* can cover almost all of the same material as feedback.
- It tends to be much faster and more efficient than feedback.
- Feed*forward* can be a useful tool for managers, peers and team members.
- People tend to listen more attentively to feed*forward* than feedback.

Organizations do not necessarily need to abolish traditional feedback practices that are often part of performance management processes. But try a more positive "yes/ and" mindset. For example: Yes, it is good to formally manage performance, and your organization will benefit by encouraging an increase in positive, strengths-based and forwarding-looking feedback practices.

Resources

Love 'em or Lose 'em: Getting Good People to Stay. Berrett-Koehler Publishes, Inc., ©2004.

"Try FeedForward Instead of Feedback." Adapted from Leader to Leader, Summer 2002, *www.MarshallGoldsmithLibrary.com.*

Engage by Involving Employees

"No manager ever won no ballgames."

–George "Sparky" Anderson

Conduct an Internet search on phrases such as "employee involvement" or "workforce participation" and peruse the links that pop up. You will be taken on a winding journey of management philosophies and organizational research from the past 50 years in areas such as the empowerment and motivation theories of Argyris and Likert, participatory management findings of researchers such as Marchant and Lawler, Quality Circles and Total Quality Management (TQM), formal employee involvement programs and corporate citizenship-driven volunteerism.

Several common threads run through this broad collection of literature:

- The positive impact of employee involvement on organizational dynamics such as communication, trust and collaboration.
- The clear links between the quality of involvement and employee motivation and engagement.
- The organizational value that comes from unleashing employee ideas in areas such as process improvements and decision making, and the organization's internal and external images.

Definitions of Involvement

The word involve is defined in several ways:

- Sharing the activities of a group;
- a connection of inclusion; and
- a sense of concern with and curiosity about someone or something.

When organizations successfully enhance the quality of employee involvement, there is a commensurate enhancement of group connection, inclusion and access to the interests and natural curiosity of the workforce.

Employee involvement is described in many ways, depending on a writer's viewpoint. Consider two such descriptions:

- A variety of management practices centered on empowerment and trust that are designed to increase employee commitment to organizational objectives and performance improvement. (*www.dictionary.bnet.com*)
- Creating an environment in which people have an impact on decisions and actions that affect their jobs, and a management and leadership philosophy about how people are most enabled to contribute to continuous improvement and the ongoing success of their work organizations. (*www.humanresources.about.com*)

A Core Principle

Both of the descriptions above include key elements of employee involvement. At the root is this core principle: Your employees will be more committed to your organization when they are involved and invested in ways that are useful to and valued by them and the organization. In a study using data from member firms of the Society of Human Resource Management (SHRM), Freeman and Kleiner found that "a much larger proportion of EI (employee involvement) participants … look forward to going to work (as opposed to not caring one way or the other or wishing they did not have to go); are more loyal to their employers; trust that their company will keep its promises to them and other workers; and view their firms' program for dealing with the workplace problems as very effective." Clearly, programs designed to involve employees have a positive impact on general workforce engagement levels, and, depending on the type and visibility of involvement programs, on the attraction and retention of talent as well.

Ways to Involve Employees

Below are descriptions of some of the involvement approaches in use today. Some may be very familiar to you, and some may represent new ideas. Regardless, they are reminders of investments you can make now to involve employees in the enterprise.

Quality Teams

Emerging from the TQM movement, organizations form quality teams focused on continuous improvement. The initiative may include training for managers on quality-related skills such as statistical analysis, analytical problem solving, TQM and/or Six Sigma's quality measurement tools.

Suggestion or Complaint Systems

This type of involvement program is simply a way for employees to suggest improvements or lodge complaints on which the organization may choose to act. Formats might include the obvious suggestion box approach, employee presentations of ideas to management or feedback to supervisors and executives on their performance. To sustain the efficacy of this sort of program, the workforce must trust that the process is taken seriously and appropriate actions will follow. If attention wanes on the part of leadership, such programs lose participation and impact.

Employee Involvement in EI Program Design

This may sound redundant, but it is a serious approach. What could be better than involving employees in involvement program design? This begins a dialogue around what is most important to employees and to the organization; it also builds awareness and ownership across the workforce.

Employee Satisfaction Process

Many organizations invest in yearly or semiannual employee data gathering practices. (For more on this topic, see Chapter 49: Measure Employee Perceptions.) A high-impact response to this practice is to involve employees in taking action as members of special project teams.

Special Project Teams

Often, these projects are directly related to themes from annual employee satisfaction or opinion surveys. Organizational leaders, along with employee representatives, select projects that are important to the workforce and to organizational outcomes. A cross-section of employees and managers are selected to collaborate on the project. Following is a sample of possible special projects:

- Create outstanding ways to involve employees in bringing new talent on-board.
- Build a professional development process or career path guidelines.
- Create innovative and implementable employee recognition alternatives.
- Provide input on a user-friendly performance review process.
- Brainstorm on new products or services.
- Design flexible hours or alternative work arrangement programs.

Action Learning Teams

Action Learning, according to the American Society for Training and Development, is "a group effort that involves solving real problems, focusing on acquired learning and implementing systems-wide solutions." High-potential leaders and employees in key positions are formed into teams and provided a challenge that the organization wants to overcome or resolve. The choice of problem or challenge is important; it must be compelling and significant. Depending on the type and scope of the business, chosen projects may have:

- regional or global implications
- actual and strategic importance
- risk taking possibility
- potential for quantifiable payoff

Action learning programs require executive sponsorship and active support, expert training and coaching on action learning processes, and access to key company information and/or market data. They might also involve presentations to executive decision makers, reflection sessions on what has been learned and measurement of tangible or intangible outcomes. While action learning can be a resource intensive approach, the payoff can be extraordinary. Some benefits of a well-executed action learning approach include:

- Leadership, team and interpersonal skill development.
- Increased two-way communication between experienced and less experienced leaders and access to key operating information.
- Exposure to high-level decision-making processes and increased perspectives on how to decrease costs or grow revenue through strategic action.
- Analytical and conceptual skill building.
- Solutions for complex organizational problems.
- Relevant organizational learning.

Employee Contributions & Volunteerism

Many organizations believe that an important part of their brand is to give back to society, with contributions running the gamut from monetary charitable gifts to executive sabbaticals in nonprofit organizations. The Center for Corporate Citizenship describes it this way: "Employee volunteerism is an important component of corporate citizenship that gives employees an opportunity to be personally involved in a company's commitment." This type of approach is directly related to the quality of an organization's external brand and, therefore, valuable in attracting talent.

Some volunteer programs are designed to provide professional growth experiences to future leaders. For example:

- Safeco's Building Skills Through Volunteerism matches employees with volunteer opportunities to help them develop professional skills. Employees use an Intranet site to identify the kinds of volunteer activities that can help build competency in a desired area. The experiences are integrated into their personal development plans and are considered in reviews and potential career advancement.
- Timberland established a Path of Service Program in 1992. It includes a 40-hour paid benefit per year for employee volunteerism and also includes a service sabbatical during which employees may spend 1 to 6 months lending their talents to nonprofit organizations in supporting civic issues. (Source: "Employee Involvement: A Key Element of Corporate Citizenship," The Center for Corporate Citizenship.)

Boiling It Down

For any of these approaches to work, ensure that the following three things are in place:

1. Key leaders, i.e., those who would be instrumental in initiating, resourcing and following up on programs, must see this investment as a high priority. They must believe that the ability and interest to contribute innovation resides in the workforce, and that it is the leader's job to create the conditions that unleash that capacity.

2. The program is compelling to employees. The goal or focus of the program represents something that is valued by the workforce. This boils down to three possibilities: the ability to control or positively impact quality of work life; organizational outcomes of value; or contributing to the greater good.
3. Involvement programs have value to the organization. The process or outcomes of the program have a measurable impact on financial results, talent depth, organizational image, or other dimensions of value to stakeholders.

"The key to gaining a competitive advantage will be the ability of leaders to create an adaptive, learning environment that encourages the development of intellectual capital," says Warren Bennis of the USC Business School. "Leaders will be those who learn how to create environments that release the creative power of individuals."

Resources

"Action Learning" Info-line training resource from the American Society for Training & Development, 2001.

"Action Learning; Real Work, Real Learning. What Works Online: 2001," 1st Quarter, American Society for Training & Development, 2000.

"Public Administration Review," Participative management and job satisfaction: lessons for management leadership. 2002.

"What I Wish I Knew," *www.teambuildinginc.com.*

"Who Benefits Most From Employee Involvement: Firms or Workers?" *www.nber/ sloan/freeman.html.*

30

Communicate Times Ten

"Without credible communication, and a lot of it, the hearts
and minds of the troops are never captured."

–John P. Kotter

Those who review the results of employee satisfaction surveys observe a common theme consistently bubbling to the top of employee wish lists–more and better communication. The request to communicate is so frequently and persistently drummed into leaders' ears that it is sometimes hard to hear any longer, yet employees want more information virtually all the time. Is this a reasonable expectation? And if you must communicate more and better, what difference does it really make to your organization?

Studies in 2003/04 and 2006/07 by Watson Wyatt led to the following conclusions:

- 56 percent of workers in a highly engaged employee group reported receiving monthly communication from senior management.
- 42 percent of employees with low engagement say communication is annual or never.
- Shareholder returns for companies with the most effective communication were more than 57 percent higher over a 5-year period than companies that did not communicate as effectively.
- Firms that communicate effectively are 4 1/2 times more likely to report high levels of employee engagement.
- Firms with highly effective communication are 20 percent more likely to report lower turnover rates.

Organizational leaders operate under the extreme, energy draining challenges of rapid decision making, increasing competitive demands, technology challenges and need for differentiation in the marketplace, all the while needing to keep people informed of what is happening and why. As John Kotter suggests in "Leading Change: Why Transformation Efforts Fail," leaders tend to underestimate the need to communicate new visions and changes by a factor of 10. Your business strategies will succeed only if you bring the people along with you. To achieve increased employee understanding, ownership and commitment through communication, leaders must increase the quantity and quality of organizational messaging. If you think you are already communicating with your employees at an optimal level, your organization is one of the very few that does.

The Content of Organizational Communication

Leaders have multiple goals to achieve through what is communicated: new organizational strategies and execution plans, business successes, new competition, new opportunities, changes or bad news, employee news or milestones. In times of extreme and rapid change, communication becomes even more crucial. Employees want to know the who, what, how and why of organizational life, and leaders serve them well by planning and delivering messages that are authentic and engage the hearts and minds of employees.

Effective Approaches to Consider

This chapter offers some reminders and hints about the dos and don'ts of organizational communication.

Know What You Want to Say & Demonstrate

Sometimes a new organization vision or set of strategic drivers needs to be introduced, explained and reinforced. All leaders and managers should be able to summarize the vision or other key messages in short, compelling statements and to make them personal. Finally, leaders demonstrate commitment by repeating the message in different forms and living it through their choices and priorities.

Use Different Channels of Communication

By relying too heavily on one channel of communication, you under use the rich communication options available today. In "Leading Change: Why Transformation Efforts Fail," John Kotter says, "In most successful transformation efforts, executives use all existing communication channels to broadcast the vision. They turn boring, unread company newsletters into lively articles about the vision. They take ritualistic, tedious quarterly management meetings and turn them into exciting discussions of the transformation. They throw out much of the company's generic management education and replace it with courses that focus on business problems and the new vision. The guiding principle is simple: Use every possible channel, especially those that are being wasted on nonessential information."

Consider using any combination of the following channels to communicate your message.

- internal Intranet websites and resources
- the organization's Internet website
- e-mail
- message boards
- blogs
- voicemail
- newsletters
- videos
- annual reports

- company events
- public speeches

- team meetings
- coaching sessions

Encourage & Train Managers

Use a cascading approach to roll out key messages. Managers and supervisors are the key link to the front-line workforce. Provide training on the opportunities and channels they should use to get out the messages, and have them practice. Urge your managers to use communication tactics already at their disposal such as planned conversation time with employees face-to-face, and performance discussions linked to strategic expectations and teachable moments. Managers should also be encouraged to listen to and pass along the issues and questions that employees have on their minds.

Listen to Employees–Communication Is a Two-Way Street

Listening happens on the individual supervisor level and should also happen at the organizational level. Surveys, interviews, focus groups, employee suggestion channels and department meetings all offer opportunities to hear what is on the minds and hearts of employees. Ask them what they are concerned about, and be sure to respond in clear, authentic ways, without defensiveness.

Hold a Compelling Event & Make it Safe

Gather your employees together in a large virtual meeting or a series of live sessions to say what you need to say and hear what you need to hear. Jim Harris relates an example of this in his book *Getting Employees to Fall in Love With Your Company,* "Motorola, the telecommunications giant, holds quarterly face-to-face town meetings in which executives share the latest company news. They realize, however, that many employees may not speak up in such large group settings out of a sense of apprehension or embarrassment. So, after the town meeting, the executives hold what they call 'rap session' break-out meetings with much smaller groups of employees to more effectively solicit two-way interaction."

Hear & Respond to Build Trust

In the August 2007 issue of *HR Magazine*, James McDermott, director of HR for the Nuclear Regulatory Commission, says, "As soon as we hear something from the staff they are having a problem with, we jump on it. We tell them we hear them, and we let them know what we are going to do and then we follow through and get it done. The worst thing you can do is come in and glad-hand everyone and say you are going to do this and do that, but then nothing happens."

Word & Deed

To be effective, leaders must become a symbol of what they are asking others to know and do. When key organizational messages are lived out by the actions and priorities of top management, the workforce begins to believe, trust and adapt to the new realities. More importantly, the internal and external brand of an organization resides in what the leaders and their followers do and say. "Communication comes in both words and deeds," John Kotter says, "and the latter are often the most powerful form. Nothing undermines change more than behavior by important individuals that is inconsistent with their words." (Source: "Leading Change: Why Transformation Efforts Fail")

Additional Tactics

Use these additional tips as a checklist to enhance your own communication efforts:

- Plan and schedule communication initiatives.
- Link the communication program to business goals and key concerns.
- Realistically assess resources and select the right communication approaches to fit constraints.
- Meet with employees regularly to build and sustain relationships, get suggestions, stay informed and communicate follow-up actions.
- Avoid being defensive in the face of natural employee venting.
- Educate employees in business issues to provide the big picture.
- Integrate all aspects of the communication program.
- Connect communication efforts to reward and recognition systems.

(Adapted from "Corporate Communications: Closing the Communication Gap; The Employee Relations Game," Johnson et al, *T+D* magazine, 1992.

Whether it is an effort to communicate change, good or bad news, or organizational brand messages, it is important to communicate more often than you think is necessary to know what your workforce is thinking and feeling. The best communication starts and ends with an understanding of the needs, concerns and desires of the workforce you seek to attract, engage and retain.

Resources

"Corporate Communications: Closing the Communication Gap; the Employee Relations Game," *T+D* magazine, Dec 1992.

"Debunking the Myths of Employee Engagement," WorkUSA Survey Report. Watson Wyatt Worldwide, 2006/2007.

Getting Employees to Fall in Love With Your Company, AMACOM, ©1996.

The Heart of Change: Real-Life Stories of How People Change Their Organizations, Harvard Business School Press, 2002.

"Leading Change: Why Transformation Efforts Fail," Harvard Business Review, 2007.

"The Six Characteristics of Highly Effective Internal Marketing Programs" Executive White Paper developed by the Forum for People Performance Management and Measurement. *www.performanceforum.org.*

Part Eight

Train for Today's Needs

31

Link Training Investments
to Business Drivers

Leaders who are directly responsible for the success of training and development in their organizations must remember that a clear link should exsist between learning programs and business outcomes. Here is a sampling of observations from such leaders.

> "The primary way we've elevated training is to align the company's strategic goals with training initiatives."
>
> –Sara Mills, vice president of learning and development, IKON

> "Pick something important to the business–something strategic–give it 100 percent focus, and follow it through to the end. A spotty approach–where you try to do something for everyone–almost never shows dramatic results."
>
> –Karen Petersack, associate dean, Technology School, Unisys University

> "The most important thing any training department can do is to solve a business problem. The metrics of success were about the business outcomes desired and had nothing to do with traditional training metrics such as number of students trained."
>
> –Tom Kelly, vice president of Internet Learning Solutions, Cisco Systems

The training lexicon in use today can be confusing. Even the word training has fallen out of favor somewhat due to its limiting connotations as evidenced by the statement, You train dogs, you educate people. The American Society of Training and Development (ASTD) now refers to this field as workplace learning and performance (WLP). ASTD believes this is a more useful and holistic descriptor of the field because it explicitly connects learning–and all of the activities that support learning–to the improvement of individual, group and organizational performance.

Conducting learning programs with no positive impact on individual or organizational performance is an empty, resource-draining activity. Organizations that are experiencing high performance today may rationalize that learning programs are unnecessary, yet without investing in future focused learning and development, these organizations are likely taking a high-risk approach. Learning initiatives must fulfill needs for current job skills and for future talent and performance needs, and they must be linked directly to key drivers of the business strategy whenever possible. Put another way, an organization's learning and development activities should disproportionately invest in the people that execute on the business strategy.

Signs that your learning and development programs are not strategically linked to your business strategy include the following:

- Overall, there is diminished interest in attending training events.
- Managers frequently pull participants from training due to higher priority activities.
- Leadership spends more time squeezing the training budget or requesting proof of training value than on identifying, collaborating on and supporting learning programs.
- A lot of employees receive a lot of generic training with little relevance to their jobs.
- Employees only value training as a way to put a check in a box for their next promotion.

An Example of Learning Linked to Big Business Initiatives

As reported in the April 2007 edition of *T+D* magazine, Ferrellgas set out to remake itself through the introduction of a $65 million, technology driven initiative that would link and integrate its key business processes as it provided service to customers. This was not a time to shortchange the training effort, since the new technologies and systems would only be effective if employees understood and used them. A well-managed training project began with employee input, needs assessment, definitions of new responsibilities and development of curricula that covered each element of the technology and how to use them. The company was persistent in following through on this investment, even through the stops and starts that are inevitable in large projects. Then, after several pilot programs, a full deployment took place in 2005. The company achieved unprecedented gains in operating efficiency and customer service with much credit going to the robust training program implemented prior to deployment.

Another Example of Learning & Strategy Linked

China International Trust and Investment Corporation (CITIC) has a sophisticated training philosophy that is linked directly to its organizational mission and role: To be China's economic window to the outside world and to act as a laboratory for its economic and social reform. This requires its people to be versatile. Versatility training for staff is the company's most strategic talent development task. CITIC clearly defines what employee versatility looks like and then creates learning processes in a variety of ways. In fact, it structures jobs so that lower-level employees focus on technology, mid-level employees get a mix of technology and business experiences, and senior employees have comprehensive knowledge across business lines. (For more on CITIC and other strategic organizational learning examples, see "The Talent Solution: Aligning Strategy and People to Achieve Extraordinary Results" by Edward L. Gubman.)

Two Ways to Link Learning & Development with Business Strategy

Think of the two processes described below as two ends of a continuum of actions that can link strategy and learning initiatives. Depending on the size, culture and appetite for learning programs in your organization, either of these approaches (or something in between) might be championed successfully.

Talk with Key Stakeholders & Act

As learning professionals transition into the role of chief learning officer (CLO), an effective first step is to initiate business conversations with executives and key stakeholders to learn about their business, their strategic objectives and workforce needs. CLOs can identify training needs based on these conversations and then formulate approaches and programs that may meet those needs, coordinate the resources required to deliver the programs and assess the impact through evaluation and ongoing conversations with constituents. In smaller organizations this may be the most cost effective way to plan an inaugural learning and development foundation on which to build.

Analyze Human Capital Readiness & Invest in Strategic Job Families

In medium to large organizations, the scale of learning and development needs would quickly escalate if equal learning and development investments were made in all employees at all levels. Difficult decisions must be made to focus on highest priority needs. All too often, it is the squeakiest wheel that gets the learning grease in organizations, whether or not the training request can be linked to business strategy. In a Harvard Business Review article titled "Measuring the Strategic Readiness of Intangible Assets," Robert Kaplan and David Norton outline a thorough process to identify the learning and development actions that will make the most difference. At a very high level the process would include the following eight phases:

1. Clarify the key business objectives and drivers of success based on the organization's strategy.
2. Identify the strategic processes that must be in place (the organizational capabilities) to execute on the business objectives.
3. Name the key, strategic positions or strategic job families that are critical to the execution of the strategy.
4. Define the skills or competencies that are required for each job family or pivotal position.
5. Assess the number of employees within each job family required to successfully implement the strategy.
6. Assess the strategic job readiness within each job family by gathering input from those who can best assess current performance levels.

7. Initiate talent management activities (such as hiring, out-placing, and learning and development activities) where readiness is low.

8. Identify measures, monitor impact and report changes in organizational capital readiness.

What Does This Have to Do with Employee Attraction, Engagement & Retention?

Prospective employees are interested in the types of learning and growth opportunities an employer offers. Being known as an employer that provides good learning and development clearly helps in competing for best talent.

A leading factor in employee engagement is access to learning and development programs. An often-mentioned theme in exit interviews, conversely, is the lack of support for professional development.

A key retention issue in many organizations is the challenge of holding onto the leaders of tomorrow and the key executives who are good at growing and retaining talent. When learning and development resources are used to invest in retaining these future executives, the organization is likely to have an embarrassment of riches in its talented workforce for years to come.

Resources

"Chief Learning Officers Link Training and Business Goals," Workforce Management. *www.workforce.com.*

"CLOs Ponder Critical Business Challenges," *T+D* magazine, August 2007.

"Fix the Disconnect Between Strategy & Execution," *T+D* magazine, August 2007.

"JCPenney Links Training to Strategy." *www.workforce-performance newslines.com.*

"Management Training: Make your business its own corporate academy for management training and development." Thinking Managers, *www. thinkingmanagers.com.*

"Measuring the Strategic Readiness of Intangible Assets," *Harvard Business Review,* February 2004.

"State of the Industry in Leading Enterprises: ASTD's Annual Review of Trends in Workplace Learning and Performance," ASTD, ©2006.

"The Strategic Impact of Corporate Learning," CloMedia. *www.clomedia.com.*

"Synergizing HR and Training," *T+D* magazine, June 2007.

The Talent Solution: Aligning Strategy and People to Achieve Extraordinary Results. McGraw-Hill, ©1998.

"View From the Top," *T+D* magazine, April 2004.

32

Manage
Performance

"Appraisals are where you get together with your team leader and agree
what an outstanding member of the team you are, how much your
contribution has been valued, what massive potential you have and, in
recognition of all this, would you mind having your salary halved."

–Guy Browning, British humorist

Overview of Performance Management

Performance management is the means by which an organization assesses
performance, develops its employees and aligns its workforce around the
organization's goals. It usually includes several separate, albeit related, activities
such as performance planning and goal setting, professional development
planning, performance appraisal/measurement and performance review. Often,
a performance management process is set up as an annual cycle linked to an
organization's compensation and/or promotion processes. In fact, a majority of
organizations that conduct formal performance management primarily use it
for making compensation and promotion decisions. Other purposes for formal
performance management programs include:

- employee learning and development
- goal alignment
- resource planning
- identification of top performers
- separation decisions

How Valuable Is Performance Management?

It seems easier to find people who view performance management as time and
energy draining, anxiety producing and often something to dread, than it is to find
those who view it as a valued, essential process. We expect a lot out of performance
management, yet it often fails to fulfill those expectations. In fact, when the
misalignment between expectations and reality is too great, organizations must
respond to demands for major overhauls. A book has been written on this topic
called *Abolishing Performance Appraisals: Why They Backfire and What to Do Instead.*

OnBoard Consulting surveyed managers and human resource professionals about their performance management systems. Fifty-six percent of line managers believe their performance management processes are not valuable. Also, more than 50 percent of those surveyed responded either neutrally or unfavorably that their system:

- Helps employees build their skills and competencies;
- is consistently applied across the company;
- uses a rating scale that enables managers to differentiate levels of performance accurately;
- helps to build a high-performance culture; and
- provides useful data that drives leadership development initiatives.

Performance Management as an Employee Engagement Tool

Employees' attitudes about their employer are formed by how they view the organization. The primary lenses through which employees view their organization include:

- how involved they are in important work
- career opportunities
- selection practices
- performance management
- training and development

Clearly, how an organization manages performance touches on each of these, either directly or indirectly. If performance management is conducted in suboptimal ways and if the systems around it are not robust, then it can impact the level of workforce engagement.

In fact, in some organizations performance management is administered in ways that can lead to substantial workforce disengagement. Managers claim they do not have enough time and often procrastinate in completing the process. Employees are often asked to appraise their own performance in unreasonable ways, perceive inequity in the performance ratings and are dissatisfied in meager rewards doled out. In other words, the practice of managing performance may actually hinder employee engagement and retention of your top performers, especially when done poorly.

The focus of this chapter is to suggest ways to avoid the practices that may make performance management disengaging and additional ways to support and even enhance employee engagement and retention through performance management.

Problems & Pitfalls

Replacing Conversations with Computers

Technology can take some of the pain out of the process. It can even allow supervisors and employees to conduct performance appraisals, feedback, performance reviews and goal-setting without ever actually talking to each other. While this may save time, it seems unlikely that this face-less approach has a positive impact on employee engagement or retention without meaningful supportive performance conversations.

One Trick Pony (or Wrong Trick Pony)

A serious flaw in some traditional approaches to performance management is focusing on one outcome rather than on multiple outcomes of value. For example, being primarily focused on organization level goal-setting (not a bad thing in itself) with little or no focus on personal goal setting would be missing the opportunity to assist individuals in aligning their own development with valued organizational needs; an engaging activity. A similar problem is focusing the whole effort on a disengaging outcome such as linking performance ratings to insignificant pay increases, rewards that are not valued by employees, or outplacement actions.

User Unfriendliness

When the steps that managers and employees must take are overly complex, the process is likely to be completed with only sporadic quality and timeliness.

One Driver

If the process is designed to be driven only by the supervisor, it may be viewed as overly dictatorial or parental. Conversely, when sole ownership is given to the employee, it may be viewed as leadership abdication without direction or support. It is far better to craft a process that is truly collaborative, driven by supervisors and their employees in equal share.

Backward Looking

It is less engaging for employees to be judged by looking back on the year's performance or to find that their past performance has been assessed against mysterious criteria about which they were unaware.

Disengaging Outcomes

A 2005 article titled "Keeping the People" cited several causes of employee disengagement. Some of these relate to poorly administered performance management activities such as:

- being passed over for promotion
- an unexpectedly low performance rating
- a lower than expected pay increase or none

Lack of Consistency

A study done by the Institute for Corporate Productivity and HR.com found that only about 20 percent of respondents indicated that a majority of employees received quality performance appraisals. When performance is managed and rewarded unevenly or inequitably, employees notice. This reduces workforce engagement levels.

Ways to Be More Engaging (or Less Disengaging) While Managing Performance

Engage Performers on the Individual Level

Have More Performance Conversations

Employees say they want feedback and support for their development. Your highest potential employees want to know how they are doing and what they could do better to contribute now and to grow in their career. This happens first and best through conversations that supervisors should be holding frequently with employees. In fact, this is the primary job of the supervisors, to help employees flourish in their performance. It is in these conversations, and resulting activities, that employees will find reasons to be loyal and committed to their supervisor and their organization. During a 12-month performance cycle, there is ample opportunity to:

- discuss goals
- explore developmental options
- provide coaching and teaching that helps employees
- discuss ways to improve performance
- identify strengths that an employee could use to further their contribution or career, and
- plan for promotion

Manage Employee Expectations

Disengagement can occur when employees are surprised by the process or outcomes of performance management. Leaders are well advised to be realistic about what employees can expect regarding career support, goal achievement, compensation policies, promotion potential and other performance related topics.

Involve the Employee in the Process

The best performance management programs create an expectation of collaboration between the employee and supervisor. An employee's role may include setting career and development goals, pursuing developmental opportunities, keeping records of accomplishments and providing feedback to the supervisor.

Ask for Upward Feedback

Consider asking for feedback from your employees on how you can best support their success and improve your performance in managing their performance.

Be quick with Good News

Avoid creating a climate where your employees only hear about it when they are doing something wrong. It is an old cliché, but an effective one; catch them doing something right, and thank them. This, too, is performance management.

Be On Time

Employees will view performance management as a low priority when supervisors miss deadlines. This quickly downgrades the level of engagement.

Provide Effective Ongoing Coaching & Feedback Throughout the Year

The best supervisors are those who see each day as a chance to support the growth and effectiveness of his or her workforce. A highly respected manager once said that he sees nearly every interaction with employees as a coach-able moment. Then when yearly performance reviews are conducted, they become a summary of coaching and feedback conversations held throughout the year.

Include Development Plans for the Future

Help employees envision future career expansion and collaborate on forming a plan to help them get where they want to go.

Engage Performers on the Organizational Level

Develop Clear Job Descriptions

The foundation upon which to set goals and provide feedback is the set of job standards and expectations that supervisors confirm with employees as they engage in the work.

Provide Effective Orientation & Training

All employees should understand how the performance management process works, what it is for and what they should do to get the most out of it. Supervisors should be effectively trained in setting goals and expectations with employees, collaborating appropriately, holding effective and engaging performance conversations throughout the year, and providing constructive and positive feedback.

Hold Supervisors Accountable for On-Time Completion

Some organizations have withheld annual manager pay raises and bonuses until performance reviews are completed.

Provide Training & Development Options

When supervisors and employees collaborate on creating development plans, they will automatically seek solutions to the identified needs. The organization must have a way to respond to these needs, whether through tuition reimbursement programs, an aligned curriculum of learning programs, developmental opportunities or e-learning access.

Design Effective Compensation & Recognition Programs

One outcome of performance management should be something of value to each person who contributed to the organization by meeting or exceeding goals.

Create Clear Career Paths & Growth Needs

As supervisors and employees discuss future goals, know what options are available for the individual's advancement and what he or she should be able to know and do to progress to new positions.

Monitor Quality & Consistency

On a department or organizational level, increase equity and effectiveness by tracking the quality of appraisals, the timeliness of completion and the perception of employees about the process. Feed this information back to the management team and enhance the practices that will aid in workforce engagement and create value to the organization.

Resources

Abolishing Performance Appraisals: Why They Backfire and What To Do Instead. Berrett-Koehler Publishers, ©2000.

Harvard Business Review on Appraising Employee Performance. Harvard Business School Press. ©2005.

33

Create the
Development Process

According to numerous surveys in various industries, the number one reason why employees remain with an organization is the presence of good career growth and development opportunities. The Hay Group's study in 1999 of 500,000 employees was one of the first of its kind; it confirmed that the main reason people stay with or leave an organization are the career growth, learning and development opportunities. Today value creation is centered on people more than on hard assets as in the past. The fact is that investing in an employee development process is a wise investment. Below is a simple but helpful model to guide you through the six steps of a development process.

Figure 33.1

Step One–Identify Leadership Attributes Required

The first step in developing talent is to identify a set of leadership attributes or criteria that your organization agrees exemplifies your desired brand. Classic sets of criteria and competencies include such characteristics as human capital developer, strategist, talent manager, results driver, etc. In fact, in *Leadership Brand: Developing Customer-Focused Leaders to Drive Performance and Build Lasting Value,* Dave Ulrich and Norm Smallwood suggest that most organizations have a 65 percent overlap in leadership competencies. The other 35 percent is the branded leadership. Some companies choose to customize leadership attributes while others use a more generic set. Regardless of which you choose, it only makes good sense to start the development process by detailing the desired attributes you will use as your measuring tool and then making sure that everyone is familiar with these attributes and how they will be used. It is from these attributes that the process then continues.

Step Two–Assess Capabilities of Current Workforce

The second step is to measure each individual's proficiency on the chosen leadership attributes. This can be done in a variety of ways. The preferred method is the multi-rater approach, which includes self-rating, supervisor rating and at least two other supervisor peer colleagues. These ratings are completed in advance and then discussed in a facilitated meeting with the supervisor and peer-level and above colleagues. Each leadership attribute is discussed and a consensus rating is agreed upon. The designations used are:

- **S–real strength.** The individual clearly excels in this area.

- **E–effective.** Although not yet a real strength, the individual is competent in the use of the skill or knowledge.

- **D–development area.** The individual clearly needs additional time to master the required skill set.

Once this step is completed, a profile of the strengths and development areas is created.

Step Three–Assign Promotability & Readiness

The third step is to assign promotion and readiness ratings. Given the consensus evaluation of the individual in terms of strengths and development areas, make a determination on the appropriateness and readiness for promotion. This rating is all about the individual's readiness to assume responsibilities not presently part of his or her role, not the readiness of the organization to provide such a role. For example, someone might be rated ready now for the next level promotion although there is no actual position open. This allows the organization to see if they have an undersupply of talent in certain areas or possibly an oversupply, leaving them vulnerable for someone to pick off that talent.

At this point, assign each individual one of the following codes:

- **Well placed**–not ready at this time but will continue to grow and develop in the present position.

- **Expandable now**–then ready within 12 to 18 months for promotion.

- **Ready now**–immediately ready to assume a higher level of responsibility.

- **Blocker**–not ready now or in the near future for promotion and presently blocks a key development job for future talent.

- **Questionable performer**–presently demonstrates questionable performance in the position; could be in the wrong job or working for the wrong person.

Once these have been assigned, you have created a department, division or organizational portfolio that might identify common areas that need development. This leads to the next step.

Step Four–Identify Development Needs

The fourth step looks at the profiles and determines areas of development that appear to be most common. When these are identified an organization-wide strategy can be created. For example, a department assesses 20 individuals against a set of nine leadership attributes. The two attributes requiring the most development are customer relationship skills and multi-dimensional communication ability, which would suggest a more global development approach than an individual one. The organization might then choose to engage in a broad training and development initiative to improve the customer relationship skills and communication skills of the entire organization, not just to provide individualized development.

By identifying which needs can be developed through an organization-wide initiative versus those to develop on a more individual basis, you can do a better job of targeting the right development.

Step Five–Target Development

The fifth step is to target the right development. Targeting should take into account the individual's current proficiency on the leadership aspects that are critical to performance. Many organizations try to build the perfect leader who demonstrates real strength in all the leadership attributes. However, in reality most people have some areas of leadership in which they can excel and other areas that will be a long-term challenge. Be sure to target development of the attributes most critical to the defined role and not on those that are not critical to success.

The idea of targeting is exactly that. Take into consideration all the elements for a particular individual and use identified strengths to help support and build the attributes that need extra attention. It is easier to expand on an identified strength than it is to develop a weakness.

Targeting allows you to look at the needs of the organization and those of the individual and determine how you can marry the needs of both in a planned and managed manner.

Step Six–Create Development Plans

The sixth step is to build a development plan. This is considered one of the hardest aspects of the talent development process because it involves creativity as much as it is data driven. The plan should take into account the variety of options available as well as the cost and criticality of the position and person. Development of leadership attributes can be done on the job; through formalized education, seminars and workshops; individual study; on-the-job coaching and other means suggested in Chapter 42: Select Development Options That Fit.

Finally, it is important to include the individual in the process of creating the plan. Often individuals themselves have good ideas as to how they might be able to develop a certain attribute, and those who are more involved in creating a plan will be more engaged in carrying out that plan.

The plan should include the following elements.

- **The development goal.** What is the specific end that the development plan should work toward?

- **Action steps/milestones.** What specific actions will be taken?

- **Proof.** How will you know if the goal has been attained?

- **Dates.** By when?

Summary

This cycle should be repeated every 12 to 18 months. Use the same method as the initial assessment so a measurement of improvement can be tracked. Many times companies will feel good about going through the process the first time but shy away from reassessment. They might feel that they need more time to determine if progress has been made, or they prefer to use anecdotal evaluation of the development activities. However, the best way to determine if you are getting a return on your development investment is to measure progress, which can occur on both an organizational level and an individual level. Here are some ways to measure:

- The number of individuals assessed in the process.
- The number of development plans completed.
- The number of development plans implemented and progress evaluated.
- The number of employees who increased their readiness from year one to year two.
- Retention of talent from the individuals assessed.
- The number of promotions and expansions compared to the number suggested in the year one session.

Remember the old saying: –*That which gets measured, gets done.* This is meant to underscore the fact that if something is important to your business, it should be monitored and measured for optimum business results. The Talent Development Process works best when implemented as outlined here and then measured as to the progress made in creating a leadership pipeline that is developed and ready as future business requirements demand.

Resources

Human Resource Planning and The Center for Creative Leadership has articles and research supporting the Talent Development Process and development options.

34

Focus on Transitions

The Importance of Career Transition Points

Ask business leaders this question: "What was the most difficult time period in your career?" The answer you would likely hear most often is: *When I was promoted to manager for the first time.* According to Matt Paese, vice president of executive solutions at Development Dimensions International (DDI) and co-author of the "Leaders in Transitions" study, making the transition into management requires "a personal transformation and self-awareness that are not required at more junior levels."

A lament often voiced by new managers is that they did not receive any training after they were promoted and no one told them what it would be like. Many new managers also report that it took them at least a year to get an idea of what was expected of them and to feel that they were being effective. Indeed, it is during and just after these transition points that your most talented people may feel least supported and are at risk of becoming disillusioned about the organization.

The Leadership Pipeline: How to Build the Leadership-Driven Company examines how organizations can grow and build a pipeline of talent that is able to pass successfully through career transition points. It is at these managerial transition points that bottlenecks can occur and high potential leaders can flounder for a variety of reasons. New supervisors often struggle in their first year, and even seasoned supervisors, business unit leaders and executives can experience a sense of ambiguity and abstraction as they progress through these levels. For some, the required abilities are not in place to begin with, which may cause leaders to go off track. When this happens, some recently promoted leaders may feel as if they have fallen victim to the Peter Principle, i.e., they have finally risen to the level of their own incompetence. Perhaps they just need some additional support to navigate these transitions.

The organizational capability of getting leaders through transition points effectively is a huge asset. The need to build this capability is even more urgent in a time when organizations everywhere are finding it exceedingly difficult to grow or hire enough experienced leaders to meet current and future needs.

Newly promoted leaders often struggle because each step of the leadership ladder brings with it a more demanding and ambiguous environment in which multiple agendas and interests compete. DDI's "Leaders in Transition" study (which gathered data from nearly 800 leaders), as reported in the August 2007 edition of *T+D* magazine, made the following conclusions:

- Few leaders report making transitions effectively, though executives report feeling more effective than lower level leaders.
- As leaders make transitions, the biggest shifts in effort are in the areas of communicating, planning and team building.
- In the United States, influence and money top the list of motivations for people to take on leadership roles.
- Few leaders feel that organizations are doing the right things to prepare their future leaders.
- The most important people to help leaders through transitions are one's boss and colleagues or peers.
- The skills that leaders said would help them most included coaching, building strong teams, influencing and dealing with complexity or ambiguity.
- Significant changes in the political network, job complexity and human dynamics of their work cause stress for new leaders.

Helping New Supervisors

As suggested previously, the first transition from individual contributor to new supervisor is often the most challenging. It is easy to ferret out the reasons for this. People enter the workforce after selecting a career they think will be enjoyable and rewarding. Some may choose scientific research for a large pharmaceutical firm for the intellectual stimulation and to discover new compounds that help society. Others may choose sales because they enjoy interacting with people every day. Still others may choose a career that allows their creative juices to flow. Yet, many organizations rapidly promote their top talent to supervisory positions, regardless of whether a person has shown a propensity or desire for supervising others. Suddenly (and it does feel very sudden for some) these successful researchers, sales people and creative specialists are expected to coach, delegate, provide feedback, understand politics, act strategically and make decisions that affect the work lives of others. It quickly becomes clear that a new supervisor must give up those things they have enjoyed most about their work as an individual contributor. This can be a very jarring new reality. In fact, more than one executive has asserted that *as leaders gain more responsibility, they are doing less and less of what they have been educated and trained to do*. No wonder newly promoted supervisors report feeling:

- Lower confidence and self-esteem;
- high stress levels;
- inclined to keep doing the work they have been doing rather than delegating it;
- isolated or abandoned; and/or
- less than competent.

Clearly, helping new supervisors survive this key transition period is a necessary focus for most enterprises. Consider doing the following in an effort to support your newly promoted supervisors:

- Develop and implement basic supervisory skills training. This training should focus on topics such as how to delegate, how to manage performance, EEO guidelines, how to lead teams, how to leverage human resource expertise for a wide variety of workforce issues, interviewing and selection skills processes, etc.
- Help new supervisors expand their perception of what it means to move from individual contributor to supervisor.
- Help new supervisors let go of the things they need to jettison.
- Link new supervisors to more experienced mentors to get them through their first year.

Ideas for Helping Future Leaders Navigate Transition Points

What can organizations do to keep their pipeline of managerial talent strategically flowing? Create an executable framework of leadership transition management. Be clear about the competencies, skills and conceptual shifts that must be supported through training and developmental experiences.

Select new leaders appropriately. As the article "Leadership Blues" suggests (*T+D* magazine, August 2007), organizations should avoid making the common mistake of relying too heavily on past performance to predict a candidate's ability to make a successful transition. This is a three-pronged effort:

1. Make your promotion criteria clear and tied into performance evaluation processes.
2. Communicate to managers and executives the need to coach and mentor their protégés on upcoming career transitions.
3. Communicate the expectation to employees that they should hold conversations with their supervisors on how to prepare for the next steps in their career.

Provide mentoring and career coach services to high-potential leadership talent. These services may be provided by executives who have the competence and desire to do it, or by expert internal or external resources.

Aid leaders in developing competence to deal with ambiguity and complexity. Often, executives bemoan the lack of strategic thinking demonstrated by their less experienced leaders. The ability to think strategically, handle ambiguity and deal with complexity might be honed in several ways:

- **Executive education programs that bring in organizational leaders from a variety of industries and regions.** Outside education programs offered by colleges and universities are often designed for expanding perspectives and facilitating cross-organizational dialogue that aids high-order analytical thinking.

- **Significant job change.** Organizations might accomplish this through a program of job rotation. By reassigning future leaders to new departments, regions or countries, individuals can expand their awareness and knowledge of the organization through a wider variety of perspectives. Similarly, by being flexible and supportive of alternative career paths and reinforcing the need for cross-department talent sharing, organizations can help future leaders seek and try out new experiences as a way to sustain their interest and retain their talent.

- **Provide outlets for new leaders to share their concerns and anxieties.** This can often be accomplished through training programs in which peers are able to discuss their frustrations and challenges and through effective mentoring and counseling as part of the transition process.

- **Take the mystery out of new roles and responsibilities.** Organizations show support for leaders in transition by helping them assimilate with the team. A leader assimilation process can be used to rapidly facilitate information sharing between leaders and their constituents by asking and discussing questions in an open dialogue. These discussions are often more effective when an experienced and neutral facilitator is involved. (See Chapter 24: Assimilate New Leaders for more ideas on this topic.)

Help leaders in transition jettison and accept. At each new level, leaders must give up some things they liked about their former position and accept things they might not like about the new position. A mentor or boss can discuss with the newly promoted leader what he or she experienced while going through the same transition and lessons that were learned. The boss or mentor should also help the newly promoted leader identify and let go of those activities on the job that will need to come off their plate so that new opportunities can be pursued. Providing guidance on how to accept new opportunities, grow the required knowledge and knowledge network, and connect with new stakeholders will help the newly promoted leader move away from old behaviors and quickly focus on the priorities of the new position.

Engage and retain your top talent by ensuring that leaders transition from each managerial level to the next with a minimum of stress and an optimal level of effective support. The best organizations build a freely flowing pipeline of talent. Newly promoted leaders who feel valued and supported during career transitions– times of new challenges and greater stress–will be more engaged and committed to their employer. Therefore, helping leaders navigate career transition points is a critical engagement and retention strategy for top talent.

Resources

The Leadership Pipeline: How to Build the Leadership-Driven Company, Jossey-Bass, ©2001.

35

Develop Strengths

"Build on strengths. Think about what you're good at. How can you do more of it and how can you do it better? If you work only on weaknesses, you're going to die one of these days a perfectly mediocre human being."

–Buck Blessing

"A manager's task is to make the strengths of people effective and their weaknesses irrelevant."

–Peter Drucker

To what extent do you agree with this statement: *At work I have the opportunity to do what I do best every day?* The Gallup organization has gathered responses to this statement as part of its Q12 diagnostic for more than 30 years. Further research confirms what enlightened leaders have known for years; the best way to flourish in your own career and to manage and develop talented people is to understand, build and leverage talents and to focus less on fixing weaknesses. As Warren Buffett once told a roomful of college students, "If there is any difference between you and me, it may simply be that I get up every day and have a chance to do what I love to do, every day. If you want to learn anything from me, this is the best advice I can give you."

Authors and researchers on organizational effectiveness and positive organizational psychology such as Martin Seligman, Donald Clifton, James Harter, Mihaly Csikszentmihalyi, Peter Senge, Peter Drucker and Marcus Buckingham have raised awareness that a focus on strengths when selecting career paths and developing talent is far superior to a focus-on-weakness approach. This is true on an individual and organizational level.

The Data Is in

In "Investing in Strengths," Donald Clifton and James Harter share study results linking employee engagement with on-the-job use of strengths. "In a study of 10,885 work units (307,798 employees) in 51 companies, work units scoring above the median on the statement: *At work, I have the opportunity to do what I do best every day* have 44 percent (1.4 times) higher probability of success on customer loyalty and employee retention, and 38 percent (1.4 times) higher probability of success on productivity measures."

This is good news for those organizations that have already aligned employee talents with job requirements. But what of those work units where a low percentage of employees agree that they are doing what they do best every day? Is there benefit to helping these employees develop their talents and use their strengths more often? Several research projects positively link strengths-based development interventions with employee engagement and results. One large study in hospitals found significant improvement in employee engagement over a 3-year period. In an automobile industry study, two groups were formed with one group (the study group) receiving a strengths-based approach to development and the control group receiving no strengths-based development. Results indicated that the study group (n = 48) grew in engagement by significantly more (d = 0.72) standard score units than the control group (n = 207). Additionally, the study group grew in productivity by 50 percent more than the control group did.

What a Strength Is

In *Now, Discover Your Strengths*, Donald Clifton and Marcus Buckingham define a strength as: *Consistent near perfect performance in an activity.* People build strengths by leveraging talents and acquiring skill through fact gathering and practice. This concept boils down to the formula:

Talent	(Naturally recurring patterns of thoughts, feelings or behavior)
+ Skill	(Facts and lessons learned related to a talent)
Strength	(Consistent near perfect performance in an activity)

What Are My Talents?

Nearly any well-facilitated feedback mechanism will help you discover more about your gifts, talents and abilities. Here are several methods that you can use to further hone in on what you do best.

- Ask your friends and colleagues how they would describe what you are doing when you are at your best.
- Review past performance assessments and identify the themes of positive feedback you have received.
- Take personality type or behavioral style self-assessments such as Myers-Briggs Type Indicator®, a DISC theory-based tool such as Extended DISC®, StrengthsFinder 1.0 or 2.0, FIRO-B® or any of a wide variety of communication, leadership or thinking style inventories. Use two or more of these diagnostics to triangulate themes and patterns related to preferences and other positive talent dimensions.
- Keep a log of activities in which you engage on the job over several weeks. Identify those activities that you enjoy and are fulfilling and those activities that you do not enjoy and are not fulfilling. The activities you enjoy probably point to areas where you have natural preferences and talent.

The Argument Against the Focus-on-Weaknesses Approach

Clifton and Buckingham describe several misleading assumptions about human potential, such as: *Each person can learn to be competent in almost anything* and *each person's greatest room for growth is in his or her areas of greatest weakness.* They distinguish between the concept of true development and the mere practice of fixing weaknesses. And while it is important to respond to specific failures in performance through remediation, *this isn't development,* they say, *it is damage control.* And by itself damage control is a poor strategy for elevating either the employee or the organization to world-class performance. As long as an organization operates under these assumptions, it will never capitalize on the strengths of each employee.

Tom Rath, author of *StrengthsFinder 2.0* (and Donald Clifton's grandson) shares research data suggesting that weakness-based management is better than nothing, but not nearly good enough. "The tough math is this: If your manager is ignoring you, the odds of you being negative and miserable on the job–what we call *actively disengaged*–are four in 10. If your manager focuses on your weaknesses, things get a lot better. The odds of being actively disengaged are only two in 10. But if your manager focuses primarily on your strengths, the odds of being actively disengaged are just one in 100."

Strengths-Based Development Strategies

As a leader in your organization, you can take action on several levels: developing your own talents and strength, coaching and developing others through strengths-based approaches and elevating your organization's practices away from a focus on fixing weaknesses and toward practices that focus on leveraging the strengths of your talented people.

Develop & Leverage Your Own Talents & Strengths

We offer the following guidance to focus on strengths and manage weaknesses in your approach to self-development:

- Identify a talent theme (or area of preference based on style or type) and build a strength around it that helps to meet or exceed job requirements.
- If you have identified the activities you love to do on the job, and that are fulfilling to you, plan on how you might use that talent more on the job over time. As Marcus Buckingham suggests, you should find ways to do the things you love to do more every day and over time move away from those things you loathe doing.
- Identify a strength (a job activity you do well) and capitalize on it. Be more visible in your approach to doing it. Seek ways to use it more often.
- Identify a development need and transform it to a midrange skill. You will not be fulfilled by forcing yourself to excel in an area that is not of interest to you.

- Compensate for a weakness by adopting strategies to work around it.
- Address lack of experience in an area by seeking out new opportunities. Seek experiences in an area that will help you gain knowledge and skills that are of interest to you.

Coaching & Developing Others

Consider the following ideas for helping others develop and leverage strengths:

- Provide feedback on the person's talents and strengths as you see them. Point out what he or she does consistently well on the job.
- Help your employees develop careers that will move them toward their areas of interest and potential strengths.
- Follow this principle: Goal setting and development planning are about leveraging strengths to contribute value to the business. Weaknesses can be handled through other means–outside of the performance assessment process.
- Model goal-driven, strengths-based development by doing it yourself. Openly communicate your plans with your employees.

Encourage Strengths-Based Development Practices in Your Organization

Your organization's leadership practices and human resource processes should be aligned and focused on strengths-based activities to maximize the contributions of your people. As Marcus Buckingham puts it, when leaders say that their people are their greatest asset, what they really mean is–our people's strengths are our greatest asset. So what can you do?

- Examine the depth and breadth of your leadership pipeline for ways to enhance strengths-based alignment.
    - –Ensure that there is a good fit between the talents and interests of new employees and expectations of the job and career progression.
    - –Provide training to supervisors on how to apply strengths-based performance management practices.
    - –Ensure that the performance management process is not purely focused on assessing and fixing skill gaps but links organizational goals to the true talents and strengths of individuals that execute on those goals.
    - –Identify high-potential future leaders and enhance their strengths through developmental options that are more (not less) aligned with their existing set of strengths and talents.
    - –Promote individuals who have the strengths and predisposition to excel at the next level.
- Provide feedback mechanisms that emphasize identifying themes of talent and ability.
- Do all that you can to create viable career path alternatives. Provide reasonable career options that allow people to continue doing what they do best and to grow in ways that are fulfilling to them rather than disengaging.

Summary

According to Clifton and Harter, "The strengths-based organization does not ignore weaknesses, but rather achieves optimization, where talents are focused and built upon and weaknesses are understood and managed." This is analogous to the business axiom that organizations need to understand and leverage their core capabilities in order to achieve differentiation and win in the marketplace. Strengths-based organizations help their employees understand and leverage core capabilities to win in their careers. And in doing so, these organizations help their employees flourish in work and in life. As Peter Senge wrote, "To seek personal fulfillment only outside of work and to ignore the significant portion of our lives we spend working would be to limit our opportunities to be happy and complete human beings."

Resources

12 Elements of Great Managing, Gallup Press, ©2006.

Go Put Your Strengths To Work, Free Press, ©2007.

Positive Organizational Scholarship: Chapter 8–Investing in Strengths. Berrett-Koehler Publishers, ©2003.

Now, Discover Your Strengths. Free Press, ©2001.

StrengthsFinder 2.0. Gallup Press, ©2007.

36

Focus on
Key Positions

"The only thing worse than training your employees and losing
them is not training your employees and keeping them."

–Zig Ziglar

The challenge that enterprise leaders face all over the globe is acquiring and keeping
a full pipeline of talent. Because of this, a chief fear in many organizations is losing
talented individuals who are currently demonstrating peak performance. Ratchet
this need up a notch by considering the impact of the employees who are in key,
strategic positions. These are truly the people you do not wish to lose. (For more on
key, strategic positions, see Chapter 10.) The conclusion is quite simple; hold on to
your top performers, especially those in pivotal positions. Accomplishing this feat is
the complicated part.

Learning & Development for Those in Key Positions

The article "Royal Treatment: How to Engage Key Talent" reminds us that one of
the ways to motivate key talent is through professional development and leadership
training: Professional development opportunities consistently rate as one of the
top three reasons why employees choose to stay with their employers. Companies
should consider these programs as an investment and a significant vehicle for
keeping a competitive edge."

The authors of *The Workforce Scorecard: Managing Human Capital to Execute
Strategy* assert that to be competitive in the marketplace, organizations need to
build a differentiated workforce strategy that is supportive of their unique go-
to-market strategy. One hallmark of a differentiated workforce strategy is that
development investments are targeted at the 'A' players and 'B' players with 'A'
potential. The focus is on the use of competency growth models and development
opportunities that focus these current and future 'A' players on 'A' positions. 'C'
players receive few, if any, development resources.

Types of Positions Drive Training Strategies

As an example, one company in the supply chain business identified the frontline supervisor as a key position, because frontline supervisors are in daily contact with the hourly workforce. In this business, the highest operating cost factor is warehouse labor. Fluctuations in hourly labor productivity directly impact profitability. Therefore, frontline supervisors are in the position to maximize profits by retaining and guiding a reliable workforce. This organization has invested in a set of customized, locally held training programs to enhance the supervisory skills of their frontline supervisors in order to enhance the level of engagement and loyalty of the workforce. These targeted training areas include interviewing and on-boarding skills, communication skills, positive coaching practices and proper use of incentive programs.

At Disney, the position of trash remover was found to be crucial in sustaining the entertaining and customer service oriented environment for which Disney is famous. Training and performance support for these workers transformed the way in which they performed this critical job.

Leaders in a medical products industry identified the R&D scientist as a key position to execute on their strategy to develop differentiating products for their market. The first challenge in this case was to assess how to better invest resources in effectively staffing open R&D scientist positions with specialists in strategic technologies. The next challenge was how to develop broader capacity in the R&D team. The primary developmental approach was to provide job enrichment opportunities and remove barriers to external professional development and access to thought leaders and cutting edge technologies.

Training & Development Strategies for Disproportionate Investments in Key Positions

Leaders and chief learning officers may need to make tough decisions on how to best allocate learning and development resources. As suggested in Chapter 31: Linking Training Investments to Business Drivers, training resources and programs should be linked to the key drivers of your business strategy. By extension, this means that the people who receive the largest percentage of investment in learning and development should be those who are in key, strategic positions to execute on that strategy.

A common piece of advice given by personal financial planners is to pay yourself first. Similarly, an organization should pay itself first, by banking on the development of its most crucial employees and positions. This differentiated learning and development strategy is made real by accomplishing the following:

• Apportion development dollars to key strategic performers and above average performers who have high potential.

- Provide engaging, valued development assignments
for individuals in key strategic positions.
- Ensure that there is a clear competency model, career path
and growth options for people in pivotal positions.
- Top leaders own the career management of individuals in key positions.
- Leaders are rewarded for developing strategic talent.
(Adapted from *The Workforce Scorecard*.)

Ways to Invest in Key Positions

As suggested in Chapter 42: Select Development Options that Fit, there are a variety of approaches to talent development and training, some of which represent a high return on the time and resources invested and some with a lower return on investment. It is especially true that development approaches should be custom crafted for employees in key positions, because fruitful and valued development is a key reason why top performers choose to stay.

Top talent likes to work with top talent; so investing in developmental and performance enhancing resources for strategic job families will create a virtuous cycle for the retention of top talent. Here are some things to consider when crafting your learning and development strategies for key positions:

- Create the capability for rapid access to performance enhancing information and resources. Some organizations do this by tagging current industry developments and best practices and pushing this information to individuals in key positions who need it. At minimum, individuals in the position to execute on strategy should have access to contact names, phone numbers, e-mail addresses, websites and databases from which they can extract accurate, cutting-edge and timely information.
- Do a rigorous assessment of competence in key positions. As recommended in Chapter 39: Map Out Competencies, organizations should clearly identify the critical competencies and organizational capabilities that link to business drivers. Having accomplished this, the next step is to assess how well individuals are performing in key positions against those competencies. The goal is to link top performing individuals (or style 'A', players) in these key positions, enhance the skill and knowledge of high potential performers (or B players) and remove low performers (or C players). Since top performers like to work with top performers, it is a high-risk strategy to delay removing poor performers who are currently in key positions.
- Send them forth and clone their learning. Some high performers value the chance to connect with other experts in their field through professional conferences, state of the field education and other thought leadership gatherings in the industry or specialty. Remove barriers to outside gatherings. When your top talent returns, invite them to summarize and share new knowledge and insights through events such as small group presentations, white papers and proposals.

- Support individual self-development through research. Encourage advanced development in areas that are of value to the organization and to the individual's professional depth. Projects such as this might be put in the context of action learning, where groups of key employees embrace and explore solutions around key organizational challenges with the support of expert coaches and executive team interactions.
- Use other creative developmental approaches that go slightly beyond traditional training.
    - –Ask employees in key positions about the areas in which they are interested in exploring deeper knowledge or gaining firsthand experience. Collaborate on building a customized approach for gaining the desired knowledge and experience.

Summary

Ask yourself these questions when examining your practices for developing talent in key positions. Does your organization:

- Have a process to identify key employees and positions whose performance is critical to accomplishing the business strategy?
- Have an effective performance management program that includes career and professional development options for key positions?
- Regularly review key jobs at all levels to ensure that they provide a balance of challenge and growth?
- Use mechanisms to better understand the concerns and needs of key employees and high performers?
- Effectively encourage key employees and high performers to generate and carry out new ideas and techniques?
- Differentially reward and invest in key employees and high performers?

If your answer is no to any of these, you have identified a high-gain opportunity to create value by investing in the development and retention of your talent in key, strategic positions.

Resources

The Workforce Scorecard: Managing Human Capital to Execute Strategy, Harvard Business School Press. ©2005.

"Royal Treatment: How to Engage Key Talent," Workspan, July 2002.

37

Manage Knowledge by Leveraging Leaders to Teach

This chapter responds to five interrelated concerns of organizational leaders:

1) winning in the marketplace;
2) retaining and leveraging the significant skills and knowledge of experienced leaders before they leave;
3) creating a deeper bench of future leaders;
4) aligning workforce performance to business needs; and
5) engaging and retaining top talent.

A high-gain response to these concerns is to have leaders who are engaged in teaching and learning and to integrate teaching and learning into your business operating practices.

Why Should Leaders Teach?

Leaders are teachers. They teach every day through what they say and don't say, by what they do and don't do. The question really is, do you want them teaching accidentally or in a purposeful and planned way?

The point of view of this chapter draws heavily from the ideas of Dr. Noel M. Tichy as outlined in *The Cycle of Leadership: How Great Leaders Teach Their Companies to Win*, and from those organizational leaders who have implemented leadership practices in concert with his ideas. Tichy is a professor of organizational behavior and human resource management at the University of Michigan and in the mid-1980s was head of GE's Leadership Development Center in Crotonville, N.Y., Tichy says, "In teaching organizations, leaders see it as their responsibility to teach. They do that because they understand that it's the best, if not only, way to develop throughout a company people who can come up with and carry out smart ideas about the business."

BD Medical's CEO, Ed Ludwig, says, "Teaching gives me the opportunity to talk to people about where we are going, about our journey to become a great company. Frankly, I don't think the role of a teacher is optional for a CEO in today's complex, multifunctional, multinational, technology organization. It's part of the job. And it's a fun part."

Key Reasons Why Leaders Should Teach

When leaders teach:

- Strategic information is shared, enhanced and acted upon. Making employees smarter leads to greater success.
- Their knowledge is passed on. Leaders leverage hard-won knowledge from their own experience by sharing it.
- Leadership bench strength is deepened. Leaders-as-teachers report expanding their own knowledge and leadership skills when involved in explicit teaching. And the potential of future leaders increases when teaching occurs.
- It aligns workforce performance. Clear priorities and practices are communicated to align each employee's activities to organizational objectives.
- Workforce engagement and retention improves. Leader-teachers report a strengthening of their own loyalty to the organization. And learners are impressed that leaders take the time and energy to get involved with employee growth and success thus engaging key employees.

In What Ways Do Leaders Teach?

Leaders demonstrate what is most important through every interaction by what they are doing and how they are doing it. This is teaching at a tacit level. Leader-teachers are convinced that there is value in teaching at a more explicit level. Below are some examples of leaders in action as teachers.

- Georgia Pacific's former CIO Chuck Williams transformed the IT group to become a marketplace differentiator by developing a compelling, teachable point of view, developing leader/teachers on his staff and cascading the teaching through personal stories, team building, carefully crafted coaching sessions and business dialogue.
- Larry Bossidy led AlliedSignal Inc. to become one of the best performing companies by teaching senior leaders about strategy and spending a large amount of time teaching a growth mindset to employees.
- Executive team members and other functional leaders at Johnson Controls serve as faculty for their 5-day Transitions: Managers of Managers program. Executive faculty members are selected by exemplifying strategic competencies and by their desire and credibility to teach key business topics.

Concern #1: Winning in the Marketplace

To win in business today Tichy says, "the issue is going to be who is best at generating knowledge, harnessing the energy of words and making sure that it is targeted to the most productive issues. The winners in the future will be organizations that are big, fast and smart. And they will be that way because they will be Teaching Organizations."

Many executives dedicate themselves to the role of teacher because they have found it pays off in the organization's performance and innovation.

- Andy Grove of Intel believes that companies with leaders at all levels who can spot trends and have the courage to act will prosper while other companies falter.
- Roger Enrico, former chairman and CEO of PepsiCo, demonstrated his teaching commitment through deep involvement in a 5-day leadership program. The program resulted in some of the biggest business ideas that PepsiCo has had in the past several years.
- Joe Liemandt, CEO of Trilogy Software, believes that his entry-level employee boot camp has become a primary research and development lab helping Liemandt reinvent the company several times in the rapidly changing software industry.

Concern #2: Retaining & Leveraging the Significant Skills & Knowledge of Experienced Leaders

Some organizations invest a lot of time and expense in building computer-based solutions for managing knowledge. These expensive system-building projects may be required but are often plagued by issues such as obsolete, hard to retrieve information and an inability to move at the speed of business.

By having leaders teach, information is focused and shared at the speed of the human brain. In fact, when executives explicitly teach their deeply embedded, contextualized, experience-based knowledge to others, that information is no longer at risk of being lost due to retirement or other exits from the organization. The business knowledge residing in the brains of your top talent becomes shared knowledge.

As Frank Guide of BD Medical puts it, "As for myself as a teacher, I'm enjoying having this venue to pass along the experience that I've gained over the past 26 years at BD."

Concern #3: Creating a Deeper Bench of Future Leaders

In *The Cycle of Leadership*, Tichy asserts, "As I have said for many years, a company's success is directly tied to its ability to create leaders."

Gary Cohen, president of BD Medical, participates in sessions of BD's leadership development program as a teacher. "That enables me to gain insight on people who might have significant future leadership potential," he says. "The individual interaction around learning and development is a…two-way learning process for me, and provides a unique opportunity to sense the future potential for leadership roles."

Concern #4: Aligning Workforce Performance to Business Needs

When leaders teach, they better align workforce performance. According to Tichy and Chris DeRose in *Launching Cycles of Leadership*, "Companies that are serious about building alignment use carefully designed processes to engage tens or hundreds of thousands of people and to encourage teaching, coaching and open discussion."

For example, Royal Dutch/Shell used a process called Focused Results Delivery to engage leaders in teaching and to engage employees in applying new ideas in critical projects. This approach provided common goals and processes to thousands of Shell employees.

Concern #5: Engaging & Retaining Top Talent

Executives who are deeply committed to and involved in teaching and leadership development are also deeply loyal to the organization itself. These leaders do not suffer from present-eeism (the on-site version of absenteeism). As Jay Glasscock, VP of operations at BD Biosciences, puts it, "Each time I teach a BDU class, I'm reenergized to lead and reminded of the potential that lies within all of us when intellectually challenged."

Also, the level of engagement across the workforce improves. Gary Cohen says this about the BD University experience: "I'd also say that an even more meaningful benefit is that when leaders participate…it makes participants feel important and appreciated. Many are surprised that our highest-level (and often busiest) executives would stop their other activities to devote so much time to associate development."

Good Ideas to Apply as You Seek to Teach

- Formulate your teachable point of view.
- Use your organization's business operating cycles as teachable moments. Consider how the operations planning process, budget reviews, performance appraisal and other processes may provide these opportunities.
- Establish the teaching-learning competency as a component of your promotion criteria.
- Create a cadre of effective leader-teachers. Recognize and reward them.
- Use key leaders when on-boarding new and experienced hires.
- When responding to employee opinion or engagement surveys (a significant way to learn and teach across the organization), involve various leaders and cross department representatives in forming and preparing response teams.

Summary

Larry Bossidy, a consummate leader-teacher, asserts that you can find out how you are doing as a leader by asking yourself about the people you are leading. "When you retire, you won't remember what you did in the first quarter of 1994 or the third," he says. "You'll remember how many people you have developed–how many you helped have a better career because of your interest and dedication to their development. When you're confused about how you're doing as a leader, find out how the people you lead are doing. You'll know the answer."

Resources

The Cycle of Leadership: How Great Leaders Teach Their Companies to Win, HarperCollines Publishers, ©2004.

"Launching Cycles of Leadership," *Optimize* magazine, August 2002, CMP Media LLC. 2002. *(www.optimizemag.com/issue/101/pr_leadership.html)*

"The Thought Leader Interview," *Strategy + Business* magazine, Issue 30.

"The Leadership Engine: How Winning Companies Build Leaders at Every Level," *Harper Business,* 1997.

"The Teaching Organization," *T+D* magazine, July 1998.

"Those Who Lead, Teach," *T+D* magazine, October 2007.

38

Leverage Technology for Blended Learning

Learning in organizations serves at least two purposes:

1. to create workforce competence for achieving high individual performance and business outcomes, and
2. to engage and retain talent by providing professional development support.

Learning and development programs will most effectively attract new talent and engage and retain current employees when learning happens in ways they value. Yet, one size does not fit all, and formal classroom training is insufficient. According to a recent U.S. Department of Labor study, informal learning accounts for at least 70 percent of what employees learn about their jobs. Learning and development must be a continuous process that happens both inside and outside the corporate classroom, and through individual and group interactions with each other and with technology.

The topic of electronic learning (e-learning) or web-based training (WBT) can seem daunting. But, according to one expert in the field, e-learning is not really that different from the time-tested university education model: i.e., attend a lecture, do homework and take a test. However, the lecture may not be a person talking to a room full of people, the homework may take any of number of learner-driven experiences and the test can also take a wide variety of forms.

Technology in service to learning is a hot topic, and one reason may be the promise of huge financial savings. Studies have shown that well executed e-learning programs can realize from 100 percent to over 2,000 percent positive return on investment (ROI). (See "E-Learning Strategies for Success" in the May 2004 edition of *Chief Learning Officer* magazine.) As any e-learning specialist will tell you, the time and expense of a complex e-learning initiative can be quite extensive and yet the program may fail to deliver expected results, especially if the project does not take into account how people learn or are motivated to change behavior. For these reasons, most learning professionals have come to realize that a blended approach to learning will likely be more robust, more engaging and more likely to deliver results.

What Is Blended Learning?

Blended learning simply refers to the use of multiple approaches in achieving a learning objective. At the very basic level, this type of approach blends synchronous and asynchronous learning activities. A group of learners meet (live or virtually) at the same time and location (synchronous) to gain information. Individual learners can do homework, research and practice on their own time schedule (asynchronous) to explore the information. As you can imagine, this can take an almost unlimited number of forms using a wide variety of learning technologies and channels. Examples of different approaches are provided later in this chapter.

The Strongest Argument to Blend Learning

Think about the makeup of your workforce. Organizations of nearly any size will have distinct demographic groups working side by side: baby boomers (born between 1943 and 1960), gen Xers (born between 1960 and 1980), and millennials born between 1980 and 2000). In an article titled "Training Tomorrow's Workforce" (*T+D* magazine, April 2007), the authors observe that "younger generations have different communication styles, work habits and attitudes about technology. Many gen Xers and virtually all millennials never have known a world without computers, an Internet connection, cell phones and iPods. These technologies influence everything from how they choose to communicate and learn in the workplace, to their expectations of flexible work hours and easy access to real-time data. To successfully manage this multigenerational workforce, workplace learning and performance professionals will need to provide training and technology that fits both the learning styles and lifestyles of this diverse workforce."

Myths of Web-Based Training

If you ask business leaders about e-learning, you almost certainly will uncover strong opinions, and some may be negatively disposed to the promise of e-learning. This may be due, in part, to a disconnect between existing beliefs and the actual experience of e-learning. Learning professionals may find themselves in the position to dispel some often-held myths about web- based learning.

- **Myth #1:** WBT will save (or make) you money. The biggest misconception about web-based training is that it is cheap. In can take a huge amount of time, talent, training resources and money to switch to the web.

- **Myth #2:** All classroom learning can be converted to the Internet. This myth can drive leaders to push for a total conversion effort of classroom training in order to save money. Yet some content simply does not work as an online experience. Money is spent but competence is not grown.

- **Myth #3:** The number of web-based participants can be unlimited. In fact, you should limit the number of online participants and push toward a sense of community, especially when synchronous learning is part of your blended approach.

- **Myth #4:** Online learning lacks the social element found in the classroom. Just because people are not sitting together does not mean that individuals and groups cannot interact. This is especially true for gen Xers and millennials in the workforce and can be greatly enhanced by emerging technologies and platforms such as discussions forums, blogs, online chats and wikis.

Note on terminology

Blog (a shortened form of web log) is a website where entries are written in chronological order and commonly displayed in reverse chronological order. Blog can also be used as a verb, meaning to maintain or add content to a blog. A Wiki is a piece of server software that allows users to freely create and edit Webpage content using any Web browser; it is a unique tool that allows the organization of contributions to be edited in addition to the content itself. A familiar example of this is Wikipedia.

- **Myth #5:** WBT requires less time. The online workload should take approximately the same amount of time as in the classroom and might even take more.

- **Myth #6.** WBT is suitable for all trainers and participants. In reality, learning specialists must know the needs, learning styles and goals of the trainer and participants prior to creating e-learning courses.

- **Myth #7:** Online learning is better. Web-based learning is no better or worse than instructor led training. (Adapted from "Rethinking Web-Based Learning," *T+D* magazine, January 2005.)

Warnings to Heed

In "The Illusion of e-Learning: Why We Are Missing Out on the Promise of Technology," Frank Greenagel provides some useful warnings:

- Many e-learning developers seem unaware of how people learn, or they continue to use flawed models of adult learning as evidenced by the rampant proliferation of boring, low impact courses built today.
- Too often, the features of the technology platform are driving the instructional strategy. The focus should be on creating an engaging learning experience that contributes to the organization's objectives.
- We need to accept the fact that the development cost of good e-learning is high and that the effectiveness of courses must be measured as carefully as one measures cost savings.

The World of Wireless

The conversation about how to leverage e-learning often assumes the use of computers and traditional keyboards as part of a blended experience. Add to this the advent of wireless devices (cell phones, PDAs, iPods and the like) that allow more freedom than ever before. Consider the following observation from "Wireless Wonders" (*T+D* magazine, March 2006).

> *The advent of wireless and handheld devices … means that Internet-based applications and functionality can be delivered to the smart phones, PDAs and cell phones. This is important because this means that content typically delivered through a portable computer can now be pushed through the aforementioned devices. From a training perspective, this creates endless possibilities for delivery of learning and performance content.*

Clearly, the world is changing around us and furnishes learning professionals with new tools to push learning to where the learners are and to the tools they use.

Examples of Effective Blended Learning

To meet the demands for information exchange and rapid learning across a global organization, Caterpillar, Inc. created Knowledge Network, which blends the features of knowledge management and virtual communities to facilitate access to up-to-date information (validated by community managers) and allows members of virtual communities to post questions and respond to queries from other community members.

St. Aubin, Haggerty & Associates, Inc. has built blended learning capabilities into "The Effective Interview," a two-day intense workshop for senior leaders and key hiring managers used to align organizational hiring criteria and practices. The companion online program simulates pre-interview planning and observation practice along with downloadable tools, a quick-reference guide and an online mastery test. Following online completion, participants receive real-time feedback on observed interviews by expert coaches.

In its push to be on the cutting edge of the retail industry, Target uses a cutting-edge approach to learning as it experiments with new collaboration tools such as blogs, wikis and podcasting while retaining some traditional features of organizational learning. (Adapted from "Five Innovated Examples of Blended Learning," *Chief Learning Officer* magazine, September 2007.)

CDW uses blended learning as a critical strategy to enhance performance. The organization developed Wired, a comprehensive technology skill development program containing online assessments to drive customized learning paths and self-paced e-learning. Wired also can provide synchronous distance learning to reach remote employees and online performance support tools. (Adapted from "Five Innovated Examples of Blended Learning," *Chief Learning Officer* magazine, September 2007.)

The Challenge & the Opportunity

As these examples demonstrate, effective blended learning often blurs the line between work and learning, creates technology-enabled collaboration and information sharing, and optimizes the link between new information acquisition and on-the-job performance.

As stated in "Training Tomorrow's Workforce" (*T+D* magazine, April 2007), *Blended approaches will require training staff to assume new roles, design instructional content in new formats, and be more skilled in the use of new technologies.* The options for innovative blended learning approaches will rapidly increase in the years to come, a growth made possible by new technologies that have still not arrived on our radar screens.

Resources

"Case Study: Blended Learning at Wells Fargo," In Practice, an online publication of ASTD. December 2004.

"Five Innovative Examples of Blended Learning," *Chief Learning Officer Magazine*, September 2007.

"E-Learning Strategies for Success," *Chief Learning Officer* magazine, May, 2004.

"Rethinking Web-Based Learning," *T+D* magazine, January 2005.

"Training Tomorrow's Workforce," *T+D* magazine, April 2007.

"Virtual Communities at Caterpillar Fosters Knowledge Sharing," *T+D* magazine, June 2004.

"Wireless Wonders: The World of Wireless Learning is Liberating," *T+D* magazine, March 2006.

39

Map Out
Competencies

When you earnestly believe you can compensate for a lack of skill by doubling your efforts, there's no end to what you can't do.

–Poster caption from Despair, Inc.

Many organizations and talented individuals are good at doing a lot of things. Unfortunately, some time-honored activities continue to be carried out long after their usefulness has expired. These obsolete capabilities get in the way and do not contribute to employee engagement because they are not linked to the important results of the business. One executive who had recently joined an organization to head up the quality function tells of receiving competently produced reports containing quality information that were of no strategic use to him or to anyone else in the organization. It was just something the staff had always done. This is a small example of a larger truth: As an organization leader, you need to be able to describe and map out the individual competencies and organizational capabilities that are crucial to future performance.

Competencies & Capabilities

Competencies are traits that must be present in an individual and used in appropriate ways to successfully achieve work outcomes. In an article titled "Competency Based or Traditional Approach to Training?," competencies are further described as: *A person's knowledge, skills, thought patterns, mindsets, social roles or self-esteem. Without the use of competencies at the correct strength, performance of any kind is impossible.* Some organizations use the acronym KSA (knowledge, skills and attitudes) to refer to the required competencies for a specific position.

Dave Ulrich and Norm Smallwood integrate the concept of individual competencies into their concept of organization capabilities. They define capabilities as: *The collective skills, abilities, and expertise of an organization.* Organizational capabilities are built through focused hiring, training and development; performance management; communication and other leader-driven practices. In this chapter, competencies will be used to discuss the tools and concepts related to individual level activities and capabilities as organizational level capacity.

Competencies & Competency Modeling

A competency is an active description of a skill set or output expected of a performer, accompanied by several behavioral descriptions that are likely to be associated with the competency at a particular employee level. For example, a competency modeling project at Sharp Electronics resulted in sets of competencies for a variety of positions. Below is a partial description of one competency for one position.

Position: Sales Director

Competency: Understands and encourages staff to use all aspects of products, services and the market to increase business.

1. Knows the factors affecting zone markets.
2. Encourages staff to gather and communicate competitive information.
3. Provides tailored sales direction.
4. Develops strategies that will affect the business at district and zone levels.
5. Develops business plans that anticipate market opportunities.

Note that the behavioral descriptors progress from performance that might be expected of a less experienced sales employee to the behaviors expected of a sales director. Each subsequent descriptor incorporates all prior behaviors on the list. Frequently, competency models are built around shared core competencies that run across all functions and positions. Specific functional competencies (such as sales skills within the sales function) and behavioral descriptors by level are then added.

The Value of Competencies & Competency Models

The business driver for producing competency models is that they serve to align your talent pipeline; to hire new employees, to manage performance, to assess candidates for promotion and to conduct focused succession planning. For employees seeking to progress in their career, well designed and communicated competency models help them map their path to a successful career by understanding what is expected of them and pointing the way toward developmental activities.

Building a Competency Model of Your Very Own

In general, a competency modeling process consists of the activities depicted in Figure 39.1 on the following page. At each step of the way, the core competency modeling team should analyze the new data and document conclusions.

Step 1: Planning and business analysis. Facilitate discussions with business leaders to identify business drivers, environment and high-gain application for a competency model.

Step 2: Interviews with senior executives. Interview senior executives with thought provoking questions that will assist in crystallizing competencies, such as the following:

• What is unique about this organization that makes us successful today?

Figure 39.1

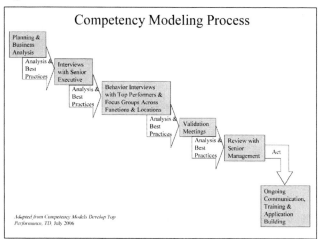

• Which of these must we retain going forward?
• Where do you believe this organization struggles today?
• Think of leaders who have impressed you and are successful. What are they doing that is different from average leaders?
• When you have seen a leader struggle or fail here, what seemed to be the main causes?

Compile and analyze results from this step and consider how best to organize the information for the next step.

Step 3: Behavior interviews with top performers and focus groups across functions and locations. Build out behavior descriptors for each competency by interviewing top performers and conducting focus groups.

Step 4: Validation meetings. Validate your findings through key stakeholder discussions.

Step 5: Review with senior management. Present the final modeling process to top executives for final buy-in and action planning.

Tips for Effective Implementation of Competencies

Based on anecdotal evidence and the article "Competency Models Develop Top Performance" about Sharp's experience, below are some lessons learned:

• Be clear about the set of needs for which you are developing the competencies and determine the set of key owners and users.
• Avoid over complicating the scheme you are populating with gathered information. As one of our clients warned, a project like this can seem like a human genome project.

- Employee participation in the competency model development process creates good awareness and broader ownership of outcomes. The Corbett Accel Healthcare Group formed an advisory board made up of high potential leaders in each functional area and location. This team drove the process of identifying the business drivers, competencies and developmental activities for progressive levels within each functional area and key positions.
- Prepare and facilitate timely training to managers and employees.

A Word About Organizational Capabilities

Dave Ulrich and Norm Smallwood, in the article "Capitalizing on Capabilities," define capabilities as "the collective skills, abilities, and expertise of an organization…They represent the ways that people and resources are brought together to accomplish work." When done well, competency models are integrated into your leadership practices so that the organization enhances its overall capabilities to deliver required results.

Figure 39.2 illustrates a way to think about competence and capabilities.

Figure 39.2

Organizational Capabilities Table		
	Individual	Organizational
Technical	1 An individual's functional competence	3 An organization's core competencies
Social	2 An individual's leadership ability	4 An organization's capabilities

Ulrich and Smallwood explain the table as follows: The individual-technical cell (1) represents a person's functional competence, such as technical expertise in marketing, finance or manufacturing. The individual-social cell (2) refers to a person's leadership ability—for instance, to set direction, to communicate a vision or to motivate people. The organizational-technical cell (3) comprises a company's core technical competencies; for example, a financial services firm must know how to manage risk. The organizational-social cell (4) represents an organization's underlying DNA, culture and personality. This might include such capabilities as innovation and speed.

They go on to describe why these distinctions are important. "Organizational capabilities emerge when a company delivers on the combined competencies and abilities of its individuals. An employee may be technically literate or demonstrate leadership skill, but the company as a whole may or may not embody the same strengths. (If it does, employees who excel in these areas will likely be engaged; if not, they may be frustrated.)"

Ulrich and Smallwood have identified a list of 11 core capabilities that well managed companies tend to exhibit.

- **Talent.** We are good at attracting, motivating and retaining competent and committed people.

- **Speed.** We are good at making important changes rapidly.

- **Shared mind-set and coherent brand identity.** We are good at ensuring that employees and customers have positive and consistent images of and experiences with our organization.

- **Accountability.** We are good at obtaining high performance from employees.

- **Collaboration**. We are good at working across boundaries to ensure both efficiency and leverage.

- **Learning.** We are good at generating and generalizing ideas with impact.

- **Leadership.** We are good at embedding leaders throughout the organization.

- **Customer connectivity.** We are good at building enduring relationships of trust with targeted customers.

- **Strategic unity.** We are good at articulating and sharing a strategic point of view.

- **Innovation.** We are good at doing something new in both content and process.

- **Efficiency.** We are good at managing costs.

Summary

Individual and organizational competencies are considered key success factors because they map out what is needed for the organization to be successful. You will want to align your key success factors with strategic organizational success factors to create a clear and engaging career map for your top talent.

One way to think of organizational success factors is to be clear about your organization's leadership brand: i.e., the exceptional abilities of managers and leaders that are geared to fulfill customers' and investors' expectations. (See Chapter 4: Creating a Leadership Brand, for more on leadership brand.) In "Building a Leadership Brand," Ulrich and Smallwood recall a workshop where leadership competency descriptions were collected from several firms in diverse industries, and then the firm names were deleted from each list. Workshop attendees were not able to distinguish the firm or industry from which the competency descriptions came. The conclusion? "By focusing on the desirable traits of individual leaders, the firms ended up creating generic models. And vanilla competency models generate vanilla leadership." Your model of leadership competency should emerge from what your leadership brand requires of all managers and leaders.

Resources

"Building a Leadership Brand," *Harvard Business Review*," July-August 2007.

"Capitalizing on Capabilities," *Harvard Business Review*, June 2004.

"Competency Models Develop Top Performance," *T+D* magazine, July 2006.

"Competency-Based or a Traditional Approach to Training?" *T+D* magazine, April 2004.

Part Nine

Retain:
Develop for Tomorrow's Needs

Plan for
the Future

"There are many methods for predicting the future. For example, you can read horoscopes, tea leaves, tarot cards, or crystal balls. Collectively, these methods are known as 'nutty methods.' Or you can put well-researched facts into sophisticated computer models, more commonly referred to as *a complete waste of time*."

–Scott Adams

Businesses today face significant challenges in putting the right people in the right jobs with the right leaders. And if leaders do not improve their ability to predict their future and build the workforce capabilities accordingly, resilience will be lost.

Magnitude of the Problem

According to the Bureau of Labor Statistics, by 2010 the United States will have 10,033,000 more jobs than people to fill them; by that same year, more than 25 percent of the current working U.S. population will reach retirement age. CLO Magazine reports that 77 percent of companies said they do not have enough successors to their current senior level managers already working in the organizations.

The Global Human Capital Study was released in October of 2007–the result of collaboration between the Economist Intelligence Unit and IBM Institute for Business Value. In the study, 400 human resource executives from 40 countries provided input. Report findings included:

- 75 percent of HR executives say they are concerned about their ability to develop future leaders.
- 52 percent of HR executives say a significant workforce related challenge facing their organization is the inability to rapidly develop skills to address current and/or future business needs.
- More than one-third of study participants state that their employees' skills are not aligned with current organizational priorities.

Are We Running Out of Talent and Energy?

Many organizations have already witnessed departure of talent without being able to replace these workers. When more are walking out your door (due to retirement or greener employment pastures) than coming in the door, it puts a strain on the active workforce. How might this impact engagement?

An employee engagement researcher gathered information linking engagement and personal energy at work. Energy was found to be an important determinant of both individual and firm performance. Her research found that "leaders are reporting personal energy levels at work to be lower than where they say they are most productive." She found that when "leaders and managers are feeling confused, distracted and overworked, their employees are doing much worse...The research shows that a decline in leader energy predicts reduced employee energy scores." As organizations ask managers to do more with less, growing a pipeline of effective leaders to drive business success in the future becomes much more difficult. Not only do managers seek other employment options, their employees become less effective as energy is drained from the system.

What Is in Your Future?

A 2004 U.S. Department of Labor study identified three major trends that will shape the future at work: shifting demographic patterns, the pace of technological change and the path of economic globalization. Key implications related to workforce planning are:

- Employees will work in more decentralized, specialized firms and employer-employee relationships will become less standardized and more individualized.
- Slower labor force growth will encourage employers to adopt approaches to facilitate greater labor force participation among women, the elderly and people with disabilities.
- Greater emphasis will be placed on retraining and lifelong learning as the U.S. workforce tries to stay competitive in the global marketplace and respond to technological changes.

Know What You Need

You first need to know more precisely what you require in your future workforce. Refer to Chapter 12: Forecast Changes in Market and Business, for frameworks to analyze future needs. Given constraints caused by limited talent pools, you may need to respond in novel ways to your future workforce needs assessment. First, you may have to ramp up your capability to access internal talent.

Know What You Have Now

Responding to a pending workforce talent crisis will require your organization to be resourceful at tapping into internal talent. The rapidly morphing face of business brings with it demands for nimble workforce movement and resilience; it often requires organizations to quickly fill open positions with competent individuals when none seem to be available. Some organizations do this by more frequently searching for the right talent outside of the organization. While this can work well, it comes with a higher risk that the person either does not really have the competence to hit the ground running or will not excel in the firm's culture. A lower risk, higher return strategy is to fill open positions with competent internal talent who have proven track records of performance.

The problem for many organizations is that information on employee competence and experience is not readily available; they have not built the capability to track and move talent where it is needed most. Following are two accounts of what sample organizations have done to polish up their crystal ball and more efficiently access and move internal talent.

Terry Lundgren is CEO, chairman of the board and president of Macy's. He talks about his involvement and perspective on Macy's talent processes. "We look at the org[anization] charts for every division to see who is at the top and who the backups are for various roles. In some cases, we go down three levels. Then we drill down into their qualifications. The information we use is all electronic now, starting with the organizational charts and including the whole history of the people we are looking at–their bios, their job histories, and their strengths and development needs. We can click our way through it all and easily fine-tune potential teams. It's very cool. One of our challenges, as we grow larger, is to maintain the ability to know what people can do so that we can encourage their careers, give them developmental opportunities, and put them in the right jobs at the right time."

"Polish Your Crystal Ball" (*T+D* magazine, November 2007) chronicles the Nuclear Energy Institute's turnaround in improving the recruiting and retention of competent employees. The article concludes that–by maintaining an inventory of current competencies, consistently revisiting the conversation with executives, embracing strategic context, and putting some incentive behind competency forecasting, your organization can polish up its crystal ball and generate better information to fuel effective succession planning.

Creative Talent Pipeline Approaches

To achieve a higher level of resilience in meeting the workforce requirements of your organization's future, consider seeking innovative solutions to traditional approaches. Some of those approaches below are already used extensively in some industries and may be new avenues for talent enrichment in your industry as well.

Leadership depth-building
- Build leaders who exemplify your leadership brand. Select, groom and promote managers and leaders on the basis of individual capabilities that reinforce

the leadership brand. By linking individual abilities and the organization's brand capabilities, you create an engaging level of alignment. GE, Johnson & Johnson, Disney, Boeing and PepsiCo do this to develop such deep leadership talent that they become leader feeders into other organizations.

- Create an organizational structure that aligns best with strategy execution, not with the interests of current executive team members. Avoid the temptation to mold your executive positions and reporting relationships to the specific talent spectrum of incumbents. Create the structure strategically first, and coach leaders in transitioning to the correct roles.
- Do effective succession planning. See Chapter 41: Right-Size High Potential Leadership Programs for more ideas on this topic.
- Create a strong pool of leaders who are willing and able to coach and teach.
- Create an organization of generalists rather than specialists. Make job rotation part of the culture. It should be a transparent, cross-department and cross-business unit process for creating deep leadership talent.
- Ramp up your commitment to mission-critical training and development for key, strategic positions.

Partner with Local Learning Institutions

- Grow students as prospective employees. Some organizations have tackled the problem of obtaining skilled workers by partnering with local colleges and universities in training students to meet required skill needs. An organization assists the educational institution in training faculty, purchasing technologies and developing materials. On the other side, the institutions benefit from increased enrollment, and students in these programs have clear incentive to learn well to gain employment with the sponsoring businesses.

Leverage Your Close-to-Retirement Employees

- Conduct retirement planning. Track experienced workers and collaborate on how best to leverage their knowledge as they plan their futures. Bring back retirees into coaching, mentoring and independent contractor roles.
- Be inviting to deeply experienced employees as they near retirement, and leverage their knowledge and experience. The good news here is that many workers nearing retirement age do not plan to retire in the traditional sense. An AARP article on hiring older workers concludes, "Sixty-nine percent of (baby) boomers surveyed in a recent AARP study indicated their plans to remain in the workforce past traditional retirement age–perhaps into their 70s or 80s." Organizations that value older workers' experience and willingness to work are able to take a big bite out of the talent gap.

Maximize & Optimize Diversity

- Examine the gender and diversity balance of your leadership pipeline. Ensure that talented minorities in the workplace have equal access to all positions, including leadership positions. Accelerate your support of diversity in the leadership team.

Contract & Part-Time Workers

- Use a part-time workforce to meet the ebb and flow within your business cycle. Let go of the bias that all work must be done by full-time employees. Embrace the capacity for workers who can contribute value in support roles. Create a nuclear organization that can direct the work of independent contractors to fulfill the brand and strategy of your organization.

Creative Sourcing & Focused Hiring

- Tighten your hiring practices. Filling empty chairs with warm bodies can no longer be a solution. Every new hire must fit your business needs, hiring criteria and be a viable candidate to fill the next higher position.
- Create an employee referral bonus program.
- Creative incentives for leaders and managers to mine their professional or technical networks for talent.
- Leverage technology such as Internet job sites and online screening and analysis tools.
- Examine the job descriptions of pivotal positions to identify skills or experience that could be taken off the required-for-hire list and can be gained on the job or taught relatively easily.

Be Flexible

- Establish effective flexible work arrangements. Creating flexible options for talented employees is undoubtedly becoming a requirement for keeping talented workers.
- Adopt a more flexible and informal work environment to be more inviting to today's entering workforce, the millenials. They are interested in life-work balance (note the order of priority) and are even less interested in being micromanaged than baby boomers and gen Xers.

Summary

As comedian George Burns once said, "I look to the future because that's where I'm going to spend the rest of my life." A bright future for your organization requires bright thinking and planning now so you have the right talent doing the right things as your future challenges and opportunities rapidly become current reality.

Resources

"Employee Engagement: Beyond the Fad and into the Executive Suite," *Leader to Leader*, No. 44, Spring 2007.

"The Future at Work–Trends and Implications," Research Brief 2004. *www.rand.org.*

"Hiring Older Workers: A Solid and Sound Investment Proposition," Article by AARP. February 2006. *www.aarp.org/research/international/perspectives/feb_06_ olderworkers.html.*

41

Right-Size High Potential Leadership Programs

What organizations want sounds simple: The right talent in the right place at the right time. This would be easier if business stood still and markets stopped changing. But what do you do when the business keeps growing or changing? Managing your portfolio of leadership talent is, and will continue to be, a crucial organizational effort. Chapter 33: Create the Development Process, outlined a talent development process. This chapter will focus on two activities that are also directly linked to strengthening your leadership pipeline:

1. High potential leadership development; and
2. succession planning.

Synchronize Leadership Development & Succession Planning

Leadership development in many organizations often refers to two levels of activity:

1. Elective generalized management skill programs for new and middle managers, and
2. Focused experiences for a select group of high potential future leaders.

Both aim at increasing the breadth and depth of leadership talent.

Succession planning is about building an approach to identify and develop candidates for success in top leadership positions. Often, succession planning and implementation involves top executives (sometimes in conjunction with the board of directors) in targeting, assessing and developing players who are their likely backups on the bench or on deck preparing to enter the big game.

Leadership development, high potential leader programs and succession planning are different elements along a continuum of leadership pipeline fulfillment. As suggested in "Developing Your Leadership Pipeline" in *Harvard Business Review*–Succession Management must be a flexible system oriented toward developmental activities, not a rigid list of high potential employees and the slots they might fill. By marrying succession planning and leadership development, you get the best of both: Attention to the skills required for senior management positions along with an educational system that can help managers develop those skills.

Ownership of Leadership Development & Succession Planning

While the supporting roles for managing the leadership pipeline may vary from organization to organization, it is crucial that the ownership reside at the highest levels possible. Without dedicated executive sponsorship and involvement, these initiatives are either doomed to failure or easily trumped by other programs of the month. For example, Robert Lawless, CEO of McCormick & Company, holds an annual session with his board of directors and the vice president of HR. He says the purpose is to "review development needs, goals, objectives, performance, and the recent training and development for the top people in the organization." He then cascades the process through the organization.

Who Are Your High Potential Performers?

First, you and other leaders must adopt a mindset of talent differentiation. As an article in *Workspan* magazine states it, "The truth is that some employees are simply more valuable than others. The employees who help a company execute its business strategy, the ones who *operationalize it*, are its key talent. If they leave, there is a financial impact on the business. And if they go to the competition, the impact is double."

Here are ways to examine your organization to identify high potential talent.

- Identify the mission critical positions or job families that drive the execution of your business strategy. (See Chapter 36: Focus on Key Positions, for more ideas on this.) Then identify the above average and stellar performers in those mission critical positions.
- Consider linchpin positions. These are jobs that are essential to the long-term health of the organization or provide key developmental experiences to those who are in the position. Incumbents in this position should be developed and moved further to make room for other talent.
- Identify people selected by incumbent executives as viable successors.
- Identify additional risk-to-lose employees (those who may be in positions other than mission critical positions).

Employ the following nomination exercise to engage executive team members in identifying additional high potential candidates and to create a useful, cross functional dialogue around talent sharing. In smaller organizations, this process may be useful to generate or expand your list.

High Potential Nomination Exercise
1. Each executive lists four people who have demonstrated enough potential to assume an executive or senior management position but who do not report within the executive's own organization.
2. Nominations should include anyone who has not been listed already in a discussion of high potential employees and backup successors.

3. Criteria to use:
   - demonstrated behaviors cause you to feel he or she has a great deal of potential
   - demonstrated ability to operate with senior management
   - demonstrated desire to operate at a senior level
   - minimum 12-month tenure in the organization
   - If you had to take your best guess, and stand behind it, who would you nominate from the list?
4. Then each executive uses the same criteria to nominate no more than two individuals from his or her own area of accountability.

Some organizations conduct an analysis of talent by rating them on current performance and future potential. See Chapter 33: Create the Development Process, for further information on rating performance and potential. The result of such an analysis can be summarized in a portfolio matrix such as the one shown in Figure 41.1.

Figure 41.1

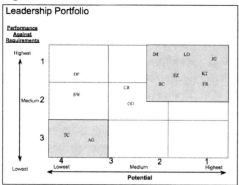

For individuals who are plotted on the top left of the matrix, you should consider the key actions to be taken to engage and develop their leadership capacity. For those individuals falling in the bottom left quadrant, you should also take action that will mitigate the negative impact that lower potential performers may have in blocking higher potential employees from gaining new experiences.

Succession Planning

The process of succession planning involves identifying and developing candidates for success in fulfilling an organization's key roles. This process is often shrouded in secrecy. Some organizations have begun to build a more transparent, employee driven, technology enabled process for succession planning.

The goal of the succession management group at Eli Lilly and Company was to provide a desktop tool to–be like Amazon. Lilly's web-based succession tool is available through an icon on employees' computer desktops. According to

"Developing Your Leadership Pipeline," employees can rapidly access the portal on the company's Intranet to access job postings; in addition, "Lilly's HR managers and the succession management team can use the company's success management website to assess an employee's current level, potential level, experience, and development plans. They also use it as a general querying and reporting tool."

Whether you are able to leverage technology and create a fully transparent succession planning process or not, it is critical to have a plan and approach that meets the need for making clear succession decisions, allows for clear access to the right talent at the right time and prepares the organization to be nimble in filling key positions as conditions change.

Types of High Potential & Successor Development Programs

Launch your future leaders into well-crafted development programs that are aligned with business strategy drivers and your organization's leadership brand. At the very start, it is important to integrate individual development planning to establish goals, developmental activity plans, time frames and measures.

Often through trial and error, organizations hone the approach and content of programs that align best with their leadership brand needs. In additional to internal training offerings, high potential development programs fall into three main categories: academic, action learning or new experiences. While most organizations may have elements of all three, they tend to invest more in one than the others.

1. **Academic focused**–Partner with a well chosen educational institution. For example, Ingersoll Rand found that sending their leaders to executive MBA programs was successful in building fundamental knowledge of business management, but it came with a price. They found that many graduates opted for new careers outside of the company, or were less connected to their business and their colleagues during and after the program. They decided to partner with Indiana University's Kelley School of Business to create a 3-year custom designed MBA program with virtual components and cohort groups that met to dialogue and complete assignments. The length and depth of the program allowed high potential leaders to stay connected to their careers and take on even greater responsibilities while in the program. This approach has the benefit of tapping into the deep knowledge of faculty while remaining grounded in the business and creating a well-connected alumni group.

2. **Action learning focused**–At The Schwan Food Company, high potential candidates are selected through an assessment, interview and essay writing process. In addition to a rigorous professional assessment resulting in focused development plans, groups of high potential employees are given the task to respond to real world business issues facing the company. These projects give future leaders a firsthand taste of leadership responsibilities

to come. Schwan leaders believe this program gives team members an understanding about leadership, and "helps establish working relationships with senior executives to whom they report," according to Arnie Strebe, CEO of Schwan's University.

Often, the executive team identifies target issues for action learning projects. Executives and other leaders are then involved in reviewing and advising the work of the action learning teams. Samples of action learning projects include:
- turning around a failing business unit or region
- resolving a customer service breakdown
- designing a new business/product startup
- creating an innovative knowledge management process

3. New experience focused–Many organizations heavily invest in developing leadership talent through a variety of on-the-job experience. Job rotation, cross-functional transfers and international relocation are all aspects of this approach. Nothing works better to expand perspectives, grow a cross-organization network and get a better grasp of customer's needs than this approach. A related method is to ensure that executives spend significant time in a position that has significant customer contact. At Stryker, a key factor in assessing executive readiness is an extended assignment in a customer facing position. Procter & Gamble assigns leadership talent to brand teams for gaining vital customer and profit & loss experience. International assignments should also be considered as important job rotation opportunities. According to "Building a Leadership Brand," an international experience can give a person a strong feel for what the company represents in each of those regions, and reinforce some of the underlying and shared assumptions about how the organization relates to its customers.

Measuring Success

Take the pulse of your high potential development and succession management activities through measures that help you make effective adjustments. Some metrics to consider are:

- Number of nominations for key positions.
- Ratio of fully ready successors per incumbent per level.
- Number of managers completing development plans for high potential employees.
- Number of qualified employees placed in key positions over the past period.
- Attrition rate from the succession plan.
- Changes in ready now status.
- Ratio of women and minorities involved in program.
- Changes in women and minority ratios.

Summary

Effective leadership development and succession management is only possible with stellar executive ownership and involvement. Leaders who create cultures elevating talent building to the status of a pivotal business differentiator leave a legacy of sustained organizational success and released human potential.

Resources

"Building a Leadership Brand," *Harvard Business Review*, July-August 2007.

"Developing Your Leadership Pipeline" *Harvard Business Review*, December 2003.

"Effective Succession Planning: How to Design and Implement a Successful Succession Plan," *T+D* magazine, October 2006.

"Implementing Your Succession Plan," *T+D* magazine, November 2007.

"The Royal Treatment: How to Engage Key Talent," *Workspan*, July 2002.

Select Development
Options that Fit

"I am always ready to learn although I do not always like being taught."
–Sir Winston Churchill

"There can be no mental development without interest."
–Alfred North Whitehead

"I never let my schooling interfere with my learning."
–Mark Twain

These pundits have noticed a common theme in human development–important learning and growth can and does happen outside of traditional education approaches. And it happens best when our inherent curiosity is engaged.

Growing talent through the use of creative development strategies is an especially timely topic for leaders who are facing a variety of challenges regarding the depth of leadership talent in their organizations due to factors such as:

- Rapid growth and change requiring new leadership in new ventures;
- members of the executive team who are nearing retirement without clear successors;
- significant organizational restructuring or realignment requiring greater business acumen and management abilities across teams; and
- clear indications from employees who want more development options and programs–to retain key talent.

Development vs. Training

Training is used most often as a term for those learning activities that build skills for current, functional job responsibilities. Workplace performance and learning specialists use the word development to refer to activities that prepare key employees for positions that will be available in the future. Development options, then, are the choices that organizations have available to them to build strategic knowledge and experience that, in turn, deepen leadership bench strength.

The "2006 State of the Industry in Leading Enterprises" report sponsored by the American Society for Training and Development describes the data and themes across companies that are exemplars of great organizational learning and development or BEST organizations. Leadership development and succession planning were the focus of many BEST organizations in 2006, whether to prepare for senior management turnover, to develop managers to be better leaders, or to identify the leadership characteristics important to the organization in preparation for developing a leadership initiative. The report also indicates the average percentage of employee access to different types of development opportunities. Employee access percentages for leadership development activities include:

- knowledge sharing: 78 percent
- mentoring and coaching: 71 percent
- job rotation: 49 percent
- employee supported conference attendance: 55 percent
- tuition reimbursement: 84 percent

The practice of developing talent for the future is clearly linked to employee fulfillment, engagement and retention when done well. By ensuring that key contributors are groomed and supported in their career growth, the organization creates what Bill O'Brien, CEO of The Hanover Insurance Group from 1979 to 1991, called a *legacy mentality at the top.*

Principles of Development

The most effective leadership teams work with the following principles in mind:

- Identify the people in your organization on whom you wish to invest in deeper and broader talent development.
- Be clear on what they already know and can do, their strengths and where they need further expansion.
- Do not use just one approach to develop their leadership competence. Even the best on-site or off-site executive development program or e-learning curriculum will not meet all the developmental needs of all your future leaders.
- The leadership team and the employee to be developed equally share the responsibility for developing the capacity to lead.
- Ensure first that development planning targets mission critical positions.
- Ensure that all high potential candidates for future leadership positions (highly talented individuals at lower levels) are also targeted for clear, effective development and support.
- Development of talented employees is a high gain retention strategy when handled in ways that are engaging to the employee.
- Development of talented employees is a high gain strategy to develop bench strength–to create multiple successors for key leadership positions.
- Assessing talent and development needs requires open and frank discussions in appropriate executive and functional leadership team forums across disciplines.

- Best developmental decisions often require the softening of organizational boundaries. High potential talent is for the whole enterprise and not owned by any specific functional area.
- Plans for developing individuals should be customized to the situation and players involved. Plans may require a variety of developmental strategies to be effective.
- Top talent is engaged by new challenges. As Mihaly Csikszentmihalyi, a noted educator, once said: "Those periods of struggling to overcome challenges are what people find to be the most enjoyable times."

Development Strategies

Time and money to invest in development are not in unlimited supply. The table of development strategies (Figure 42.1) below moves from those activities that yield the highest return on time and money invested (career development discussions and plans, job placement based on development needs) to those activities that may yield less return on investment, even though some of these strategies do not come at a high price tag (motivated self-development, event-based opportunities). All of these strategies have been used in effective ways. The ones you choose to consider will depend on the business needs and the career growth interests of the talent you seek to develop.

Figure 42.1

Summary

All developmental approaches should be initiated by goal oriented, feedback rich career development discussions and planning (the first strategy above). Helping talented employees develop their capabilities for future responsibilities is not sustainable if the tone is compliance oriented. Engage their heart and mind in the endeavor. They have to want it.

A compelling explanation behind what drives people to blossom into new roles is described in "Job Sculpting: The Art of Retaining Your Best People," *Harvard Business Review*. The authors talk about DELIs (Deeply Embedded Life Interests). "Think of a deeply embedded life interest as a geothermal pool of super-heated water. It will rise to the surface in one place as a hot spring and in another as a geyser. But beneath the surface–at the core of the individual–the pool is constantly bubbling. Deeply embedded life interests always seem to find expression even when a person has to change jobs or careers for that to happen."

Resources

"Developmental Strategies for Employees and Supervisors," St. Aubin, Haggerty & Associates, Inc. (*www.staubin.net*)

"Job Sculpting: The Art of Retaining Your Best People," *Harvard Business Review*, September-October 1999.

Manage Retention & Turnover

Organizations facing high loss of talent go to great lengths developing programs with the primary goal of retaining talent. According to a 2006 study by the Society for Human Resource Management and CareerJournal.com:

In response to improvements in the economy and the job market, nearly half of respondents indicated that their organizations had implemented special processes to retain staff.

More alarmingly, 76 percent of employees responded *somewhat likely* or *very likely* to a question on the likelihood of beginning or increasing a job search as the economy and job market improves. Another source estimated that a 10 percent reduction in employee turnover was worth more money than a 10 percent increase in productivity, or a 10 percent increase in sales. These challenging times require innovative approaches, beyond what has been traditionally done, to retain your top talent.

Employee engagement and turnover are opposite faces of the same coin. When people are engaged in their work and committed to contributing value, they tend to stay longer and live your employer brand. Many chapters of this book directly address organizational strategies that make a difference in managing retention and turnover. Listed below are some of the concepts from earlier chapters in this book that point to effective retention approaches.

- Be a talent magnet and use your brand to attract talent (see Chapters 5 and 14). When you become an employer of choice, the right talent beats a path to your door.
- On-board effectively (see Chapters 20 to 24). By capturing the hearts and imaginations of new talent, you beat the vicious cycle of new hire churn.
- Build an engaging culture (see Chapters 24 to 27 and Chapter 44). Engaging leaders exemplify and support a culture in which employees thrive and are proud. Virtue, trust and respect for the individual describe engaging cultures.
- Communicate well (see Chapter 30). Employees want to be in the know. Effective, open, honest and positive communication from leaders will pay dividends in reducing turnover.

- Engage by involving employees (see Chapter 29). Employee involvement is a common and effective tool to link efforts to organizational outcomes.
- Train for today's needs and develop for tomorrow's needs (Chapters 31 to 43). Talented people desire to learn and grow. Organizations that effectively and visibly support personal growth will outretain their competitors who less clearly support it.
- Encourage wellness in the workplace (see Chapter 45). Wellness programs not only impact productivity through better health, they enhance workforce engagement levels.
- Recognize and appreciate (see Chapter 46). Employee recognition programs publicly demonstrate appreciation for employee efforts.

A focus in any of these areas can result in useful and valuable strategies for retaining talent. Additional programs that are specifically designed to reduce unwanted turnover will be discussed in the following section.

Retention Program Innovations

Below are program descriptions and examples increasingly used to retain talent. While this is not intended to be an exhaustive list of ideas (and may well miss a favorite idea of yours), it does point to innovative ways that demonstrate to employees that you care about their well-being and want them to stay. An effective innovation will be built on one or more of these core employee messages:

- We want to express our appreciation for the value that you bring.
- We want to make your work life and personal life easier.
- We want to help you enrich your own life in ways that you value.

Better Service Awards

Organizations give gifts to employees for length of service. As tenure with the company increases, the value of the gift increases. Organizations are now expanding these programs to provide broader choices. To accelerate these programs, the value level of gifts can be increased and the number of service years reduced. For example, an employee may be able to select a flat screen, high definition television as he reaches a career milestone with his employer. A note of caution: Be willing to continue this program for many years to come, and do not be too cheap. This can actually be disengaging when done poorly.

A note about employee rewards and incentives in general: Rewards can hinder performance. In *Punished by Rewards: The Trouble with Gold Stars, Incentive Plans, A's, Praise and Other Bribes,* Alfie Kohn provides four reasons why, sometimes surprisingly, many reward and incentive programs are likely to ultimately fail.

- **Rewards punish.** When people know what the reward might be for certain performance, they know that punishment for failure is also possible. The stick is contained in the carrot.

- **Rewards rupture relationships.** Rewards and punishments tend to flourish in asymmetrical relationships where some people have a great deal more power than others. Power differences impede open, collaborative interactions.

- **Rewards ignore reasons.** Reward systems usually do not require any deep understanding about why people might underperform. To truly engage someone in improved performance, it is clearly important to understand the root causes of current inferior performance.

- **Rewards discourage risk taking.** For people working for a reward, the system encourages doing exactly what is necessary to get the carrot, and no more. Likely, you have heard salespeople say,–*Once I make my quota, I can finally relax.*

Health Benefits

The healthcare system in the United States seems to get more complex and costly every month. The annual analysis and decision making around health plan alternatives is becoming a headache for many organizations. However, health benefits can be a differentiator in retaining employees. Employees are putting increasing weight on the levels of benefits they have and how much they must pay for them. Retention is positively impacted if your employees can say their benefits are better and/or cost less than what they would be paying elsewhere.

Fitness Access

At Qualcomm locations, employees have access to fitness centers with weight machines, free weights, aerobic exercise equipment, lap pools, tennis courts, basketball courts or volleyball courts. Some organizations are broadening accessibility to fitness activities by forming fitness clubs for biking, hiking or sailing enthusiasts or support involvement in corporate Olympic games-style competitions.

Making Life a Little Easier

Many organizations realize that great value is gained by helping busy, often overworked employees balance the demands of their life outside of work. Many organizations supplement day care in or near their facilities. Concierge services are also becoming more commonplace, staffed by professionals who can help with a myriad of energy and time draining activities such as finding a housekeeper, attending to dry cleaning, social planning, travel, entertainment, gift buying, grocery shopping and other life errands. Typically, the employer covers the cost of the concierge service and the employee picks up the cost of products obtained.

Look for a life balance need that is special to your employee population. At Google, for example, new moms and dads are able to expense up to $500 for takeout meals during the first 4 weeks they are home with their new baby.

Employee Referrals

When employees receive bonuses for successfully referring friends for jobs in the company, it has a threefold positive impact:

1. Employees value the referral bonus itself;
2. employees are communicating your employment brand outside of work; and
3. work life improves for people who are working with friends.

Giving Back to the Community

We all want to have meaning in our work and in our life. Serving a purpose is linked to a sense of personal fulfillment. Many organizations see it as their obligation to help employees find ways to contribute in meaningful ways to the community around them. Search *www.usafreedomecorps.gov* for volunteer programs in your area. Some organizations are in industries that suggest specific community involvement programs. For example, a company with strong links to the field of oncology supports employee involvement in cancer awareness and advocacy programs.

Conduct Stay Interviews vs. Exit Interviews

Some organizations are reducing exit interviews by focusing on stay interviews. St. Luke's Hospital of Kansas City credits low employee turnover to its process of conducting random stay interviews with long-term employees, asking them why they value working at the hospital and what suggestions they have to improve the work environment.

Spiritual Counsel

As suggested by "Creative Approaches to Retention," a growing number of organizations are addressing the spiritual needs of employees by offering chaplains and chaplaincy services–at work. The Society for Human Resource Management (SHRM) white paper explains that chaplain services may range from fulfilling a simple need like having someone to talk to–to the complex need of arranging funeral services for an employee or employee's family member. Companies using these services point both to a desire to address the needs of the *whole employee*, and to a measurable positive impact on absenteeism, turnover and health insurance costs.

Innovative Relocation

It is getting more difficult for employers to get their employees to move where they may be needed most. Some organizations are increasing their level of relocation assistance in order to retain key talent by providing whole family services. Consider expanding your relocation services by offering research and information on school districts, youth activities, cultural organizations and other desired information about the new location.

Fruitful Time Off

Sabbaticals have been around for a long time–the idea of taking a long break from one's daily work in order to fulfill a specific career-related goal. Professors and clergy are two groups that have traditionally undertaken sabbaticals to deepen their understanding, rejuvenate or advance their work. Organizations in the private sector are just beginning to expand the idea of sabbatical taking as a plausible work-life balance approach for employees who have reached a certain level of tenure or responsibility. Some programs may expect industry-focused research that expands business offerings or competitive advantage while others may support the pursuit of personal development interests.

Summary

Your organization has many options to directly impact unwanted turnover. Some options will have a more significant impact than others, and some will take more effort than they are worth. The intended outcome must be creating business value through reducing unwanted turnover. Achieving this outcome requires an assessment of leadership actions, organizational practices and elements of the environment that may negatively impact retention. It also requires the organizational will to take corrective actions to keep the people you need to keep.

Resources

"Creative Approaches to Employee Retention," A SHRM White Paper, May 2000.

"Employee Turnover: Analyzing Employee Movement Out of the Organization," A SHRM White Paper November 2002.

How to Become an Employer of Choice, Oakhill Press, ©2000.

Love 'Em or Lose 'Em: Getting Good People to Stay, Berrett-Koehler Publishers, Inc., ©2005.

Punished by Rewards: The Trouble with Gold Stars, Incentive Plans, A's Praise, and Other Bribes, Houghton Mifflin Company, ©1993.

"Retention Tactics That Work," A SHRM White Paper, September 2002.

"The SHRM/CareerJournal.com 2006 Job Retention Poll," *www.shrm.org*.

Part Ten

General Retention Practices

Sustain a Climate of Respect & Inclusion

"Our commitment to diversity is a commitment to individuals and to the team. It's about creating an environment in which all associates can fulfill their potential without barriers, and in which the team is made stronger by the diverse backgrounds, experiences and perspectives of individuals. It's about giving all of us–individually and together–the best possible chance to succeed."

–Bank of America CEO Kenneth D. Lewis

Overview of Diversity in Organizations

The subject of diversity continues to be a fairly controversial topic. In today's environment we are bombarded with diversity issues in the media and rarely with a positive perspective. Immigration, language barriers, strong sentiments stemming from September 11 and sexual harassment and race discrimination lawsuits are constantly in the news. Indeed, social forces, coupled with individual cultural and life experiences, shape people's views about diversity, and discussions surrounding these issues tend to evoke a tremendous level of emotion. In the workplace, employees' views about diversity affect how they interact with peers, subordinates, supervisors and customers; in particular, how they interact with those they consider different than themselves.

From an organizational perspective, the current U.S. workforce is the most diverse in its history, and significant demographic changes in the composition of the U.S. labor force will be seen for years to come. Between 2004 and 2014, the Bureau of Labor Statistics projects an increase of 33.7 percent in the Latino/Hispanic workforce, 16.8 percent in the African American workforce and 32.4 percent in the Asian workforce. Diversity by gender, religion, age and sexual orientation will become more prevalent. It is unrealistic to expect that such a diverse group of individuals can effectively work together and contribute fully simply because they are employed by the same company. It is the responsibility of organizational leaders to acknowledge the importance of managing a diverse workforce.

One of the major challenges organizations face today is attracting, retaining and engaging a diverse workforce. In the initial stages of working with clients on their diversity initiatives, consultants often begin by asking top management what diversity means to them. The answers run the gamut of hiring more minorities and women to treating everyone the same to dealing with differences in the workplace. When asked to describe how they would create a respectful climate that allows everyone to attain their full potential, responses vary from punitive approaches for harassment on one end of the spectrum to creating fun places to work at the other. The objective of this chapter is to provide an overview of diversity in organizations and outline the process for successfully creating and sustaining a climate that values diversity and inclusion.

Definition of Diversity

"Diversity is about more than race and gender," says Xerox chairwoman and CEO Anne Mulcahy. "It's about more than numbers. It's about inclusion. Diversity means creating an environment where all employees can grow to their fullest potential."

What does diversity mean? When asked to define diversity, most will immediately reference people's physical characteristics, which are really just the tip of the iceberg in that they represent only a small part of a very large mass. Because physical characteristics are visible, they are focused on the most. Yet when people get to know one another, they are exposed to what is below the surface and begin to realize that they have much more in common than they initially thought. One way to look at diversity is to simultaneously acknowledge both differences and similarities and consider both to be equally important.

From Compliance to Valuing Diversity

In today's organizational environment, it is crucial to move beyond the legal perspective of mandated compliance, i.e., affirmative action/EEO. This legal perspective is viewed as being a defensive or reactive strategy and tends to focus on historical prejudices that have kept members of certain groups out of organizations. There is still much confusion on the issue of affirmative action and legal compliance and negative views of the numbers game.

While EEO compliance is a requisite of running an organization and not an option, managing and valuing diversity is quite different. Managing and valuing diversity is about creating a multicultural and inclusive organization that proactively embraces both the similarities and differences of its employees and customers. It promotes a desire to gain access to employees and new customer groups with the purpose of learning from their different perspectives.

Leveraging Diversity as a Resource (Competitive Advantage)

As Edward Bullock, vice president of diversity at L'Oreal USA, has said, "When everyone thinks alike not much thinking takes place. Real innovation and success can only take place and can thrive when different voices and different points of view are invited to the table. Then and only then can we all enjoy the fruits of diversity and inclusion."

Indeed, recent group and organizational studies have proven that managing and valuing diversity creates a competitive advantage in organizations. The business case for promoting diversity and inclusion highlights enhanced business processes and outcomes such as:

- attracting and hiring greater talent
- job satisfaction
- higher retention
- creativity
- problem solving
- decision making
- marketing
- adaptability
- productivity

In an inclusive environment organizational members feel they are a part of critical processes. Different perspectives are valued and in turn provide organizations with a competitive advantage. Data show that turnover and absenteeism are often higher for women and minorities and that job satisfaction is lower, but organizations with a reputation for attracting and retaining a diverse, highly competent workforce have an advantage. Organizations recognized as the best companies for women, African Americans, Latinos, and gay, lesbian and transgender employees have acknowledged the different needs of their diverse employees. They have implemented, for example, work/life programs to help balance office and home life.

In 2008, the combined buying power of African Americans, Asians and Native Americans will exceed $1.5 trillion. The Latino/Hispanic economic clout will rise to $1,014.2 billion, an increase of 357 percent from 1990. People prefer to not only work for organizations that value diversity but also purchase products from organizations that value diversity in their customer base as well as their workforce.

Process for Becoming an Inclusive Organization

Organizations that have decided to be more truly inclusive can take the following steps; the process can be sized to meet your available resources, demographics and markets.

1. **Create a vision and commitment that aligns diversity with the organizational strategy.** Sustainable diversity initiatives require a direct link to business strategy and CEO commitment. It starts at the top; without clear, heartfelt buy-in from the CEO, no company can manage diversity effectively.

2. **Establish an executive diversity council.** Internal diversity councils usually are comprised of a company's senior leadership. The most effective ones are headed by the CEO because that sends the message to the entire company of the importance of diversity to the company's lines of business. Top management needs to go beyond passively supporting diversity efforts, they must be engaged and model the commitment to diversity. At The

Pepsi Bottling Group, CEO and president Eric Foss is chair of the diversity council. Bank of America's CEO, Kenneth Lewis, is personally responsible for appointing members of the diversity council and meets regularly with employee resource groups.

3. **Establish a diversity task force.** Headed by a senior manager, the role of this team is to champion the diversity efforts of the organization. Committee members should be a broad representation of gender, race, ethnicity, religious backgrounds, age, disabled employees, and occupational groups. Their selection should be inclusive (not exclusive).

4. **Conduct an organizational diversity assessment.** An assessment of the organization includes capturing the views held by employees in the organization as well as an in-depth analysis of the human resource practices, policies and procedures. An analysis of this information will inform the organization about its current diversity status as well as establish a baseline from which to move toward becoming an inclusive organization.

5. **Develop a diversity strategy and tactical action plans.** The results of the cultural assessment are translated into a strategy with specific goals and objectives and a timeline for implementation.

6. **Establish metrics and timelines.** Holding managers accountable for keeping diversity in the forefront is critical. Wal-Mart deployed Diversity Tracker, a system for managing and reporting progress on its diversity goals. Coca-Cola ties 20 percent of management bonuses to diversity success and makes diversity training mandatory for the entire workforce. In 2005, 90 percent of the top 10 diversity companies linked management compensation to diversity initiatives.

7. **Fund and execute action plans.** Of the top 50 diversity companies recognized by DiversityInc. magazine, one of the most common shared traits is a stable diversity budget. One of the biggest concerns voiced by senior leaders is the commitment to funding in troubled economic times. The credibility of the commitment to diversity is certainly challenged and tested during such times.

8. **Reassess and renew.** Conduct a diversity reassessment in order to determine the level of success in achieving the diversity strategy. Begin the process again from the new starting point.

Summary

Creating and sustaining a respectful climate that allows everyone to attain their full potential and contribute to the success of the organization is an ongoing commitment. It is not a one-time fix.

Resources

The Bureau of Labor Statistics, *www.bls.gov.* The principal fact finding agency for the federal government in labor economics and statistics.

DiversityInc., *www.diversity.com.* The mission of this website and monthly print magazine is to bring education and clarity to the benefits of diversity.

We would like to acknowledge and thank Dr. Monica C. Gavino for contributing to this book by writing this chapter on diversity and inclusion. Dr. Gavino is on the faculty of the Graham School of Management at St. Xavier University in Chicago where she teaches MBA and undergraduate courses on diversity, and serves as Chair of the St. Xavier University Diversity Committee. She is considered the diversity expert at St. Aubin, Haggerty & Associates as she works with clients on their implementation of their diversity programs, as well as conducting our "Valuing and Respecting Differences" workshop.

Encourage Wellness in the Workplace

Lifestyle is a word that refers to the pattern of choices we make in our lives. These choice patterns become routines that are hard to break. Genetics aside, people who are healthier have made choices and built routines that lead to greater health and less need for medical intervention. Poor health, often the result of poor lifestyle choices, greatly increases the risk of disease and medical expense. For an organization, the overall health of its workforce impacts the cost of healthcare and the level of productivity.

Consider the gravity of the problem:

- More than 75 percent of the entire U.S. population does not get enough physical activity, based on the latest recommendations from the surgeon general.
- If you are a man, a tobacco user at age 24 and use tobacco your whole life, "it's going to cost $220,000 to treat you for related diseases," according to Dr. Steve Aldana, a nationally recognized wellness expert. This means that "if you spend $4.25 for a pack of smokes," he says, "the real cost of that purchase is about $40–$44.25 of which will be paid for by someone else."
- According to a National Health and Nutrition Examination Survey by CDC's National Center for Health Statistics, the percentage of U.S. adults classified as obese more than doubled between 1980 and 2000, from 15 percent to 31 percent.
- According to *Business Week*, 2002 healthcare costs for an obese person were $1,244 higher than for a person with a healthy weight.
- Obesity is a greater trigger for health problems and increased health spending than smoking or drinking. Individuals who are obese have 30 percent to 40 percent more chronic medical problems than those who smoke or drink heavily. (From "The Effects of Obesity, Smoking and Drinking on Medical Problems and Costs," *Health Affairs*, March/April 2002.)
- About 12 percent of total healthcare costs are obesity related. When you add in healthcare costs related to poor diet, sedentary living and tobacco use, "You're now sitting at 65 to 70 percent of total healthcare expenditures

within your organization," according to Dr. Aldana (as quoted in "Unhealthy Behaviors" by The Wellness Councils of America).

Which Do You Want First–the Good News or the Bad News?

As you can see, there is a lot of bad news related to the current state of health in the United States. Obesity and lifestyle-related disease is on the rise. The impact of unhealthy lifestyle patterns in today's youth has been well documented as well. Further, these same realities apply to the current and future workforce.

Yet, there is some good news. Lifestyle choices can and do change on an individual level through information, support, motivation and well-designed programs. Positive lifestyle changes across the workforce can and do benefit an organization directly. Comprehensive worksite health programs have been shown to yield from $3 to $6 return on investment for every dollar spent.

Another piece of good news is that health is now in the national spotlight. Because of this highly public focus, many tools and resources are available to leaders who want to do something about worksite wellness. For evidence, explore some of the resources at the end of this chapter for models, information, tools and other resources available through the Internet alone.

Clearly, an organization will benefit financially through well-designed worksite wellness programs and will increase its ability to attract, engage and retain employees by doing so. This view is echoed by J. Barry Griswell, CEO of Principal Financial Group: "In my view, employee health and productivity is one of the most important issues corporations face. Let me tell you why. I have a philosophy that if you want to lead a successful company and satisfy shareholders, you must start by making sure your employees are treated well. Give them the tools and resources they need to stay happy, healthy and productive. When you do that, employees in turn treat customers well. When customers are treated well, it creates shareholder value. So, to me, healthy, motivated and productive employees are a very fundamental part of doing good business and building a great company."

Getting Started on Worksite Wellness

If your organization currently does not have any sort of wellness program, a tried and true framework is offered by The Wellness Councils of America (www.welcoa.org). WCA's 7-C model–the seven benchmarks of success identifies key activities such as:

1. **Capturing senior level support.** Leaders at the top control resources, communication channels and priorities.

2. **Creating cohesive wellness teams.** Create a team of dedicated employees who represent the major constituent groups. Involve this team and its stakeholders early in the process.

3. **Collecting data to drive health efforts.** Find out what is needed and what will make the most difference to the people and the business.

4. Crafting an operating plan. Focus the program by designing program elements, goals and measurement processes.

5. Choosing appropriate interventions. Consider what will influence behavior change, select program types and design program features for maximum interest and motivation.

6. Creating a supportive environment. Supportive environments can significantly increase positive behavior changes.

7. Consistently evaluating outcomes. Measure the impact of your efforts, and identify additional opportunities.

If your organization already has some kind of worksite wellness programs in place, the goal is to improve the offerings and communication to reach a greater number of employees and achieve greater organizational benefits. Dr. Lee Handke, vice president of wellness at Blue Cross and Blue Shield of Nebraska, described what they learned when assessing the current status of their programs. "It was clear from the data that our employees didn't really feel supported in making healthy lifestyle changes. This was an eye-opener for our organization. I mean, we had been doing wellness for some years. Despite our efforts, our employees weren't seeing our attempts at helping them manage and maintain their health at work. This told us that we needed to take our program to an entirely different level."

On What Should a Wellness Program Focus?

Balanced, high-impact programs will have more than one focus. As you start out on a wellness journey, you may wish to start by implementing a program in one or two of the following focus areas and then build on early successes. The focus areas below are adapted from an interview with Dr. Handke as reported by The Wellness Councils of America.

- **Screenings.** Many tools are available to offer health screenings to employees. Screenings may range from employee self-evaluations to on-site health screenings by medical professionals.

- **Environmental wellness.** Consider offering healthier (not pricier) food choices in the corporate cafeteria, healthy snacks in meetings, on-site fitness center equipment and aerobics classes or other exercise options.

- **Education.** Many employees are unaware or poorly informed about the impact of exercise, diet and other lifestyle choices on their overall health. Employees can make better, more informed lifestyle choices through good information and education sessions.

- **Behavior modification.** Create programs that involve employees in taking control of their health. Offer programs that help people stop smoking, lose weight, exercise more and eat better. Some organizations provide health points to employees when they accomplish program goals such as losing weight or quitting smoking. Points can be redeemed for prizes or money. The best reward is better health; but money can be a more immediate incentive for many.

- **Community support.** Involve employees in wellness initiatives in the community. This illustrates the organization's commitment to wellness as a way of life and involves employees in meaningful, active pursuits.

Tips for Implementing a Wellness Program to Attract, Engage & Retain Talent

Benefits of a healthier workforce abound, and one key element that may be overlooked is that wellness programs impact your talent pipeline. A job applicant is more likely to choose an employer with employee wellness options (fitness centers, access to healthy food, etc.) than to work for an employer without wellness options. Similarly, current employees become more engaged when their employer aids them on their road to a healthier life.

Here are some tips for implementing worksite wellness programs to maximize attraction and engagement of talent:

- Get sponsorship from the top executives and create an advisory wellness team. When employees are led and represented well, they will know there are teeth behind wellness platitudes.
- Communicate it. Be transparent about your plans, programs and impact.
- Bring it to the workplace. Make programs easy to join and use.
- Use technology to stay in touch. Gather information, keep track of successes, make information available to employees, push information out to employees and measure business results through technology. Develop a dedicated wellness site on your employee Intranet.
- Keep measuring. Data enables you to communicate positive program outcomes to leadership and to employees, providing a greater sense of involvement and gratitude.
- Make it inspiring. Wellness is not another compliance program. You are helping your people reach their full potential, achieve better health and get control of their life and their sense of well-being. Use this type of language in your wellness interactions.
- Keep growing it. Reach a broader band of employees with more meaningful wellness tools. Expand the focus from internal to external programs. Involve more employees in guiding the program at various locations.

J. Barry Griswell, CEO of Principle Financial Group, talked about his personal health journey in an article titled "Leading By Example." Through exercise and better nutrition he went from 297 pounds to 246 pounds and improved triglycerides and cholesterol levels. "This is not something I did to get some numbers in order," Griswell said, "it's something I did to change my life for the better. ... Changing my lifestyle and getting back into shape has improved my life in countless ways. It relates to what we were talking about before–being able to reach one's full potential."

Summary

Imagine this: Each year your organization's wellness program impacts a greater number of employees in the same way that Griswell describes. How much more engaged will these employees be in contributing value to the organization? How would their interactions with colleagues and customers improve? How likely will they represent the organization positively to prospective employees? The answers are obvious. The opportunity is to do the right thing by helping your people do what they have always wanted to do, attain and sustain a healthier lifestyle.

Resources

"America On the Move," *www.americaonthemove.org*.

"Health Promotion: Sourcebook for Small Businesses," Wellness Councils of America and Canada, 1998.

"Healthier Worksite Initiatives," Center for Disease Control and Prevention, *www.cdc.gov/nccdphp/dnpa/hwi/index.htm*.

Infinite Wellness Solutions, *www.infinitewellnesssolutions.com*.

National Business Group On Health, *www.wbgh.org*.

"Planning Wellness: Getting Off to a Good Start, 4th edition" Summex Health Management, ©2005.

The Wellness Councils of America, *www.welcoa.org*.

46

Recognize & Appreciate

"Appreciate everything your associates do for the business. Nothing else can quite substitute for a few well-chosen, well-timed, sincere words of praise. They're absolutely free and worth a fortune."

–Sam Walton

Large companies seem to believe that recognizing employee contributions is important; important enough to spend in excess of $100 billion each year on gifts and rewards, believing that this makes employees feel wanted and respected. In an article called "Closing the Recognition Gap" (*www.management-issues.com*), Jerry Pounds cites a 2005 employee recognition survey by the National Association for Employee Recognition that found 90 percent of the 614 organizations surveyed had an active employee recognition program. Yet when the Gallup organization surveyed 4 million workers on topics of recognition and praise, they found that two-thirds of employees feel they received no recognition on the job in the previous 12 months.

In our experience recognition programs in organizations could be described as having form without substance. The focus of this chapter is to better understand the substance of employee recognition and appreciation, and the qualities and practices a leader should consider when seeking to enhance employee engagement through true recognition.

The Substance of Recognition & Appreciation

Have you noticed that the word recognition is made up of the root word cognition? Cognition means the mental process of knowing or perceiving something. Recognition means that we have perceived or come to know something again. Recognizing employees means that we have come to know their value and are prompted to action with sincere appreciation.

So, recognition is simply the message to an employee that–*I recognize your contribution of value to this organization. I appreciate the effort and the success you are helping us have and I view you as an essential colleague in this business. I appreciate you. Thank you.* Why is this powerful? When people get this clear message (through words, actions, responses and even gifts) that their hard work is noticed and appreciated and that someone values them at work, it has a plethora of positive effects. People respond with more effort when they know it is appreciated. They are grateful and begin to feel more obligated to be responsible and helpful. Others who observe acts of appreciation elevate their positive perceptions of the manager and organizational culture.

About Rewards

The concept of employee rewards goes hand-in-hand with recognition. A thank you and a gift often carry more weight than a thank you alone. A reward could be a gift of words or it might be an elaborate program of money or other gifts of value. Often, organizations provide gifts without being clear about the performance that is being rewarded, which is an empty exercise. In fact, reward and incentive programs can quickly become an assumed and expected part of the compensation package and do not increase engagement of employees significantly. When rewards and recognition are sincere expressions of appreciation for specific, valued contributions, the activity becomes engaging.

Make note: Recognition and reward activities in an organization are not compensation. Rosabeth Moss Kanter, an author and professor at Harvard Business School, says, "Compensation is a right; recognition is a gift." The compensation and benefits received by employees are merely the agreement between the organization and the employee about what is rightfully expected for doing the work. Recognition and reward is specifically linked to actions of value and are sincere expressions of thanks.

What Works Best?

Be clear about what you are recognizing (the specific contribution of value to the organization), and provide a reward (words, money, awards, tokens) that is valued by the receiver. As a leader, it is best to:

- **Own the recognition.** The thank you for this contribution message should come from a specific person that is in the position to clearly understand why the employee's efforts make a positive impact.

- **Simplify and connect.** Be clear about what is appreciated, i.e., the specific individual or team effort that is valued and why it is valued. The reward (whatever it might be) should be clearly linked to the recognition. In others words, there should be no space between the recognition and the reward.

- **Know what they value.** In some companies, the most heartwarming gift is a framed award plaque for the employee's workspace. Other employees might just want a personal thank you and do not place a high value on pomp and circumstance or gift certificates. For some, money or gift cards may be the only way to get your message through that your really do appreciate their efforts. It is nearly impossible to sincerely express appreciation without knowing what your employees value.

Why Aren't Leaders More Effective in Engaging & Retaining Employees through Recognition?

In the hectic atmosphere of everyday work life, it becomes easy to skip thanking others. Following are some of the most common excuses leaders make to justify not showing their appreciation:

- People are already paid very well to do a good job; that should be enough.
- Our bonus or incentive program provides enough motivation.
- The organization has limited resources for doing this. It costs too much.
- I am concerned it will become expected all the time. I do not want to set a precedence.
- I do not know how.

We Already Have a Recognition Program. Do We Have to Do More?

Think of recognition and reward activities at two levels: organizational and personal. Many organizations create recognition programs that provide options for how managers can reward their employees. These organization-wide programs are helpful to leverage resources, but they only go part of the way. Even if your organization has a great rewards program, you can and should do everything you can to personalize and maximize recognition activities.

Here are some ideas for maximizing employee engagement through recognition.

- Take time, not (just) money.
    - Taking a small amount of time to note important dates like birthdays or company anniversaries and accomplishments can often go further than money alone. Four out of five employees say that intangible rewards like praise and verbal recognition for their work are valuable. (Maritz Research Poll, November 2004.)
    - Remember that cash rewards have no real lasting value, cannot be greatly enhanced and may come to be expected as part of the compensation package.
- Plan and execute.
    - Target specific behaviors that are actual contributions of value to the organization and that you wish to recognize.
    - Communicate this target and then recognize clearly.
    - Adapt your recognition strategies based on what the receiver values and what the situation may require.
    - Make it timely. Recognize behavior as soon as possible to sustain credibility and make connections clear.

- Nurture a culture of recognition.
  - Develop your managers and team leaders. Give them clear guidance, tools and communication approaches to help them be sincere recognizers of talent.
  - Select and promote employees who appreciate the efforts of others and are passionate about recognizing the contributions of their people. This should be a key criterion for your promotion process.
  - Assess your recognition activities. Continually evaluate what is working and what is not. Do what is possible to support managers in sincere recognition processes.

"Gratitude is not only the greatest of virtues, but the parent of all others."

–Cicero

How Can Individual Managers Do this at Low Cost or No Cost?

Scan this list, and then decide which of these would work well in your environment, be valued by the recipients and be relatively easy to orchestrate:

- verbal praise or congratulations at a group meeting
- send a personal note of thanks
- Post-it notes in a workspace or on a paycheck
- an e-card or computer certificate of appreciation
- a feature about the employee or team contribution in a department or company newsletter
- a recognition bulletin board hall of fame
- doing the employee's least favorite task for him or her
- a half or full day off as a thank you
- an award pin for the employee to wear
- a traveling trophy (a token of thanks that "travels" to different recipients' work spaces)
- treating the employee to lunch
- allocating additional responsibility
- special assignments or challenges
- offering flexible hours
- cross-training opportunities
- asking for his or her opinion and involving the recipient in unique, valuable ways

Summary

Whatever you do, try to do something different that has not been done before to show your appreciation. And remember the words of William Arthur Ward, American scholar, pastor and teacher:

"Flatter me, and I may not believe you. Criticize me, and I may not like you. Ignore me, and I may not forgive you. Encourage me, and I may not forget you."

–William Arthur

Resources

www.recognition.org.

www.motivationonline.com.

1001 Ways to Reward Employees, Workman Publishing, ©1994.

Recognition, Gratitude & Celebration, Crisp Learning, ©1997.

Secrets of a Successful Employee Recognition Systems, Productivity Press, ©1995.

How to Recognize and Reward Employees, American Management Association, ©1994.

Innovative Reward Systems for the Changing Workplace, McGraw-Hill, ©1994.

Maximizing the Impact of Recognition: An Approach to Rewarding Employee Contributions, Worldatwork, 1998.

The Cycle of Leadership: How Great Leaders Teach Their Companies to Win, Collins, ©2004.

47

Zero Tolerance for Disengaging Behavior

In his book *Good to Great: Why Some Companies Make the Leap … and Others Don't,* Jim Collins illuminates the double-edged sword of holding on to underperformers. "Letting the wrong people hang around is unfair to all the right people," Collins writes, "as they inevitably find themselves compensating for the inadequacies of the wrong people. Worse, it can drive away the best people. Strong performers are intrinsically motivated by performance, and when they see their efforts impeded by carrying extra weight, they eventually become frustrated. Waiting too long before acting is equally unfair to the people who need to get off the bus. For every minute you allow a person to continue holding a seat when you know that person will not make it in the end, you're stealing a portion of his life, time that he could spend finding a better place where he could flourish."

Collins is writing here about transforming an organization from good to great by getting the right people first, then deciding where to drive the bus—the directions to pursue for the business. The concept also applies directly to the subject of employee engagement, i.e., some employees do not perform because they are actively disengaged. Leaders should have zero tolerance for individual and systemic sources of active disengagement.

What Does Active Disengagement Look Like?

Using Gallup's work in this area, there are three types of employees:

1. **Engaged employees.** They work with passion and feel a profound connection to their company. They drive innovation and move the organization forward.

2. **Not-engaged employees.** These people are essentially checked out. They are sleepwalking through their workday, putting time—but not energy or passion—into their work.

3. **Actively disengaged employees.** They are not just unhappy at work; they are busy acting out their unhappiness. Every day these workers undermine what their engaged coworkers accomplish.

At some point in your career you have probably worked with someone who was noticeably disengaged from his or her work and employer. The damaging behaviors demonstrated by such employees may include undercutting the decisions of the management team, rampant procrastination, persuading others to hide information or misinform, creating fictions, creating obstacles to customer service or even sabotaging someone else's work. Fomenting anti-organization, anti-collaboration rebellion can create a toxic environment for larger numbers of employees and work groups. Some toxic environments might be explained by poor management or poor systems, but they are often the result of one or more actively disengaged individuals who find the time and expend the energy to damage relationships and productivity in the workplace.

A warehousing and distribution company that hired a consulting firm to improve operations and management processes at one of its facilities provides a graphic example of one worker's ability to create a toxic environment. The primary reason for this project was a concern on the part of management that the workforce was talking about bringing in a labor union. An interesting discovery was made during the analysis portion of the project. The union scare was tracked down to one disgruntled (and underperforming) worker in one building on one shift who was actively pushing pro-union activities among his shift mates. Of course, when workers' rights are being violated, labor unions may help protect those rights. In this case, however, no one would have benefited–the actions of this individual were solely self-serving, a hallmark of active disengagement.

Statistics on Actively Disengaged Employees

In 2006, the Gallup Management Journal reported that of all U.S. workers above 18 years of age, about 20.6 million or roughly 15 percent–were actively disengaged. The lower productivity of actively disengaged workers costs the U.S. economy about $328 billion.

Responding to Active Disengagement

Organizational leaders must demonstrate zero tolerance for those people in their organization who are behaving in ways that create toxic relationships or a toxic climate because of their disengagement–especially if the actively disengaged employee is someone with significant supervisory, managerial or customer facing responsibilities. You should not ignore, condone, collude with, reward or promote disengaged individuals. Similarly, if you find groups of actively disengaged employees, examine the organizational systems and processes in that work unit for plausible root causes and then deal with those causes. You should have zero tolerance for actively disengaged managers and for systems that create disengagement.

On an individual level, what can leaders do when actively disengaged behaviors become known? The answer depends a great deal on factors such as:

- The types of behaviors that have become damaging to relationships and the business;
- the employment level of the person;
- the type of protections and rights available to the person;
- the existence (or nonexistence) of performance data over time; and
- the clarity of the employee handbook on required business behavior.

Choices are available for dealing with actively disengaged employees; zero tolerance means that action must be taken. Your choices boil down to two: either reconnect or remove the actively disengaged employee. The best course of action is not always obvious and might not only involve individual-level actions. The interventions below are listed in order of escalating severity.

- **Explore the reasons behind the behavior in a concerned, respectful way.** The Gallup Employee Engagement report showed that 80 percent of actively disengaged employees "strongly disagree that their relationship with their manager is one of their strongest personal relationships, compared to 15 percent of engaged employees." It would seem that working harder to form a more open, trusting and supportive relationship with disengaged individuals may reduce their level of disengagement, especially for those who are seeking to air their concerns and be better understood.

- **Provide coaching on alternatives to disengaging behaviors.** For example, if the employee has been overly cynical about current changes in the workplace when speaking with other staff members, it may help to provide them with other response options. Show them how their actions are detrimentally impacting you and others. Suggest more positive ways to deal with ambiguity. Involve them in something that you and they value regarding the change effort.

- **Be clear on consequences if disengaging behavior continues.** This standard performance improvement strategy, when done well and sincerely, can turn some behavior around. This intervention is often supported by a performance improvement plan document that spells out goals, timelines and consequences for noncompliance. This is less a strategy to make actively disengaged employees more engaged, and more a strategy to begin the documentation process in preparation for transferring or exiting the individual.

- **Follow through on consequences if behavior does not change.** When a performance improvement plan has been discussed and documented, be sure you are ready and willing to make the tough choice if and when the time comes.

- **Move the person to a position that may be a better fit.** In the spirit of full disclosure (and not passing problems to others), this type of move should only be made with full involvement of leadership in the new area. Also, this option should only be taken if it is crystal clear that the causes of active disengagement of the employee will no longer exist in the new position, and that the talents and strengths of the person will be better utilized.

- **Withhold rewards.** When a person demonstrates active disengagement, he or she should not be considered for promotion or other types of rewards until things have changed.
- **Exit the actively disengaged employee.** If an employee remains actively disengaged, he or she should be given the opportunity to flourish somewhere else. Acting as quickly as possible to remove an actively disengaged person is even more important when he is at a higher level in the organization, handles customer interactions or has significant responsibility for strategic business results. As Dave Ulrich said in an interview in *Strategy & Leadership* magazine, "The most strategic human resource decision a company could ever make is to help place its poorest performers with a competitor–and hope they stay a long time!"

Group Disengagement

You may find that you have a higher level of actively disengaged people in specific units of your organization. If so, consider whether this might be caused by the organization's systems or by accidental cultural norms. Explore the possible root causes of group disengagement by asking questions like these.

- Has too much change occurred too quickly, with no hope of stabilization or no end in sight?
- Have disruptions been foisted on talented employees with little preparation or communication?
- Is there extreme ambiguity about the future?
- Has communication about the future been adequate or inadequate to manage employee engagement?
- How difficult is it to surmount barriers to performance?
- Is it unreasonably difficult for people to make progress in their work?
- Have you lost hard working people who have not been replaced, thereby requiring otherwise engaged employees to shoulder overly broad areas of effort?
- Is access to information onerous?
- Are there patterns of inequity in employee treatment, such as favoritism?
- Are there signs of active disrespect in the work setting?
- Have leaders lost touch with the cares, concerns and contributions of their people?
- To what extent have the good contributions of employees gone virtually unrecognized?

Consider seeking the assistance of internal or external organizational development specialists. Conduct interviews, focus groups and surveys with representative members of the work unit to identify the sources and symptoms of the situation. Executing plans to resolve systemic disengagement may also require the alignment of leadership actions and human resource processes.

Summary

When groups of nonmanagement employees are actively disengaged, look at the systems. When a higher-level leader is actively disengaged, remove the source of disengagement or remove the leader to another position or out of the organization.

The authors of the two haiku below seem to be disengaged; clearly their talents are being underutilized. You do not want to find self-expressions like this on the desktops of your employees.

"Pried my thumbnail off
With a staple remover
Just to stay awake."

"Today is payday–
For one brief, shining moment
It all seems worthwhile."

Resources

Good to Great, HarperCollins Publishers Inc., ©2001.

"Getting Personal in the Workplace: Are negative relationships squelching productivity in your company?" *The Gallup Management Journal.* 2004. *www.gallupjournal.com.*

"Gallup Study: Engaged Employees Inspire Company Innovation," *Gallup Management Journal,* 2006.

48

Assess Organizational Practices

Organizations survive and grow based on their ability to provide products and services that others will buy at a price that represents a positive return. The drivers behind building loyal customers are described in the well-known service-profit chain model. As recapped in "Putting the Service-Profit Chain to Work," seven fundamental propositions emerge from the links in the service-profit chain:

1. **Customer loyalty drives profitability and growth.** A 5 percent increase in customer loyalty can boost profits by 25 percent to 85 percent.

2. **Customer satisfaction drives customer loyalty.** Xerox found that its very satisfied customers were six times more likely to repurchase company equipment than were customers who were merely satisfied.

3. **Value drives customer satisfaction.** An insurer's efforts to deliver maximum value include funding a team that provides special services at the sites of major catastrophes. The company has one of the highest margins in its history.

4. **Employee productivity drives value.** Southwest Airlines deplanes and reloads two-thirds of its flights in 15 minutes or less; pilots fly an average 20 hours more per month than competitors. Fares stay low while service remains high.

5. **Employee commitment and loyalty drives productivity.** One auto dealer's annual cost of replacing a sales rep who had 8 years of experience with one who had less than a year was $432,000 in lost sales.

6. **Employee satisfaction drives commitment and loyalty.** In one company study, 30 percent of all dissatisfied employees expressed an intention to leave, compared to only 10 percent of all satisfied employees. Moreover, low employee turnover was found to be closely linked to high customer satisfaction.

7. **Internal quality drives employee satisfaction.** Service workers are happiest when they are empowered to make things right for customers and when they have responsibilities that add depth to their work.

Internal quality is created by organizational investments in practices that increase employee commitment and loyalty by improving their perception of the organization. This, in turn, increases the retention of talent and the occurrence of extra effort behaviors from your workforce. A model that describes the dynamics of value creation is illustrated in figure 48.1.

Figure 48.1

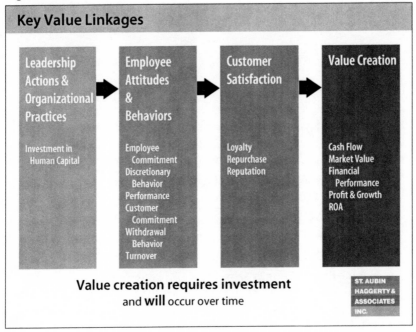

Many insights can be derived from this model. One is that you get very little traction from trying to improve the organization by merely doing employee attitude surveys. In most cases, when organizations have gathered employee opinion data, the leadership team quickly realizes that they are missing information on the root causes behind the data. The questions they ask sound like this:

- What causes the across-the-board desire for better communication from the top?
- Why do we have lower scores in some areas regarding the performance management process?
- What is behind the data trends regarding retention and an employee's likelihood to leave?
- What is causing the employee perceptions about manager approachability or favoritism?

Without better understanding the answers to questions such as these, the likelihood is higher that leader driven responses will be ill directed because they would be based on assumptions or leaps of logic from ambiguous, symptomatic data.

Identify the Practices that Influence
Your Internal Employer Brand

Prior to conducting employee opinion surveys, it is important to first identify the practices that influence your internal employer brand the most. As stated in Chapter 1: *Internal branding is about building an image in the eyes and minds of the current workforce and the prospective employment pool that this organization is a good, if not excellent, place to work.*

Further, leaders who wish to maximize this process of creating organization value are advised to gather information in two areas that go deeper than most employee opinion surveys:

1. The organizational practices where you are doing well and where you are not.
2. The practices that influence your outcomes the most.

Some of the key leadership and human resource practices that should be assessed include:

- employee involvement
- career opportunities
- training and development
- selection practices
- performance management

By linking the perceptions of each of these practices to an employee's view of the organization through statistical analysis, a picture forms of the practices that can be leveraged to increase the employee's perception of the organization and the human resource function. This in turn has a beneficial impact on employee attitudes resulting in beneficial employee behaviors such as intention to stay and extra effort. These two factors constitute employee commitment–a deeper bond between employee and employer than is connoted by the concept of employee engagement.

Why is this important? Most organizations cannot undertake to recast every possible management process into a world-class practice. The time and resources are simply not available. When organizations rely solely on best practices data to overhaul their processes, they are much more likely to misappropriate resources for process improvements that make very little difference to moving the scale of employee perception or commitment. Each organization has a unique, differentiating value proposition and unique workforce. Undifferentiated organizational improvements are likely to be suboptimizing. The one size fits all approach to adopting best practices is a no-win concept, or at best operationalized mediocrity.

For example, not everyone can do what GE does in creating an embarrassment of talented leaders. One company is undertaking a valiant effort to create a leadership institute for key positions and high potential managers. The project team struggles to balance a strong desire to emulate GE's renowned Leadership Development Center in Crotonville, N.Y., against the limited resources and experience within the organization.

Each organization has unique levers that can be pulled to impact employee attitude and behaviors. A surprising trend is that the practice of pay for performance tends to have less impact than some organizational leaders assume. Practices that appear to trend higher in the data include performance management processes and employee involvement.

Responding to the Data

Christopher Cowdray facilitated significant value creation within London's prestigious Claridge's Hotel by focusing on the leadership and human resource practices that would have the greatest impact on employee commitment and ownership of the customer service encounter. A 360-degree feedback system was introduced for managers to gauge morale. Recruiting was focused on hiring individuals with attitudinal as well as functional competence. An employee appraisal program and rapid promotion system was installed. With these and other improved organizational practices, the hotel's selling price was recently set at £300 million, tripling the original purchase price of an estimated £100 million within 5 years. This represents an organizational value increase of approximately £500,000 per employee–true value creation.

Summary

When you seek to connect with what is on the minds and in the hearts of your employees, first seek to identify the organizational and human resource practices that reinforce your employer brand and thus have the largest impact on engaging and retaining your top talent. Then, it takes leadership and organizational will to make the procedural and cultural adjustments required to have any sort of positive impact. Transparency and proactive communication aid greatly in this effort. Once you have put in place the enhanced practices that will make the biggest difference, measure the impact through organizational scorecards or engagement dashboards. And you may want to continue assessing employee engagement levels. For this, use a customized or well-selected employee survey tool, the subject of the next chapter.

Resources

"Bringing Your Employer Brand to Life Through Your Organizational HR Practices". Gavino and St. Aubin, 2007.

"Putting the Service-Profit Chain to Work," *HBR OnPoint*, Harvard Business School Publishing, 2000.

49

Measure Employee Perceptions

Jack Welch, former CEO of GE, once said, "The three most important things you should measure in a business are customer satisfaction, employee satisfaction and cash flow." He later amended this list: "No, it should read: the three most important things to measure in a business are employee satisfaction, customer satisfaction and cash flow," noting that employee satisfaction is fundamental to the growth of any service company in efforts to strengthen its customer loyalty.

Capture the Flag

Does your leadership team possess information on the perceptions and ideas of your workforce? Does your workforce have the opportunity to communicate their opinions and be more involved in the business? Disconnectedness between leaders and employees is reminiscent of an old game played at summer camps called Capture the Flag.

On a typical sunny afternoon at camp, 80 or so rambunctious, pre-teen campers were divided into two teams. Each team was given half of the camp and a flag to plant somewhere in its territory. The goal was to sneak across enemy lines, capture the opponents' flag and carry it back into your territory without being tagged and put into prison. For those who chose to immerse themselves in the game, the experience was exhilarating and full of intrigue, secretiveness and playful anarchy. For those who were disconnected from the activity, the game afforded the opportunity to sneak off somewhere to enjoy a little peace and quiet. The game was typically won by the intrepid souls who heroically applied their gifts of speed, diversion and guile to foil their opponents' defenses and carry the flag home to victory. Most participants in the game did not know what they should be doing to help win the game and tended to wander around aimlessly or hide out and wait for it to be over. Some participants were either rankled or grateful to spend most of the time languishing in prison. Some did not learn the game was won until someone told them—perhaps hours later.

Capture the Flag is a metaphor about organizations that do not measure employee perceptions. In these organizations, leaders may not know what the troops are doing or how they are feeling about participating in the game. They may wonder why the troops are not more engaged or feeling a greater sense of urgency. Some leaders may overly rely on the most talented combatants to engage the enemy and come out victorious through speed and innovation. Employees may perceive that their leaders are so focused on beating the competition that they turn a deaf ear to the needs and ideas of the troops. Managers may be unclear how to use resources to gain advantage and wonder what role they should be playing to help win the game. And most organizational members are not clear if they are winning the game or not.

Employee Surveys Are Ubiquitous

Enter the phrase employee opinion surveys into your Internet search engine and see what happens. A recent Google search showed 1,810,000 hits for that phrase. The first several pages were links to articles or external providers of surveying resources. In an age where these types of tools can be harnessed in powerful ways and survey resources are readily available, it does not mean all surveys are useful or that frequent employee opinion gathering is just more of a good thing.

Guiding Principles for Employee Surveys

Organizations survey their employees more frequently then ever, but often do very little with the results. The authors of *The Workforce Scorecard: Managing Human Capital to Execute Strategy* include employee surveys as a viable method to measure workforce success and engagement in the organization. But they offer some warnings. "Over time, if you use the same measures, managers might gain additional insight by comparing how these responses vary from period to period. It's nice to know that there has been a 15 percent gain in workforce commitment, or perhaps you will be concerned by a 10 percent decline, but what does it mean? What important management question does it answer? Is there a compelling business case that links these results to bottom-line performance? The problem with employee surveys is not the form of the measure; it's the motivation for the measure."

The following principles will guide you through the effective administration of employee surveys:

- Establish clear priorities for benchmarking and assessing trends in employee perceptions by first doing an organizational practices survey. (See Chapter 48: Assess Organizational Practices for more on this topic.)
- Select an employee survey tool that will measure the dimensions that will have the greatest impact on employee commitment and extra effort behaviors based on high gain organizational practices.
- Communicate results in compelling, employee valuing ways.
- Make your response visible through involvement and status reporting.

Types of Employee Surveys

The wide variety of employee survey types reinforces the notion that organizations often do not know precisely what to measure and that the business of surveying employees is booming. As a sampling, you can purchase or create surveys to focus on areas such as:

- engagement
- culture
- satisfaction
- customer care
- climate
- development
- improvement

Going Inside or Outside

The decision of whether to do your own survey or to use outside help is an important one. There are many factors involved in the decision; below are some considerations for each approach.

Using Internal Resources
- Do you have the survey expertise internally to manage and analyze survey data?
- Is normative data (internal organization data compared to data from other organizations) of significant interest to you? If so, do you have relevant normative data available to you without using external providers?
- Do you have the technology and bandwidth to administer the survey and process data?
- Do you have the time to devote to compiling, analyzing and communicating the results?
- Is it likely that your response rate will be negatively affected if internally handled?

Using External Resources
- Are you able to identify an external provider who is willing and able to work with your requirements, not theirs?
- Does the external provider have useful normative data, if this is something of value to you?
- Does the external provider have the technological capabilities to administer the data gathering and data analysis process?
- Do they have the capability to conduct all necessary phases of the survey process, including executive presentations of the data and conclusions, within the timeframes you require?
- Is it likely that the response will be positively affected by externally administered surveys?
- Is your budget sufficient to cover the total cost of using an external provider?

The What of Employee Surveys

Peruse the websites of external providers of employee engagement surveys, and you will find many commonalities and variations regarding topics and questions. Here are some of the more common areas that employee surveys target:

- morale
- job security
- commitment
- working conditions

- opportunity for career growth
- relationship with supervisor
- employee involvement
- communication
- workload
- training and development
- performance appraisal
- perception of the leadership team
- satisfaction with the work
- quality

The How of Employee Surveys

A high response rate for your survey is desired. Some ways to get a higher response rate include:

- Using outside providers to handle the data confidentially.
- Preparing the respondents on the purpose, timing and use of the survey.
- Being clear on who owns the survey so the communication and coordination of survey participation is a priority.
- Ensuring that executives understand the importance of their involvement in the process.
- Doing presurvey work such as creating survey sponsors within work units, communicating a specific plan to report survey results and addressing confidentiality concerns.

Some Common Mistakes in Conducting Employee Surveys

- **They take too long to complete.** While it is good to have valid and reliable scales of questions, some surveys take an inordinate amount of time to complete. When word gets out to the employees, response rates suffer.
- **Using multiple dimensions in a single question.** Each question should ask for a response to one factor, not more. Multiple factor questions beget useless data.
- **Asking questions for which there is no actionable resolution.** This issue is endemic with many employee survey questions. For instance, most surveys include items on salary and compensation. Usually these are the items that trend the lowest. But what is the cause behind it? What can you do additionally that you are not already doing to carry out your compensation strategy?
- **Asking legacy questions.** You should only ask questions that help benchmark or provide trend data for those key organizational practices that will make the biggest difference in supporting your internal employer brand.

Planning Your Process

When preparing to administer a survey, the questions below may help avoid ill-conceived approaches:

- How many employees will be surveyed? Will you cover the whole population or a representative sampling?
- What are the various methods that will need to be used for survey administration? (Internet, Intranet, e-mails, paper-based, focus groups, phone protocols, etc.)

- Which employees can have computers and e-mail addresses?
- How many locations will be involved?
- If paper-based surveys are used, how will results be compiled and coded?
- What time period is best?
- Who will sponsor and drive communication and survey reminders?
- Will you need to translate the instrument into other languages?

Responding to the Data

Organizations are quite right to be concerned about raising employee expectations by asking their opinions on work-related topics. If your organization does not have the will to take significant action in response to the data, by all means, wait to survey employees until a more opportune time. However, a powerful way to engage and reengage employees in the important work of improving the organization is to get them involved in follow-through actions after processing their input. When the organization has identified the practices that positively reinforce its internal employer brand and continues to measure employee perceptions of those organization practices, it is prepared to face virtually all future challenges and to succeed.

Summary

From *The Leadership Challenge: How to Keep Getting Extraordinary Things Done in Organizations,* a sign on the Northern California coast–*Never turn your back on the ocean*–is used as an analogy for remaining vigilant of external realities and not getting too caught up in admiring the *beauty of your own organization,* thereby risking disaster. The reverse can also be true. Leaders can get so caught up in keeping their eyes glued to the ocean (or in capturing the flag of market share and profitability) that they lose track of where the troops are, what they are doing and how they might create more value to the organization through increased commitment and creative effort. Do not lose track of the troops.

Resources

"The Workforce Scorecard," Harvard Business School Press, 2005.

"Leadership Actions and Organizational Practices Diagnostic," St. Aubin, Haggerty & Associates, Inc. *www.staubin.net.*

50

Respond–
Invest in Talent

An Effective Response Is Necessary

As has been stated in a variety of ways in this book and other publications on the topic, business today is facing (or soon will face) leadership and talent shortages at epic levels. If your organization is slow to polish its employer brand and to focus on retaining your current top talent, your opportunity to win the game may soon be lost.

As described in Chapters 48 and 49, organizations can effectively identify high impact investment opportunities by first diagnosing the leadership and human resource practices that make the biggest difference in retaining talent. Then they should gather employee perceptions about how they are doing in aligning practices with their intended employer brand. As described by Gavino and St. Aubin, "Internal branding is about building an image in the eyes and minds of the current workforce that the organization is a great place to work. At the heart of internal employer branding is the understanding of what it is like to work for a company and what drives an employee's desire to keep working for that company."

It is a good and positive thing to gather data. However, when the organization's response to employee opinions is not well communicated or makes no perceivable difference in the employees' work lives, the effort is a poor investment and may even lower engagement levels. So, first make sure you have the capacity and willingness to respond effectively, starting at the very top of your organization.

The Service-Profit Chain Revisited

The service-profit chain model revolves around the concept that customer loyalty is only truly achievable over the long haul by employees that are committed. And this happens only when organizations make discretionary investments in their employees. How employees perceive the quality of their employer is most often impacted by the quality of human resource (HR) related practices. Managing the organization-to-individual interface is challenging, and the greater challenge is in deciding which investments to make to improve employee attitudes.

This challenge is expressed well by Gavino and St. Aubin: "What has been difficult for HR leaders in many organizations…is to justify the funding required to invest in and enhance all of the organization's HR practices at any give time. During difficult economic times requiring budget cuts, it is not feasible or realistic to expect organizations to make substantial investments in every area of HR. Therefore, understanding which organizational HR practices have the most significant impact on the organization is a must. This is quite different than just improving in areas that need attention. Oftentimes the actions taken are simply reactions to HR areas that don't score very well in employee surveys. The focus and investment is placed solely on the basis that these HR practice areas appear to need improvement. The important step that is missed is first determining which HR practices influence, for example, the organization's internal brand the most."

Organizational HR Practices

As Figure 50.1 suggests, effective investments in the right organizational HR practices will advance your internal employer brand with employees and, in turn, positive employee commitment levels and retention of top talent.

Figure 50.1

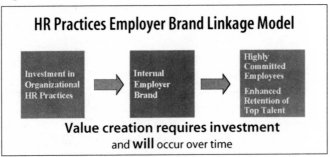

Creation of value requires ongoing investment in order to turn goals into reality. This means that organizations need to continue to target their investments in human capital by targeting the right practices and measuring the impact of those investments. It requires an ongoing feedback loop of assessment, investment responses and further assessments.

The HR Practices Pyramid

The human resource function of an organization is responsible for many of the activities and processes that impact employee perceptions of the organization. The practices of the HR function are of three types:

1. transaction (or non-discretionary);
2. traditional (or discretionary); and
3. strategic (or transformational).

See Figure 50.2 for an illustration of these levels.

Figure 50.2

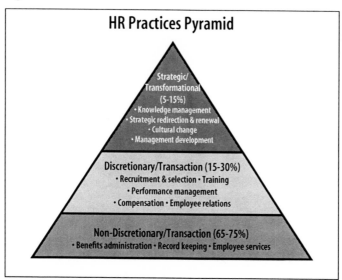

1. Transactional HR Practices

Non-discretionary practices are transactional in nature. Transaction practices include keeping good employee records, administering benefits and compensation accurately, and providing other HR related transactional services. The sample processes in Figure 50.3 are nondiscretionary in that all organizations need to do these things in order to be in compliance with basic employment requirements.

Figure 50.3

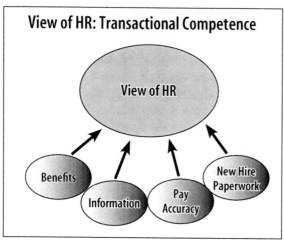

An important insight into transactional HR practices is that employees expect you to get this level right. If mistakes are made at the transactional level, employees' perceptions of the organization plummet. When it is done right at this level, expectations are merely met. In other words, you can tarnish the perception of the organization through poor service and inaccurate records, but you cannot improve employee perceptions beyond a basic level of acceptability. Transactional processes are a hygiene factor in organizational life, nothing more. It is important to get this level right so you can earn the right to focus on other levers for improving your internal employer brand.

2. Organizational HR Practices–Discretionary

Any practice that impacts the quality of your employees' working life and their perceptions of the company could be targeted for investment. Use an analysis process that, at a high level, assesses which of the practices, summarized in Figure 50.4, have the most powerful impact on employees' perception of the organization and the organization's employer brand.

Figure 50.4

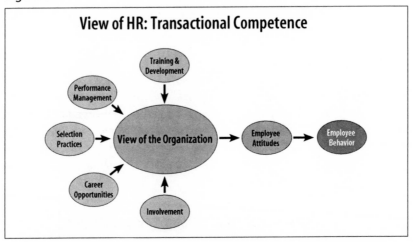

As this model depicts, the practices around employee involvement, career opportunities, selection practices, performance management processes, and training and development have a direct impact on an employee's view of the organization. By investing in the practices that most influence those views, attitudes about employment in the organization also change. This change drives behaviors such as customer service actions, extra effort and intention to stay with the organization.

Examples of Responses

An organization wanted to install a pay for performance program. Based on evidence that the organization's performance management and promotion processes were much more powerful in determining how employees viewed the organization, they conducted a deeper assessment of employee perceptions and discovered that even informal feedback and performance assessments were greatly valued by employees.

As Gavino and St. Aubin concluded, "Given that resources allocated to HR tend to be limited, clearly it is important to know the incremental value of different HR practices, before moving forward on programs intended to enhance all practices across the board, or investing in the practices that won't have the level of impact as others would."

A national logistics company conducted an organizational and HR practices assessment using a variety of surveying methods, asking questions about employees' views of the organization, level of commitment, intention to stay or leave, staffing practices, training, development, pay for performance, performance management, career opportunities and involvement. Through data analysis, it became clear that the practices having the most significant effect on the internal employer brand were career opportunities, selective staffing practices and involvement in decision making. This helped guide organizational leaders to invest in strategic practices in these areas. Another finding showed that the hourly labor force, a significant operating cost component, perceived the organization through the lens of the relationship with their direct supervisor. When the relationship was good, attitude and intention to stay was high, and when the relationship was poor, the reverse was true. This made clear the importance of investing in supervisory skill training for frontline supervisors in areas such as effective on-boarding, communication and coaching skills.

Summary

When you choose to advance your internal employer brand through focused investments, it is important to evaluate the impact of those investments and to make ongoing adjustments. When done well, this is what happens–initial investments in the right organizational HR practices improve employee perceptions, attitudes and behaviors. Positive employee behaviors drive higher customer loyalty levels creating business value through lower costs and higher profitability. With sustained profitability, the organization can and should reinvest in its workforce to continue being a great place to work, where clients know they will receive high quality products or services and this virtuous cycle continues.

Resources

"Bringing Your Employer Brand to Life Through Your Organizational HR Practices". St. Aubin and Gavino, 2007.